WEST POINT HONOR ROLL

THE FATHER—Sylvanus Thayer, appointed in 1817 as the fourth superintendent of West Point, who established the first real academic standards and a formal structure that prevailed well into the twentieth century.

THE ENGINEER—Eleazar Derby Wood, who drove British forces from Fort Erie at the cost of his life in the War of 1812.

THE OUTSIDER—Henry O. Flipper, who in 1877 became the first black man to graduate, was wrongfully court-martialed and driven from the army on racist grounds, and died before receiving a presidential pardon a century later.

THE PATRIOT—Nicholas S. H. Krawciw, who was born in the Ukraine and immigrated to the U.S. from postwar Germany with the dream of attending West Point.

THE FAMILY MAN—Dave Ramsay, who sent poignant letters and tapes to his wife back home before his fighter-bomber crashed on a Vietnam night mission.

Books by Tom Carhart

Battles and Campaigns in Vietnam

The Offering: A Generation Offered Their Lives to
America in Vietnam—One Soldier's Story

Battlefront Vietnam: How the War was Really Fought

Iron Soldiers: How America's 1st Armored Division
Crushed Iraq's Elite Republican Guard

WEST POINT WARRIORS

PROFILES OF DUTY, HONOR, AND COUNTRY IN BATTLE

TOM CARHART

WARNER BOOKS

An AOL Time Warner Company

WARNER BOOKS EDITION

Copyright © 2002 by Tom Carhart

Cover design by Jerry Pfeifer
Cover photos by Bob Krist / Corbis, Richard T. Nowitz /Corbis
Book design by Marleen Adlerblum

Warner Books, Inc.
1271 Avenue of the Americas
New York, NY 10020

Visit our Web site at www.twbookmark.com.

An AOL Time Warner Company

Printed in the United States of America

First Printing: August 2002

10 9 8 7 6 5 4 3 2 1

Contents

Prologue:

The Concept of Self-Sacrifice—
Arthur M. Parker III

THE WIDE EXPANSE OF GRASS HAD BEEN MANICURED to perfection. Around the rim of the Plain, and separating it from the azure sky, the lazily fluttering leaves of hardwood trees screened West Point's gray granite buildings. The sun was warm on Connie's face, and she couldn't stop smiling as the band rang brassily across the field, its heavy drum thumping through her body. It marched closer now, and the music grew louder. But no one moved as the great crowd sat in silent awe at the cream of America's youth. Before them, wearing gray coats with rows of brass buttons, white trousers, and black shako hats, and carrying rifles tipped by gleaming bayonets on their shoulders, the United States Corps of Cadets paraded past in serried rows.

It was a late Saturday morning in May 1966, and Connie's heart pounded as the next row of cadets turned in front of her. At the north end of the Plain was Trophy Point, where Civil War cannon lay in neat rows around the tall spire of Battle Monument. The ground fell sharply off from there to the Hudson River, flowing down from the north between Storm King Mountain and Constitution Island, a breathtaking view. The river was diverted sharply to the east in a giant "S" curve by the granite block atop which West Point stood and from which it got its name, then resumed its relentless path south and to the sea.

Connie was positioned between Battle Monument and Sedgwick's statue, at a spot on the northwest corner of the Plain, right where Art had showed her to stand. Most of the crowd was seated in bleachers on the side of the Plain, and just as Art had promised, she had an unobstructed view as the Corps made their last turn right in front of her to pass by the main reviewing stands before the superintendent's house.

She counted the company guidons carefully, and finally got to . . . wait, there he is . . . no, it can't . . . wait, yes it is, it's him! Her heart leaped as she raised her right arm high in the air and waved it madly. She was sure that was Art, and she was almost sure he saw her. He could make no response, of course, but they would be together within less than an hour. She was very happy, and very much in love. She could barely believe it, things had happened so fast. . . .

It had been the first weekend of February 1966, just a few short months ago. Connie Leighliter was half listening to her roommate chatter as she sat by the apartment window, watching the cars below whir by through slush and snow. Their dates for the weekend, two West Point cadets, were out on a beer run to a neighborhood grocery store, and they were waiting for a third cadet to show up for a crosstown blind date they had arranged.

A beautiful twenty-two-year-old nurse from West Virginia who had become a stewardess to see the world, Connie was in love with her life. Now living in New York, she and other stewardess friends had somehow hooked into the West Point social world. And though she had not yet been truly smitten by one, Connie was simply delighted by the company of cadets.

As they talked, a gray GTO parked across the street. Arthur Middleton Parker III, a black-haired, darkly handsome man in cadet dress gray uniform, emerged. He glanced left and right, then paused for traffic, and Connie got a good look at him. As he jogged across the street, she felt a lurch inside her chest and knew that something had just happened.

"Maybe this is the one . . ." she murmured.

"The one for what?"

She turned, smiling widely to her roommate.

"I . . . I don't know . . . maybe he's the one I've been waiting for . . ."

"Oh, don't be silly! Come on, let's get the cookies out of the oven . . ."

These three cadets were part of a West Point Literary Society. They had managed to wangle a weekend in New York in order to see *Royal Hunt of the Sun*, a play about Spanish soldiers and Incas, downtown on Saturday night, to which they would take their dates. And although Connie had a theoretical date with another cadet, as soon as he came into the apartment and they formally met, she and Art had eyes for no one else. During the postplay dinner at Mamma Leone's restaurant, they sat across the table from each other and talked animatedly, ignoring everyone else. Then when he was finally ready to take his much-ignored date home after dinner, Art insisted that Connie come along, or else he'd never find his way back. And once they were alone, they sat together in the front seat, parked somewhere in Brooklyn, and dumped their lives out into each other's laps.

Art was from South Carolina, and while he had been a superstar in all high-school sports, he found that he was only good enough to play baseball at West Point. But he was a legend in the advanced French classes, he loved Shakespeare, and he wanted to write. And as if that wasn't enough, he was also terribly gracious, the true southern gentleman.

Connie was hesitant at first, but was soon caught up by Art's open encouragement and spread her wings. A small-town girl, she had found few doors open to her, a woman come of age in the sixties. She had never wanted to teach, so she chose nursing—and there was little else in the way of professional opportunities for females at the time. But once she got her nursing degree and started working, she saw herself slipping into a rut. She yearned desperately to see the world outside West Virginia, and American Airlines beckoned. So off she flew.

The next weekend, Art invited Connie up to West Point. On a sun-splashed Saturday afternoon, he took her down Flirtation Walk, the only place on post where cadets can avoid observation by officers. A pathway along the river that wound through the boulder-studded woods, Flirty was a protected cadet reserve. Halfway down the mile-long path, there is an overhanging rock known as "Kissing Rock." If a cadet and his date walk under it, the legend goes, and they don't kiss, West Point will crumble into the Hudson River. Connie was eager for Art to finally kiss her, and under Kissing Rock, they embraced for the first time. But to her amazement, when she closed her eyes and their lips first met, Connie's head was suddenly filled with the booming and hammering of massive brass church bells.

The third weekend, Art almost casually told her he knew that, one day, they would marry. Connie wanted to protest, to pull back for air. But feeling herself falling heavily, she didn't even know what to say. So she sputtered, laughed, and said nothing.

In those days of expensive long-distance phone calls, they spoke on every Wednesday and Sunday night, and Connie became a regular weekend visitor to West Point. Soon enough, Art and she were swearing their undying love, and then she was wearing Art's class pin. On her West Point visits, she saved on hotel bills by staying in the home of Colonel and Mrs. Andrew and Billie Armstrong, who took on the role of unofficial foster parents.

And they talked more and more about marriage. Art told her that he wanted to go to Vietnam as a young lieutenant, and although he was very confident he would return unscathed, there was a statistical possibility he was wrong. And given that possibility, however slight, he thought it might be better for them both if they waited until his return. He had told her that there had been other women in his life, but he had never felt this way before. He wanted everything to be right between them, and he would not sleep with her until they were married, which Connie thought was reasonable enough. But it didn't stop there—Art didn't even want to get formally engaged until after he returned from Vietnam. Just on the off chance that he wouldn't make it, he said, he didn't want to wreck her whole life.

Connie felt a sudden and enormous impatience. She felt that this was their one chance, and they had to take it. It would be wrong, she knew, utterly wrong, to simply tempt fate and await his return, to make sure everything was safe before taking on this one great challenge and casting themselves together into the mad rush of love and life.

Art seemed serene while Connie grew anxious. As June Week and graduation approached, she confided in Billie Armstrong, who smiled in her motherly way.

"Don't worry, dear. He's so brave about doing the right thing by waiting, and that's good. But just give him thirty days alone after graduation. He'll come around."

Graduation was June 8, and Connie stayed for the four days of ceremony. Art was among 579 cadets to graduate from West Point in 1966, out of the 808 New Cadets who had been sworn in way back in July 1962. It had been a long, harrowing ride, but we had finally arrived. Yes, I was also one of those 579. Virtually all of our class was to serve in Vietnam, where twenty-eight of us would die and hundreds more be wounded. But on the day we pinned on those second lieutenant gold bars, we were ebullient, wild in celebration, our joy at having passed through this most difficult trial by fire beyond restraint. We saw no clouds in the sky of the bright future that beckoned us.

After June Week, Connie went back to New York to fly, while Art went home to South Carolina. And sure enough, just as Billie Armstrong had predicted, within weeks he was reassessing his marriage plans in letters and on the phone.

Art's first duty station was at Fort Bragg, North Carolina, with the 82nd Airborne Division. He went off to Ranger and paratrooper schools for three months, and as soon as that was over, he bought a West Point miniature engagement ring, which he gave her in December 1966. They married on March 4, 1967, and Arthur Middleton Parker IV, or "Chip," was born to Art and Connie Parker on November 26, exactly thirty-six weeks after their wedding night.

But duty called. Eight days after Chip's birth, Art and Connie and Chip packed up and went to West Virginia, where mother and child would stay with her parents while Art was gone. At the airport, Art made a special plea to her father, King Leighliter.

"Take good care of them for me, will you, King? They're going to need you."

A last kiss and hug, then Art turned and waved before entering the airplane, that magical smile drifting across his lips. As she raised her hand, Connie's heart lodged in her throat. Somehow, she knew she would never see him alive again.

Sending mail back to the States from Vietnam was a snap: No stamps were needed, and all the writer had to do was write "free" in the envelope corner where stamps normally went. But in order to write, soldiers had to have the time and the paper, pen, and envelope, which wasn't always easy. Even so, Connie and Chip got lots of letters from Art. He was an advisor to a South Vietnamese airborne battalion, an elite unit that was only sent into the toughest fighting, usually on some sort of special mission.

On January 16, Art wrote, "Time is beginning to go by fast. I long for you, Connie, to hold my son and pat our dog Demetrius. But this war is so big and important that I can't help but feel as if this is where I belong now."

At first, Art was near Saigon, the capital of what was then the independent nation of the Republic of Vietnam, or "South Vietnam," whose freedom from communist domination the U.S. armed forces were trying to defend. While he was caught up in quite a bit of combat action there, in March his battalion was moved to a region several hundred miles north, off to the west of the port city of Hue. They were there to operate against North Vietnamese regulars in conjunction with the American 101st Airborne Division.

At the time, it happened that I was an infantry platoon leader with the 101st. In May 1968, Art took an afternoon to visit the rear area of the 101st to try to see various Army officer friends he had known at Fort Bragg. Art and I had been in the same battalion of the 82nd Airborne at Fort Bragg before Vietnam, and we had been good friends before that during four years at West Point, where we were classmates. Art stopped by my battalion rear to see me, but I was out in the field on an operation when he came by. But Art wrote me a brief note, which was taken out to me on the resupply chopper a few days later. When I finally got it, we were heavily caught up in killing and bleeding and dying, eating food out of tin cans, wearing the same shirt and pants, unwashed, unshaven for weeks on end, sleeping on the ground like animals. Art's note was a welcome reminder of good times from an old and dear friend, and I truly cherished it.

But more important to Art were his wife and son. He wrote them often, and his thoughts and words from one letter in particular, which Connie has shared with me, are worth quoting here:

> I am sure I will be back in your arms soon enough, my love, but we both know I am facing some risk, and so I must say something to you. If anything happens to me and I don't come home, I want most of all for you and Chip to be happy. I truly hope and pray that you will learn to love another man as fully as we now love each other, and that you will marry him. Raise our son Chip to be the wonderful man he can be. But I want you to always remember how much we love each other right now. Nothing can ever change that. Go outside at night and look up at the stars. I will always be right there, watching you, protecting you, holding you, loving you. We have reached the summit in life and love, you and I, and we have rejoiced. There is nothing better. My body may go, but I believe our bond will live always. . . .
>
> My love, my life, words cannot express how I feel for you, admire you, love you, want you, need you. The fact that we have made a baby has to be the greatest thing in either of our lives. I now feel that we have reached a point in life of such happiness that to go higher is impossible. Can any two people ever have loved as we do?

I must go now. Take care. With all my heart I
love you.

Art

I came out of the field in early June 1968. I was to be
promoted to captain in a few days, and as I was cleaning
my rifle inside a tent, my old roommate from senior year
at West Point, Mac Hayes, came in. Mac was a lieutenant
in the same battalion, and he was going out to the field the
next day to take command of another company. But he had
some grim news.

"Did you hear that Art Parker was killed a couple weeks
ago, while you were in the field?"

I was stunned.

"What?"

"Yeah. Good old Art."

"What . . . what happened?"

"He was out in the field as an advisor to the Vietnamese
airborne, they were working right next to us, lots of contact with the NVA. They hadn't been able to get any resupply for about three days, and they were loading wounded
into the first ships when they finally got in, but they were
still under fire."

"And he got hit?"

"No, it was really strange. There were only a few
Americans on the ground, and I got told this by a guy who
heard it from one of the helicopter pilots. Their LZ was on
a slope, and twenty or thirty feet in front of Art, two
Vietnamese soldiers were walking up the hill. Art could
see a helicopter moving sideways toward them, and it was
obvious the blade was going to cut them in half from
behind. There was too much noise to yell, so he ran a couple steps and dove at them, hit them in the back, and

knocked them both down. But when he did that, apparently the blade just nicked his helmet, and he went down."

"Was that all, just one nick . . . ?"

"Yeah, but that's all it took. They got him onto one of the helicopters, and they flew him out to a hospital ship just off the coast. But he never regained consciousness, and two days later, he died."

I was shaken. Mac reached his arm around my shoulder and squeezed.

"Sorry, Tom. Art was a great guy . . ."

Then Mac was gone. I walked outside the tent and wandered around in a bit of a daze. Poor Art. Poor Connie. And they just had a baby, didn't they? Dust or smoke or something in the air brought tears, and I avoided human contact for a while. Poor Art. . . .

Chapter 1:

Foundation and Eleazar Derby Wood, the First West Point Warrior

AS SAD AS ART PARKER'S DEATH WAS, his is one of many similar stories of West Point graduates who did exactly what they were educated and trained to do—risk their lives in combat for "Duty, Honor, Country." For two hundred years, the military academy at West Point has developed these West Point Warriors, people who bravely defend America at any cost to themselves.

During the Revolutionary War, a great need was felt on the American side for trained, competent military figures. Since there were no formal schools dedicated to military studies on this side of the Atlantic, and there had been only limited opportunities for men born in this country to experience combat, generally under British colors, there was a great shortage of military expertise in the new Continental Army.

The lack of home-grown military ability was felt during the war, of course. To American revolutionary leaders, it seemed that courage was both more desirable and more readily available than technical knowledge among the unschooled masses for filling out infantry and cavalry units. That much was true, but, as they were to learn the hard way, technical knowledge was absolutely essential in the more complex military fields of engineering and artillery. There, specific technical skills and abilities were required of both officers and men for the operations of any effective field army. The presence of European military experts who filled key roles in American ranks, men like Steuben and Kosciusko and Lafayette, made the need all the more apparent.

Late in 1775, Washington made the immense Henry Knox, then twenty-six years old and nearly three hundred pounds in weight, his chief of artillery. Self-educated in the military field, Knox led a hazardous expedition to Fort Ticonderoga, New York, during the first winter and returned with valuable ordnance taken from the British by Ethan Allen and Benedict Arnold. Knox fought in many battles around New York City, and once peace was signed, served as Washington's first secretary of war.

Knox made the establishment of an American military academy a key issue, which he pressed on virtually everyone he knew. In 1783, Washington took up the cry, calling for "academies, one or more, for the instruction of the art military." Washington declared, "I cannot conclude without repeating the necessity of the proposed Institution, unless we intend to let the Science [of war] become extinct, and to depend entirely upon the Foreigners for their friendly aid."

Nothing came of this, though many prominent Americans agreed with Washington's conception. Finally, in 1799, Alexander Hamilton gave a detailed plan for an academy to Secretary of War James McHenry, and sent a copy to Washington. In the last letter he ever wrote, on December 1, 1799, two days before his death, Washington told Hamilton the establishment of such an institution "has ever been considered by me as an object of primary importance to this country," and said he hoped Hamilton's arguments would "prevail upon the Legislature to place it on a permanent and respectable footing."

In January 1800, President John Adams presented Hamilton's basic plan to Congress. They deliberated and did nothing, as Congresses sometimes do. Finally, Thomas Jefferson acted in May 1801, when he had the Army begin preparations for the establishment of a military academy at West Point, New York. In March 1802, Congress finally passed legislation establishing both a corps of engineers and a military academy at West Point.

One perhaps confusing aspect of Jefferson's support for a military academy is that it seems to conflict with the antimilitary stance of the Republican party, of which he was the national leader. The best explanation from those historians who have addressed the issue is that they have found Jefferson's position on a national military academy to be an extension of his support for a national university that emphasized the study of science. But such evasive explanations are really not satisfactory.

One twelve-month period—between the fall of 1791 and the fall of 1792—saw the emergence of truly partisan politics in the United States, with an "opposition" party challenging the one in power. The precipitant event or series of events for this was the growing influence of the Treasury over the policy of the government, of Hamilton's industrial vision and plan for national development, and the virulent opposition to these held by Jefferson and Madison. The final division was a function of the French Revolution and the resulting wars that raged through Europe. The political sentiments of the entire nation were divided into the first two major American political parties: the Republicans, who supported the French and their revolution, opposed by the incumbent Federalists, who strongly opposed them and favored the British aristocratic model.

In political shorthand, the Republicans sought a truly democratic form of government that reflected the will of the people, the government for which the Revolutionary War had been fought, while the Federalists believed in entrusting all political and economic power to the competence and good will of an aristocracy based on wealth and family connections.

And these political feelings were passionately held: the adherents of either party refused to admit the legitimacy of the other, and the constant threat of internal strife loomed menacingly.

In 1798, the possibility of American involvement in a European war grew, and the incumbent Federalists used political fears to their advantage by, among other things, expanding the military. Republicans feared that this larger army would be used by the Federalists primarily to silence their political opposition. Indeed, Army troops did crack heads and smash the presses of Republican newspapers. When the Federalists were able to pass the Alien and Sedition Acts, Republican fears seemed justified. The election of Jefferson in 1800, however, ended the immediate crisis, and he went right to work trying to realize the Republican goal of reducing the size and potential threat to freedom of the enlarged Army.

As related in Theodore Crackel's *Mr. Jefferson's Army*, Jefferson's initial reduction of the size of the standing army was brought about by the Military Peace Establishment Act of 1802. This was widely portrayed as an economy measure, but Crackel shows us that such a description was little more than a political ruse, for it was really much more.

Jefferson was able to dramatically change the political coloring of the officer corps of the Army during his tenure in office. Before he was elected, the Army numbered over 5,000 men; under the provisions of the Military Peace Establishment Act of 1802, Jefferson reduced the number to 3,289. But by the end of his term, in 1809, the number had risen again to nearly 9,000 men.

At the outset of his presidency, more than 90 percent of the officers in the Army were Federalist political opponents of Jefferson. As a result of his careful reorganization of the Army's officer corps so as to discharge his hidebound political enemies, convert the less zealous to his cause, and infuse the force with the fresh blood of his loyalists, by 1809 the numbers had reversed, so that more than 90 percent of the officers were then his solid political supporters.

Jefferson saw a military academy at West Point as a very powerful tool by which he could train and then commission as officers of his army the sons of loyal Republicans. In his eyes, it was a key agency through which he could help politically reform the Army from within. So West Point was born as part of Jefferson's successful effort to establish democracy in America.

In his attempt to establish a military academy that would train politically selected young men from across the nation, Jefferson was taking bold steps, and early success should not have been expected. Indeed, for the first fifteen years of its existence, the structural, political, and organizational problems confronted by the new military academy caused it to be of only minimal value to the leadership of the army it was intended to serve.

After Alexander Hamilton's death in 1804, Federalist political power began to fade, but it was their opposition to the War of 1812 that did the first really mortal damage to the party. The year 1815 brought the formal end of the War of 1812 and the effective end of the Napoleonic Wars in Europe. In the same year, Jefferson's Republican successor, President James Madison, called for adequate military and naval forces in peacetime, direct taxation, and a national bank—things the Republican party had previously loudly opposed. But by this time, the Republicans no longer feared that the Federalists, whose national political power had faded badly, posed a genuine threat to individual freedoms, and the personal political inclinations of army officers were no longer the central issue to the nation's leadership that they had been.

In its earliest days, West Point was not well organized, and the quality of its graduates and the value of their service to America's early army varied. One graduate, however, performed splendidly during the War of 1812 and even became a national hero at a time when heroism gave much-needed reassurance to the American people.

His name was Eleazar Derby Wood. Born in 1783, he was twenty-one when he entered West Point, and studied for only eighteen months before graduating with the class of 1806. His initial assignment was with the Corps of Engineers working on harbor defenses on Governor's Island in New York Harbor. He would later do similar work at New London, Connecticut, and Norfolk, Virginia, and he was a captain when war broke out with England in 1812. He felt that the United States had suffered great harm from the British and felt that military action was warranted. In a letter to his sister, he said:

> The period has now arrived when I am to be tested as a soldier. If I prove to be one and fortunate,

it will no doubt be extremely pleasing and gratifying to all. If I shall fall in the present conflict, you must not grieve nor mourn, but rejoice that you have a brother to lose for the maintenance and preservation of those sacred rights for which our Revolutionary Patriots bled and fell.

When he joined the staff of Major General William Henry Harrison's Northwestern Army, he was put in charge of the construction of two forts that would prove to be of crucial importance. The first of these, Fort Meigs, was to be built on the Maumee River near Toledo, Ohio. The second, Fort Stephenson, had been built near Fremont, Ohio, on the Sandusky River in 1812. But after the fall of Detroit, it had been abandoned to the Indians, who largely destroyed it. Wood's mission was to rebuild it into a defensible condition.

Work on Fort Meigs began in February 1813, when Wood had his troops build a palisaded fortress using logs that covered some eight acres. As part of the construction, Fort Meigs had seven blockhouses along the wall and positions for five artillery batteries. Construction was nearly complete in March when Wood left to begin work on Fort Stephenson. This was a much smaller fort, and it took only a matter of weeks to repair its defenses. By the middle of April, Wood was back at Fort Meigs to oversee the finishing touches.

And he was none too soon, for in the final days of April, British troops were seen on the opposite side of the river. A British artillery barrage opened up on May 1. The American artillery commander was killed by enemy fire, and Wood was appointed to take command of the artillery as an added duty. But the structure of the fort held, and on

May 4, Kentucky militia under General Clay arrived to raise the siege.

The British force, commanded by a General Procter, returned on July 21. This time, it was more than twice the size of the original besieging force. The siege again lasted only four days, and it was no more successful than it had been the last time. On July 25, the British withdrew again. Procter marched his force to Fort Stephenson, which he attacked on August 2, with both artillery and an infantry attack by the 41st Welsh Regiment. The Americans were well protected, however. The combination of artillery and small-arms fire that poured out of Fort Stephenson was devastating to British forces, and the attack of the 41st Welsh failed completely. American forces had very few losses, and this was the third attack by British forces on a fortification built by Captain Wood that had failed.

At the time, military prowess of this sort was awarded not by medals but by brevet promotion. Captain Wood became Brevet Major Wood, and he did much of the planning required for General Harrison's planned attack to retake Detroit. They would there be attacking General Procter and a British force consisting of the 41st Welsh, hundreds of Canadian militia, and thousands of Indians led by Chief Tecumseh.

Wood developed a complex plan that called for the Kentucky militia who were mounted to move north on horseback against Detroit. Meanwhile, Harrison's main force would move by boat between a chain of islands and the west shore of Lake Erie to attack Fort Malden at the mouth of the Detroit River. For this attack, the commander of Harrison's artillery force would be Major Wood. This was a very complicated plan for such a young army, and the British navy had a squadron of warships loose on Lake

Erie. But on September 10, Commodore Oliver Hazard Perry defeated them, clearing the way for Harrison's amphibious attack.

And the amphibious assault went off perfectly. But when they got there, General Procter had left nothing but ashes of the fort behind. Harrison immediately set off in pursuit of him, taking only the Kentucky militia and the artillery force under Wood. They caught up with Procter and Tecumseh along the banks of the Thames River, where they fought a major battle. Tecumseh was killed and his Indian force dissolved, the 41st Welsh was destroyed as an effective fighting force, and General Procter fled the field of battle in great haste. Harrison's victory was complete. Wood commanded the cavalry force that pursued Procter, whom they narrowly missed capturing, although they did take his carriage filled with personal papers and other possessions.

Wood next moved to the Niagara front, where he helped expand and strengthen Fort Erie. He commanded an artillery section at the Battle of Chippewa on July 5, 1814, and at the Battle of Lundy's Lane on July 25, General Brown paid him the highest compliments and promoted him to brevet lieutenant colonel.

After Lundy's Lane, American forces in the region withdrew to the protection of Fort Erie. Wood was given command of a battalion-sized defensive force, which repelled the attack of a British brigade, three or four times its numerical size, on August 15. But the British siege endured. Wood was one of those counseling a sortie to attack British forces, and on September 17, he commanded an American column that did just that. And although the sortie was successful in destroying British artillery pieces and ammunition and capturing prisoners, Wood was separated from his command, badly wounded, and captured.

A Canadian physician who was assisting the British army, a Doctor Dunlop, came upon Wood as he was being carried by a group of British soldiers. He was bleeding badly, and when Doctor Dunlop offered to dress his wound, Wood told him, "Doctor, it's all in vain—my wound is mortal, and no human skill can help me—leave me here with a canteen of water near me, and save yourself."

General Porter wrote that Wood's behavior during the sortie was "an exhibition of military skill, acute judgment, and heroic valor." General Brown said he was a man who, "brave, generous, and enterprising, died as he had lived, without a feeling but for the honour of his country and the glory of her arms. His name and example will live to guide the soldier in the path of duty so long as true heroism is held in estimation." His peers felt he deserved a lasting memorial, and a monument was erected at West Point in 1816. But even this didn't seem to quite measure up as a lasting tribute to the first widely renowned American hero of the War of 1812. And then the right opportunity came along: an eleven-pointed star fortification was just being finished on Bledsoe's Island in New York Harbor, and it was named Fort Wood in his honor. Most Americans thought this a fitting final tribute.

And it was. In 1885, the granite walls of the fort were filled in, and it became the base for the recent gift to America from France, the Statue of Liberty.

Chapter 2:

Sylvanus Thayer, the Father of the United States Military Academy

AFTER THE WAR OF 1812, national military preparedness for war was an important subject of governmental attention, and the new military academy at West Point became the beneficiary of renewed political concern.

The most important influence on West Point during its early days was Sylvanus Thayer, who spent four years at Dartmouth and graduated from there in 1807, then took only one year to graduate from West Point in 1808. He was immediately recognized by his superiors in the army as a rising star and was brevetted for gallantry in action at Craney Island during the War of 1812. Thayer was sent to France, where he studied and collected materials at the prestigious École Polytechnique.

Oxford and Cambridge at the time educated their students primarily in Greek, Latin, and moral philosophy, preparing their graduates to become preachers or politicians. Harvard, Yale, Princeton, and William and Mary had followed this tradition, but formal education in the sciences was sorely lacking in the United States. Thayer was sent to France primarily to accumulate the best materials and experience available in military and engineering fields, so that these might be applied in his new post and so dramatically raise the quality of the U.S. Military Academy.

The new (1794) École Polytechnique had a rigid curriculum based on mathematics and science applied with rigor and uniformity. And it was effective: the École Polytechnique produced France's best engineers, mathematicians, government administrators, and military officers. After the better part of a year of study there, Thayer returned to the United States and assumed his new post as superintendent of West Point in 1817.

Thayer immediately established at the Academy new standards of rigid discipline as well as a new system of education. He set up the Academic Board, which consisted of the heads of the various academic departments, and together they established a rigorous four-year curriculum that focused primarily on engineering, but also included chemistry, physics, history, geography, law, and ethics. The academic "weeding out" of the less competent began right away. Freshmen (members of the Fourth Class, or "plebes") and sophomores (Third Class) were given heavy doses of straight mathematics, an important base they would need for courses in physics and engineering they would take in their junior (Second Class) and senior (First Class) years.

One of Thayer's key academic innovations was small classroom sections of perhaps a dozen cadets per teacher, with each cadet required to recite part of the day's assigned lesson and receive a grade for that recitation on every day on which class was held—an almost sacrosanct tradition that endures to the present in some subject areas. He also set up a constantly updated ranking, by academic grades, in each of the four year-group "classes" at the Academy at any given time, with praise and other plums passed out to those at the top of the heap.

Cadets wore uniforms at all times, and civilian dress or other possessions were simply not allowed at West Point, a tradition that endured until late in the twentieth century. Because they lived in a closed world in which they took the same classes, marched together, ate together, studied together, and did little else, a strong mutual dependence grew up among the Corps of Cadets. While there was not to be a formal written honor code until after World War I, all cadets understood that they were expected to act honorably and comport themselves as officers and gentlemen. And, for the most part, they did. In the monastic academic tradition they inherited from our British and European forebears, the rewards for a celibate academic life were to be found in the mind and the spirit, not in "things," money, or possessions. Under Thayer, they were embarking on an almost holy mission of serving their nation as soldiers. It was a vocation most took very seriously, and the ceremony of commissioning after four years was seen as a form of consecration. That was partly a function of the heavily religious nature of American society during the nineteenth century, but in that isolated fortress, it is an attitude that has endured.

Thayer dramatically changed both West Point as an institution and the quality of the education of its graduates. He was to remain the superintendent until 1833, when President Andrew Jackson's personal displeasure with him brought about his resignation. But parts of both his disciplinary and educational systems remain in place at West Point to this very day, where he is still revered as the "Father of the Military Academy."

Chapter 3:

The Mexican-American War— Robert E. Lee and Ulysses S. Grant

IN APRIL 1846, PRESIDENT JAMES K. POLK baited the Mexican army into crossing the Rio Grande and killing or capturing American troops, thus justifying his "defensive" war in response. It later became clear that Polk had decided on war with Mexico when that country refused to sell California and New Mexico. The ruse over the Texas border was intended to produce a Mexican attack on American forces, an attack that would justify a declaration of war in retaliation. Polk was certain the U.S. Army would handle the war with ease and would provide the opportunity for him to force Mexico into the sale of California under pressure brought by force of arms.

There were a few bloody battles fought in Mexico, and the U.S. Army won them all. The eventual peace treaty in February 1848 ceded not only what is today California, but also Utah, Nevada, and parts of Texas, New Mexico, Arizona, Colorado, and Wyoming, all for $15 million and unpaid claims—much less than Polk had been willing to pay in 1846.

West Point had not yet established itself in the upper ranks of the Army, and it had produced none of the generals in this war. But many young graduates served as junior officers, and nearly all the West Pointers who would rise to high command on both sides in the American Civil War were blooded here: Robert E. Lee, Ulysses S. Grant, George B. McClellan, Jefferson Davis, and many more—their names and feats on other days would one day ring loud and help to spread the fame of West Point around the world.

When the Mexican-American War erupted in 1846, American forces were commanded by General Winfield Scott, who was not himself a West Point graduate. In the war, however, he became a fervent supporter of the Academy and its graduates, particularly the skill and valor of the younger officers. His quotation to that effect after the war is famous, and was apparently well-earned:

> I give it as my fixed opinion that but for our graduated cadets the war between the United States and Mexico might, and probably would, have lasted some four or five years, with, in its first half, more defeats than victories falling to our share, whereas in two campaigns we conquered a great country and a peace without the loss of a single battle or skirmish.

Probably Scott's favorite young West Pointer, the man who, more than any other, helped him win that war, was Robert E. Lee. The son by a second wife of Revolutionary War hero "Light Horse Harry" Lee, his childhood was somewhat slighted because of his father's inability to manage his finances. But he received an appointment to West Point, and in 1825 was sworn in as a cadet. And he was exceptional. During his senior year, he was chosen to fill the highest cadet post of "corps adjutant," which was awarded to the cadet who showed the finest military bearing, held a high conduct record, and had registered the best performance on the drill field. When he received his diploma in June 1829, he was ranked second academically among forty-six classmates, and he graduated without having received a single demerit during his four years at West Point. Truly, Lee was a superb example of an ideal West Point cadet and graduate.

A few years later, he married Mary Custis, his childhood friend and true love. Mary happened to be the great-granddaughter of Martha Washington and the only child of a wealthy Virginia plantation owner, and her wealth was not to become an inconvenience to the son of a financial incompetent. Lee spent the next dozen years building fortifications across the entire nation—Georgia, Mississippi, Illinois, the Carolinas. Lee was a good engineer, and his skill was recognized. Then in August 1846, Captain Lee finally received orders to report for duty in the Mexican War.

Lee was to spend twenty months in Mexico. Although he was a very junior officer as a captain, his performance of engineering duties was so exemplary that he soon was called to join the staff of General Winfield Scott, the American commander. In that role, those above him—majors, lieutenant colonels, colonels, and generals—were in awe of his intelligence and his abilities. He was thus able to advise and guide the hand of General Scott, the commander in two major operations.

When the war started, three American columns invaded Mexico. The first, under General Taylor, moved south from Corpus Christi to Matamoros, then west toward Monterrey. The second, under General Wool, moved south from San Antonio toward Monterrey. The third, under General Kearney, moved southwest from Kansas to Santa Fe, then west to San Diego.

Captain Lee was initially with General Wool, but saw little action. In 1847, he was assigned to join General Scott in a new expedition that would eventually take the national capital of Mexico City. On March 9, Scott's men began to land and besiege the fortress city of Vera Cruz. Captain Lee played an important role in placing siege artillery, and on March 27, Vera Cruz capitulated.

Scott's troops took a while to reorganize, but then they headed up the narrow road to Mexico City. But on April 12, after having moved only thirty miles, they drew fire from Mexican guns covering a pass near the town of Cerro Gordo. Scott had fewer than nine thousand American soldiers, and he was facing an army of twelve thousand Mexicans under Santa Ana in strong defensive positions.

The American drive stalled, but not for long. Captain Lee went on a personal reconnaissance and found a way around the Mexican flank, across ground Santa Ana had thought impassable. Lee was able to lead American forces through forest and heavy brush, and they were even able to cross several deep ravines, lowering the guns by rope and then hoisting them up the far side. It was difficult work, but by April 17, the Americans had artillery atop a hill on one flank of the Mexican force. When the battle opened on April 19, the Mexicans broke and fled after losing more than a thousand men. Scott's casualties were 417, of whom only 64 were dead.

The Americans continued toward Mexico City, but were delayed for political negotiations that turned out to be a ruse by Santa Ana, who was just seeking a respite. Finally, American forces found themselves only a dozen miles from Mexico City, but confronting two strong Mexican fortresses between lakes and behind a fifteen-mile-wide lava bed known as the Pedregal and considered impassable.

The key seemed to be to find a way to take or bypass the seemingly impregnable Mexican defenses at San Augustin and San Antonio, two major fortresses on the road to Mexico City. Lee was assigned that mission by General Scott, and he conducted personal, high-risk reconnaissance, both by day and by night, deep into territory held by Mexican forces. He several times had to quickly conceal himself when Mexican sentries and other soldiers came within a few feet of him at night. But he stayed hidden until they had left, then returned to American lines with plans to flank Mexican forces by surprise attacks.

Orders for the attacks followed, and Lee was with the troops as they confronted the obstacles he had warned of, such as ravines, canals, and the nearly impassable broken ground of the Pedregal. Lee showed them how to continue their advance, and during the night, while American soldiers rested, he twice crossed the two-mile-wide stretch of the Pedregal on foot. He did this to keep General Scott informed of the progress of his forces, and Lee was back with the infantry when they finally launched their flanking attacks on Mexican positions the following morning.

These attacks stormed and took the Mexican positions and utterly routed the Mexican army. Suddenly, the Americans found themselves at the very gates of Mexico City. After the fact, every general in the American force had the highest praise for Lee, and he was brevetted to the rank of lieutenant colonel for his performance. In his battle report, General Scott made the following special mention:

I am compelled to make special mention of Captain R. E. Lee, Engineer. This officer was again indefatigable during the operations in reconnaissances as daring as laborious, and of the utmost value. Nor was he less conspicuous in placing batteries and in conducting columns to their stations under the heavy fire of the enemy.

In later testimony, General Scott would call Captain Lee's actions on the way to Mexico City "the greatest feat of physical and moral courage performed by any individual, in my knowledge, pending the campaign."

Santa Ana commanded Mexican forces inside the city of around fifteen thousand men, while Scott was down to around eight thousand American soldiers. But one last Mexican defensive position outside the city walls was the castle atop the steep-sided heights of Chapultepec where eight hundred Mexican soldiers resolutely awaited the American attack.

After a heavy artillery barrage early on the morning of September 13, a three-pronged American attack went across the causeways and up the steep sides of Chapultepec. Captain Lee again was at the front, although this time he was wounded and soon had to retire because of loss of blood. General Scott spoke of him again in his dispatches, saying, "Captain Lee, so constantly distinguished, also bore important orders from me (September 13) until he fainted from a wound and the loss of two nights' sleep at the batteries." But Chapultepec soon fell, and then Americans moved toward the city gates.

And now it was time for a young infantry officer serving as a quartermaster, a man fourteen years junior to Captain Lee, to show his talents: Ulysses S. Grant.

From the earliest days of the war, Grant had relished being near the front. At the battle of Palo Alto, the first major battle of the Mexican-American War, Grant was an infantry company commander, a rapt witness of a smashing victory won by the superior American artillery. Although the Americans were outnumbered, they were able to get off some 3,000 rounds of artillery fire to the Mexicans' 750. And while American fire had smashed through the ordered ranks of Mexican soldiers, Mexican cannonballs often bounced toward them, allowing American soldiers to easily step out of the way.

And Grant had been wounded. As he sat on his horse one day, he was struck in the right shoulder by an enemy rifle bullet without any warning. The bullet went across his back, just below the skin, and exited from the other shoulder. But cowardice in the face of the enemy was so greatly reviled at home, and the fear of being marked a coward so great among soldiers, that Grant went to elaborate lengths to explain to family and friends how he had been shot in the back without running from enemy fire. Fortunately, the wound healed quickly enough without infection, and it was soon forgotten.

Then Grant had been named a temporary quartermaster, and later, to his great distress, the appointment as quartermaster had been made permanent. He began to realize that he would never get the chance to show not only his daring and courage, but also his ability to think quickly under pressure and find a way to win. But then, against all odds, perhaps that opportunity had come at last.

As Garland's brigade moved toward the San Cosme gate, Lieutenant Ulysses S. Grant was well out in front. They were moving down a double carriage road, divided in the center by an aqueduct. Grant and a dozen of his soldiers would dart in and out of the ten-foot-high arches that supported the water flowing above their heads, always taking cover from the fire of retreating Mexican forces, but relentless in their pursuit. Finally, the Mexicans massed behind a barricade at an intersection of the road. They had cannon mounted there, and their fire turned heavy.

While a few other junior American officers were content to await the arrival of their own artillery, Grant knew that the attack had to be pressed. He darted across the road and down the left side of the causeway, hiding behind houses, walls, and underbrush. Soon enough, he got completely past the barricade, and he found a way to come around it and fire from the rear on the Mexicans defending it.

He raced back to the groups of officers he had just left and explained what he had found. If he could get a dozen or so volunteers to go back with him, he explained, they could fire on the barricade from the rear while the rest of them rushed it from the front.

He was soon racing back with his volunteers following him, and just as they got beyond the barricade, they ran into a hundred infantry sent up by his brigade commander to try to make a flanking attack. This group was led by a captain, but when Grant explained his plan, he was given command of the entire force. He swiftly led them around the right flank of the barricade, and they burst on the surprised Mexicans even as the rest of the Americans attacked from the front.

The Mexicans ran like rabbits, with the Americans in hot pursuit. Grant was running at the front when they got to within a few hundred yards of the main gate at San Cosme. The Mexicans suddenly darted off to both sides of the road, and the Americans saw the black mouths of two big cannon pointed at them. Most of them got off the road as well before they fired, but then it was obvious that they could go no farther without cannon of their own. But where to place them?

Again, all the other American junior officers were content to await the arrival of a higher-ranking officer who could decide what to do next. But not Grant, who immediately raced off looking for a way to flank the Mexican guns in the gate. Finally, he got a mountain howitzer and some ammunition and a crew to serve it. They raced up a hill atop which Grant saw the steeple of a church protruding from the trees. He knocked on the door, and an old priest opened it. After Grant made a few attempts to ask politely for entry in the face of the priest's obvious resistance, Grant and his men simply pushed their way in and carried the gun up into the steeple. Once there, they mounted it facing down on the gate below, which they began to plaster.

More American guns were opening up back at the first barricade, where General Werth had arrived, but they were not terribly effective. Watching through binoculars, Werth saw the great destruction being done to the Mexican position, and then saw that there was a cannon on the steeple of a church. He asked who the gun belonged to and no one knew. Finally, he sent a captain to the church, and he brought Grant back to Werth. After the general had congratulated him he assigned another gun and its crew to go back with Grant to the church and add its fire from the steeple. Grant knew there was no room for a second gun, but he was only a second lieutenant, and he dared not counter a general. So he bit his tongue and took the gun back with him. He didn't even take it into the church, and eventually it was set up on the roof of a house. Its fire was not as effective from there as that of the gun in the steeple, but he was sort of following orders, and the general would never understand anyway.

Eventually, the fire from Grant's gun and the other American guns that had come up destroyed the Mexican defenses. American infantry took the gate at San Cosme and another as well, and they worked through the night expanding their toehold inside the city. By the next day, the Mexicans had had enough, and they formally surrendered.

Until this war, West Point had been known primarily because it was the only formal engineering school in the nation. But after our victory in Mexico, its graduates had established themselves in the national consciousness as smart, competent, and victorious military leaders, and a new image of the Academy began to emerge. West Point was not only the source of the engineers who built the railroads and bridges and canals and highways and ports, but also the crucially important source of military training for the officer corps that would lead American citizen-soldiers in war—which had been its initial purpose and justification.

Chapter 4:

The Civil War—
John Pelham and Patrick Henry O'Rorke

AFTER THE ATTACK ON FORT SUMTER, the Southern exodus really started, and by May, 1861, 65 of the 86 Southerners at West Point, out of a total of 278 cadets, had resigned. Superintendent Alexander H. Bowman was convinced that the other 21 were waiting for their states to secede, at which time they would resign, so he forced all cadets to sign an oath of allegiance. All 21 signed.

But unrest continued as the so-called "border states" hung in the balance. In August, Bowman required all cadets to sign a stronger oath that contained the words "that I will maintain and defend the sovereignty of the United States, paramount to any and all allegiance, sovereignty or fealty I may owe to any State, county or country whatsoever." Two Kentucky men refused to take the oath and were dismissed. One of these was a plebe, John C. Singleton. After he returned home, he joined the Union army and was later killed in action.

On May 6, 1861, the First Class was ordered to Washington, D.C., and later received their commissions without graduation ceremonies. These men were educated for five years according to the prolongation of Academy training that had begun in 1854, and would be known thereafter as the class of May 1861. Because of the flood of recruiting then going on and the need for officers to train them, the new First Class, the class of 1862, was commissioned on June 24, after only four years, and would be known as the class of June 1861. On June 27, the next class—the class of 1863—was warned to prepare for graduation, but a few days later, cooler heads returned and the West Point education once again lasted four years throughout the rest of the conflict and, with the exception of later wartime contractions, until the present day.

Just as those cadets who resigned to fight for the Confederacy received commissions as captains, majors, and even colonels, so the volunteer units in some Union states dangled such commissions before West Point cadets. In 1861, a number of them accepted the commissions, then sent their resignations to the superintendent. However, he refused to accept them, and no cadets were allowed to resign in order to join the volunteers. Even though Bowman allowed that cadets who accepted such commissions would probably have done better than those who actually filled the ranks in their absence, he was afraid that if he accepted one such resignation, it would be but a short time before the entire Corps of Cadets would resign to fight in the war and West Point would find that it had no students.

Nevertheless, the Civil War was one in which West Pointers clearly made their marks. In fifty-five of the sixty most significant battles, West Pointers commanded the forces on both sides, and in the other five, a West Pointer commanded one side. In the Union army, a total of 294 West Point graduates attained the rank of general in either the regulars or the volunteers, while in the Confederate army, the West Point graduates who attained the rank of general reached 151.

But at West Point itself, time passed slowly for cadets eager to join the fight, and the Civil War was quite far off.

The political effect on officers of the Union army, however, whether fighting the war or serving in some support role such as teaching at West Point, was dramatic.

As the servants of a central government, the professional soldiers who graduated from West Point would naturally have wanted a stronger national army. This meant the supremacy of the federal government and the diminution of state and local governmental powers. While it was apparent that the Democratic party's states' rights position included support for state militia and volunteer forces, the Republican position was at least amenable to the concept of a strong national army. General in Chief Henry W. Halleck, a strong Democrat until 1862, set the pace when he changed to the Republican party. At West Point, a number of cadets followed suit, but the most significant change of party allegiance was probably that of the unofficial dean of the Academic Board, Dennis Mahan, who left the Democratic party to support Lincoln and the Republicans. In 1864, when West Pointer George McClellan ran for president against Lincoln as the Democratic nominee, West Pointers were tested. McClellan had been one of Mahan's best students and had even taught under him. But this was not enough to overcome loyalty to the Republican cause, and certainly not adequate to compensate for the Democratic peace plank. Mahan roundly denounced McClellan and his candidacy, as did Halleck, Sherman, and others. Mahan said that it was shameful for the Democrats to call for an end to a struggle that was, essentially, "between right and wrong."

John Pelham

The third son of a doctor, John Pelham grew up on a thousand-acre spread in northeast Alabama. He was sworn in at West Point in the summer of 1856 and embarked on the newly established five-year program. Popular with his peers, Pelham was just embarking on manhood. He wrote to his father in 1859 that he had recently attended

> the marriage of Lt. Lockett of Alabama with a lady of the Point. He graduated last June. Rather early to take a companion! I think a young officer ought to play his hand alone for four or five years at least after graduating. He ought to rough it on the frontiers and learn whether Fate is propitious, and in what direction Fortune showers her favors. That is the road I'll take.

Pelham was only an average student, but he was a fine athlete, and he was generally considered the finest rider at West Point. In 1860, the Prince of Wales, who would later become Edward VII, king of England, visited West Point and was impressed by Pelham's masterful riding feats

Pelham was elected president of the Dialectic Society, and while he felt honored, he soon found himself refereeing hot debates over slavery, abolition, and states' rights. He grew troubled, for he saw war looming. And while he had made many lasting friends from the North, when his home state of Alabama seceded, he knew where his duty lay.

In April 1861, after Fort Sumter, he could wait no longer, and left West Point for his native Alabama, just weeks short of winning that prized diploma. He was commissioned in the Confederate army, and while drilling an artillery battery near Winchester in the Shenandoah Valley, he met Miss Sallie Pendleton Dandridge. She lived on a plantation in Martinsburg, and was probably visiting friends in the Valley. But despite his expressed desire to stay single for at least several years after he left West Point, it was soon apparent that John was in love.

Then war became imminent, and all Pelham's training and studies began to bear fruit. He came back from the Valley and his battery was placed on Jackson's left front during the battle of Manassas or Bull Run. From that position, they stayed calm and cool despite heavy counter-battery and eventually small-arms fire, and were able to break an attack against Jackson's flank by Colonel William T. Sherman and his brigade of Union infantry.

After Bull Run, Pelham was promoted to captain and commanded a battery of horse-drawn artillery under J. E. B. Stuart, the aggressive cavalry leader of the Army of Northern Virginia. All winter long, Pelham trained his men and enforced the strict discipline that led to superior battle-field performance. But he also became very close to Stuart, who was only a half-dozen years older than he and began to treat him like a younger brother. And the letters between John and Sallie were sweetened by occasional visits.

Pelham's men loved him, and in the spring, he used them to repeatedly smash Union formations during the Peninsula campaign. And he was masterfully creative, using his guns and captured Union guns to destroy loco-motives carrying Union supplies, drive off gunboats pro-tecting Union piers, and confuse Union forces generally about what force they were facing and where it was.

When McClellan moved back down the peninsula and began to embark his men for the long ship ride back north, Pelham returned to Richmond with Stuart, where he was surprised to find that he had become a much-storied hero—and that he had been promoted to major.

In the Battle of Second Manassas, Pelham was with Jackson's corps on the defensive. Jackson gave him the discretion to take his guns to the most threatened point as the Union attack mounted and help repel it. This he did very well, including rescuing and then protecting their supply wagons from an unexpected Union attack. And when Union general Pope was pressing his attack against Jackson's men behind a railroad embankment, a flanking attack from Longstreet's corps completely destroyed the Union offensive and sent them reeling in bloody retreat.

Pelham performed valiantly at Sharpsburg in September 1862, holding the left end of Lee's line and protecting its connection to the Potomac River. They had not won the impressive victory in Maryland Lee had hoped for, but when his army crossed back into Virginia, it was not pursued by the Union army under McClellan.

J. E. B. Stuart's force was then placed in a long arc that extended from Harper's Ferry to Williamsport. Stuart maintained his headquarters during this time on a spacious plantation known as "The Bower," the estate of Sallie's father, Colonel Adam Dandridge, along the Opequon River near Martinsburg. As it happened, Sallie, her sister Serena, and a niece of the colonel's named Lily were living on the plantation with him. Every day involved training, but in the late afternoons and evenings, the young officers buzzed like flies around these young beauties. But Sallie only had eyes for John Pelham.

There were formal dances in the mansion, and John and Sallie seldom danced with anyone else. They rode horses into the countryside together, rowed on the river in the moonlight, sat with each other at evening picnics or around an open fire, and often just walked through the fields hand in hand. They even borrowed a yellow wagon Stuart had captured from the Yankees to go for long rides. It was an idyllic time of young love openly flowering on a very beautiful Southern plantation.

J. E. B. Stuart noticed, of course, and he was not above asking John if all this romance wasn't going to spoil his love of fighting. John was almost wistful when he answered that he still loved fighting, but he would be happy when the war was over and he could settle down and raise a family. One evening, he gave Sallie the Bible his mother had given him when he first left for West Point. Both ignored the war in a sort of idyllic romantic trance as September slipped into October.

From October 10 through October 12, Stuart's entire command, including Pelham's artillery, rode completely around McClellan's Army of the Potomac, ranging as far north as Chambersburg, Pennsylvania. They returned to Virginia and relative quiet.

But on October 29, Stuart finally broke camp. McClellan's 110,000 men were moving toward the 70,000 under Lee, and it was time for Stuart's men to conduct some aggressive reconnaissance and learn the intentions of the Yankees.

But the Yankees were in disarray. Lincoln replaced McClellan with Ambrose Burnside, who decided to move directly south and attack Lee's forces wherever he found them. He was to find them early in December outside the town of Fredericksburg. And this was the battlefield on which Pelham was to shine his brightest.

It was here that he used the Napoleonic trick of racing his guns out between the lines of infantry, unlimbering some five hundred yards from the enemy, and firing canister and grapeshot at their lines. This would keep them from advancing, or tear great holes in their lines. In Napoleon's day, smoothbore muskets were only lethal to around two hundred yards, so that the horse-drawn artillery could unlimber and fire with impunity. In the Civil War, however, both sides were armed with rifles, lethal to six or eight hundred yards, which put Pelham and his men at great risk and kept them in constant motion.

Pelham knew this, of course, but he acted as if he were immortal. At Fredericksburg, Pelham was out in front of Jackson's lines facing the Union's 3rd Division with only two horse-drawn cannon. And he stopped their advance. He would fire a few shots, then limber up and race a few hundred yards to another position, thus dueling successfully with four Union batteries and keeping sixteen thousand Union infantrymen from entering the field of battle. Commanders on both sides were stunned in rapt attention as they watched this daring young man and his crew race across the battlefield, fire, then move and fire again, almost taunting the Yankee cannoneers. Even General Lee was moved to comment: "It is glorious to see such courage in one so young."

After about an hour, one of his guns was knocked out by a shot from a Union cannon. But Pelham kept at it, now armed with only one gun, and soon found that Jackson had rushed fourteen more guns to him to keep up the fire. Pelham withdrew a certain distance and set these guns up so that their fire would be at right angles with the fire of another fourteen guns on the ridge under Colonel Walker and cover the area across which Union troops would have to advance if they wanted to attack the Confederate line.

When the bluecoats cautiously advanced at the southern end of their line, the fire from these twenty-nine guns in their front and flank soon drove them back to their starting point. While the more serious attacks this day occurred on the Union right, where repeated assaults against Marye's Heights and the sunken road at its base were repulsed with great bloodshed, this southern part of the field was not insignificant. Pelham was able to greatly damage and confuse the Union left, which ultimately never posed a serious threat to the Confederate lines.

After that battle, the only man below the rank of general who was mentioned in Lee's official reports was Pelham, a man he now referred to as "the gallant Pelham." And from Lee, such praise was of greater value than gold.

After Fredericksburg, the Army of Northern Virginia settled into winter quarters. In the early spring, there were few contacts with the enemy. But on March 17, a Union cavalry force came across the Rappahannock at Kelly's Ford and captured Confederate pickets. Stuart brought up the 3rd Virginia Cavalry Regiment to charge them, and Pelham helped aim four artillery pieces. Then he went forward to join the 3rd Virginia in their mounted attack. But just as he approached the fighting, a Union howitzer shell exploded next to him and knocked Pelham from his horse.

At first, they thought he was dead. But after laying him over a saddled horse, someone discovered he still had a pulse. They moved him to a wagon, and he was carried to the home of friends, but he never regained consciousness. Stuart was stunned when he heard the news, and he rushed three physicians to his side. But other than make him comfortable, there was little they could do, for a piece of shrapnel described as "half the size of a cherry" had pierced his skull. Shortly after midnight, he died.

Patrick O'Rorke

The man who graduated first in West Point's class of June 1861 was Patrick Henry O'Rorke, and he was quite an unusual cadet. His parents immigrated to this country when he was only three years old, and soon after their arrival, Patrick's father died. The Irish were looked down upon, and life in Patrick's family was hard work. Even so, Patrick managed to graduate at the top of his high-school class in Rochester, New York. But with no money available, college was just not possible, so he became a stone-cutter's apprentice.

Within a few years, the local congressman came to see the principal of the Rochester public high school and asked for help. The last several young men he had appointed to West Point were the sons of political allies, but all had failed to pass the entrance exams, which was an embarrassment. He was looking for a very smart young man who could pass the exams and give promise of one day graduating. If such a young man could be found, he told the principal, a young man within the Academy's age limits for new cadets of over sixteen and not yet twenty-two, then he wouldn't care about his family's politics. Could the principal help him?

So Patrick was nominated, passed the tests at West Point, and was sworn in as a cadet on July 1, 1857. He was just under the age limit, at twenty-one years eleven months, but that didn't matter to him. The crucial fact was that, with no family money or political influence, he had been admitted to the United States Military Academy and would receive the finest military education available. He could barely believe his great good fortune!

And he did shine at West Point. At graduation in June 1861, he was ranked first in the class academically, and he also was the cadet first captain, the new designation of the highest-ranking cadet. But the most surprising thing of all may have been that he was the most popular member of his class. Given that he was a few years older than most of his classmates and got the best grades in so many subjects, it is perhaps not too surprising that so many of them looked up to him. But the fact that so many of them sought his friendship and enjoyed simply being around him tells another tale altogether.

He took his commission in the Engineers, and worked on fortifications for a while. Then in the summer of 1862, the 140th New York Volunteer Infantry was raised in Rochester. Nicknamed the "Rochester Racehorses," they wanted Patrick O'Rorke, Rochester's most famous military son, to lead them. And eventually, Patrick resigned his commission in the Engineers and became their colonel.

The summer of 1862 was a happy time for Patrick for romantic reasons. From his teenage years, he had admired from afar the pretty girl who had played the organ back at St. Bridget's Church in Rochester. As a stonecutter's apprentice, he had never felt quite good enough for her, but once a cadet at West Point, his pursuit of Clara Bishop had become serious, and as an officer, it became relentless. On July 8, 1862, Patrick and Clara were wed, and in their union, he finally found a bliss whose existence he had only vaguely suspected.

After a short honeymoon, it was back to duty, and on October 8, 1862, Colonel Patrick O'Rorke formally took command of the 140th New York Volunteer Infantry Regiment. Within a few months, he learned from his darling wife that there would be no babies awaiting his return, but fathering a large brood with Clara after the war was a dream he never gave up, and his letters to her spoke often of the family joys that awaited them.

The Rochester Racehorses were in the Battle of Fredericksburg, although their participation was primarily as a covering force for Burnside. And although they lost only one man, they had their share of being cold, wet, hungry, and scared. At Chancellorsville, they had once again mostly covered the retreat of the defeated Union army. But their discipline was good and they longed to be more in the thick of the fighting.

On July 2, the 140th was moving north into Pennsylvania, part of the Army of the Potomac under General George Meade that was chasing Lee's Army of Northern Virginia. It was a big regiment for that period of the war, numbering 526 officers and men. And as they marched, unbeknownst to them, the left end of the Union line at Gettysburg a few miles ahead and off to their left front was in serious trouble.

General Sickles and his III Corps had been told to fill in the Union line as it ran south along Cemetery Ridge. When he got there, however, he saw that the ridge fell away short of a hill known as Little Round Top, and he decided that he must move his corps forward from Cemetery Ridge to take and hold the high ground of a peach orchard and a wheat field. But after he had moved his corps forward, the two ends of the long, linear formation were no longer attached to other Union forces or any defensible terrain feature, and they were open to Confederate attack. As Longstreet's Confederate corps smashed into them around four o'clock, they were driven back, and General Meade threw in all the reinforcements he could find, desperately trying to help them hang on.

In late afternoon, the 140th could hear heavy artillery fire off to their left front, and they all knew that Union soldiers had finally caught up with at least part of Lee's army. A messenger galloped up on a lathered horse, and soon Colonel O'Rorke had his orders. He passed the word for the regiment to close ranks and bunch up, then rode his horse into a field on the side so that they could all see him and his loud voice could be heard by all.

Colonel Patrick O'Rorke told his men to uncase the colors and prepare for battle, for their moment had finally come. The left end of the Union line was just a few miles away, and they were under heavy attack from Confederate forces. The troops there needed help, and the Rochester Racehorses were being sent in to support them. Today they would not be covering retreats. Today, they would be plunged into the heart of battle and it would be up to them to make sure there *were* no more Union retreats.

A fervent cheer answered him, and he knew that the blood of his men was up.

Around four-thirty in the afternoon, the brigade that included O'Rorke's regiment was just to the north of Little Round Top and moving in an easterly direction to support Sickles when it was seen by General Gouverneur Warren from the heights. General Vincent, whose brigade was the only Union force on Little Round Top at the time, had just been killed. His left wing was strongly held by Chamberlain's 20th Maine, but the commander of the regiment holding Vincent's right wing had just taken forty-five of his men out of line and disappeared. This later turned out to have been a cowardly act, that the regimental commander had simply moved them out of the line of fire and around to a position of safety on the east side of the hill. But in trying to make his own men safe, he greatly increased the danger to other Union troops on Little Round Top. All Warren knew was that the right end of the brigade was suddenly thinned out, and when the Confederates found out what little force was left to oppose them on that side, they would very quickly storm through the thin blue line that was left and take the hill.

Warren raced down from Little Round Top and stopped the Union column, which turned out to be his old brigade from the 2nd Division of the V Corps. Their commander, General Weed, told Warren they couldn't be diverted, that they had orders from Meade to move up fast and support Sickles. But Warren had Meade's authority as well, and he was able to convince Weed that unless he got some men, the Union line on Little Round Top would collapse and the whole left wing of the Union line might be rolled up. Warren saw that Weed was torn, so he told him that if he could have the big 140th Regiment, that should be enough.

Weed thought this reasonable, and as he moved on toward the Peach Orchard with the rest of his brigade, Warren directed the Rochester Racehorses up the north face of Little Round Top. As they moved, the large stones made the going rough, so Patrick dismounted and drew his sword. "Follow me, men!" he yelled, then turned and led the way.

As they reached the crest of the hill, pandemonium could be heard just over the edge of the rocks in front of them. As Warren had feared, Confederate commanders had probed and found the Yankee weakness. Now they were directing all the force they could spare to break through the Union right on Little Round Top.

O'Rorke paused briefly and tried to form his men in a line just behind the crest. A few white-faced, blue-coated infantry lurched up over the edge and into the woods they had just left, and a loud, keening Rebel Yell told them who was coming next. Then Patrick held up his sword and his booming shout was heard by all:

"LET'S GO, BOYS!"

Colonel Patrick O'Rorke, roaring his rage at the top of his lungs, plunged downhill into the mass of butternut soldiers, and all down the line his men did the same. The shock of their sudden assault stopped the Rebels cold. And then, as their numbers swelled into the hundreds and kept pouring out of the woods and over the edge, the Confederates turned and headed back downhill to relative safety. The Rochester Racehorses had gotten there in the nick of time! They had saved the day!

But Colonel Patrick O'Rorke never saw this victory. Soon after he plunged downhill into the Rebel force, he had been hit by a rifle shot in the throat. His jugular vein was pierced, and he probably bled to death before he even realized he had been hit.

In Patrick's pocket was the cherished gold watch he had gotten from the stonecutters when he first went off to West Point. His adjutant carefully took it out and made sure it got back to Clara Bishop O'Rorke. Despite their splendid victory on Little Round Top, this was a very sad day for the Rochester Racehorses.

Chapter 5:

The Cultural War—Henry O. Flipper

DURING THE PERIOD FROM 1870 THROUGH 1887, twenty-seven African-Americans were nominated for appointment to West Point, twenty-four showed up, and twelve passed the rigorous admissions tests. Of these twelve, six lasted one semester, one lasted one year, two lasted three and one-half years, and three graduated.

The first set of African-American cadets who arrived at West Point were harshly treated. Given the widespread antipathy toward members of their race at the time, it is not surprising that white cadets resisted their admission to their ranks. While under the law they could not prevent their arrival, they could turn their backs on blacks socially. And that's just what they did. From their first arrival, black cadets were "silenced," meaning no other cadets would speak to them except on official business. The penalty for breaking this exclusion was the silencing of the perpetrator. It was a harsh time indeed, and this silencing of African-American cadets lasted until 1948. Blacks continued to be tokens at West Point until 1969, and at the turn of the century, they still make up only 6 or 7 percent of each class.

The brief stories of the first two blacks to receive congressional appointments to West Point, Michael Howard and James Webster Smith, give important insight into the commonplace racial dividing lines that existed virtually throughout American society, North and South.

Of these two, only Smith passed the admissions test, and he was the only black cadet among 230. He was badly treated by most, but insisted on standing his ground, refusing to concede that he had fewer rights than did white cadets. The result was that, within a matter of weeks, all white cadets refused to speak to Smith except on official business (reports in ranks, classroom recitations, and so forth).

Because of rigid racism, during the 19th Century, black cadets shared rooms with other black cadets or had their own rooms. In July 1873, Smith was joined by Henry O. Flipper, who would graduate in 1877 and receive his commission as the first black regular army officer. And although Flipper's later book, *A Colored Cadet at West Point*, is marvelous in its detail, he makes virtually no mention of Smith at all. There are abundant other sources, however, and we can see that Flipper learned to be a reed, not an oak, to bend but not break, as Smith had done before him.

After Smith's appointment, two other blacks had been appointed and passed the admissions test. But academics were rigorous, and if a cadet failed any course in the required curriculum, which was heavily weighted toward mathematics and the sciences, he was forced to leave the Academy. One lasted for a full academic year before failing out in math and French, while the other could only make it for one semester before failing in French. Another black entered with Flipper in July 1873, but he failed out in French in January 1874. Finally, after graduation, Flipper was "recognized" by some of his classmates, and he said that he was accepted as a friend. But later actions by some who had known him at West Point may place a shadow on that recollection.

Henry O. Flipper graduated from West Point in 1877, and in 1878, Flipper's memoir of his days at West Point, *A Colored Cadet at West Point,* was published in New York by Homer Lee & Co. Thus, by the age of twenty-one, Flipper had earned a diploma from West Point, had finished his West Point memoir, and had orders to head for the frontier, where he would command United States cavalry troops and play a role in the taming of the West.

Flipper took up his duties in January 1878, and as the only African-American officer in the entire U.S. Army, his social circumstances were strained. Despite his optimistic attitude after receiving his commission, he was to be rudely awakened to the fact that most officers of the U.S. Army in 1877 were simply not willing to accept a black officer as their full equal, no matter how intelligent, competent, and well-educated at the "right" school he might be.

Lieutenant Flipper served as an officer commanding black cavalrymen in the 10th Cavalry and fighting the Apaches in Texas. His men loved him, a few of the other white officers respected him, but most hated him and wanted to get rid of him. This hatred was caused by the fact that he was not only the first black regular Army officer, but also was a West Point graduate. At a time in our nation's history when most whites thought all blacks were vastly inferior to them, a black regular Army officer was a challenging precedent.

Many officers were secretly hoping a way would be found to get rid of Flipper, for he presented a threat of black intrusion into white officer ranks. Most officers agreed that the Army would be better served if Flipper were to somehow stumble and fall from grace on his own. And who knows, perhaps someone would help with a little push.

Flipper was fortunate in his first assignment. His troop commander, Captain Nicholas Nolan, was a widower over fifty years of age with two small children. As soon as A Troop was established in quarters at Fort Sill in 1878, Nolan went to San Antonio, where he wooed and wed Annie Dwyer. He brought his bride back to Fort Sill, and her sister Mollie came along. Nolan felt he was persecuted simply because he was Irish, and he was one of the few white officers who felt great sympathy for Flipper and went out of his way to help him. He insisted that Flipper eat with him and his wife and his sister-in-law, and so he did. Mollie and he became what he called "fast friends," and soon enough, they were going on long horseback rides together.

This is an instance of what can only be termed incredible naïveté on the part of Flipper. He believed the Army to be led by officers and gentlemen who would not "ostracize" him, and if they were so intolerant as to be unable to accept him on that basis, he preferred them to keep their distance. He tried to live according to those rules, fully acting out the role of a West Point graduate commissioned officer, assuming all the rights and responsibilities to which he believed he was thus entitled. He tried to pay no attention to officers prejudiced against him, but they were legion, and surely he was not ignorant of their feelings.

For instance, while A Troop was at Fort Elliott, Texas, the wife of one of the other officers wrote to eastern newspapers criticizing Nolan and his wife for receiving and entertaining Flipper in their quarters. In response, Captain Nolan wrote a letter of protest that was published in *The Army and Navy Journal*. This publication made a practice of reprinting official orders, excerpts from court-martial proceedings, and other military news items during the late nineteenth century, thus capturing the flavor of the social and military life of the officer corps. In Nolan's letter, he admitted his bias in favor of Flipper because, as a much-persecuted Irishman himself, he felt he shared a bond of persecution with African-Americans.

Captain Nicholas Nolan welcomed Flipper into his home, but other white officers did not. The result was that Flipper made friends with townspeople, civilians who might be white, black, Mexican (he spoke excellent Spanish), or of unknown mixed breed. Flipper was basically just an average American cavalry officer fighting the Indians on the western frontier, save only the color of his skin.

For several years after his arrival, Flipper's unit moved around to different forts in Texas and Indian Territory while fighting Indians or outlaws. In the spring of 1880, A Troop arrived at Fort Davis, Texas, where it had been transferred with two other troops of the 10th Cavalry in order to fight Victorio's hostile Mescalero Apaches. Fort Davis was less than sixty miles from the Rio Grande, and after a brief stop there, A Troop took up the chase of Victorio and his men, along with several troops of the 8th (white) Cavalry and a company of Texas Rangers.

On November 10, 1880, fierce fighting resulted in the deaths of nineteen Indians and three troopers, and Flipper was designated to read the Episcopal service over these soldiers. The American soldiers were buried where they fell, after which a rifle volley was fired and the buglers played taps. Then at the end of November 1880, Flipper and A Troop returned to Fort Davis.

There certainly must have been many other such instances while Flipper and his men were fighting both Apaches and armed outlaws. But the official records of this action, one which resulted in the deaths of three U.S. Army soldiers, and the religious service read at the burial by Lieutenant Flipper, rise to the level of compelling evidence. Whatever else this official record might show, it seems undeniable evidence that, at least on this specific occasion, Flipper had risked his life, under arms, in service to his country.

One is reminded of the words allegedly inscribed at Thermopylae: "Stranger passing by, go and tell the Spartans that we lie here, obedient to their laws." Or perhaps, more pointedly, the words of Robert E. Lee: "A call to serve one's country is a high call; a call to serve her under arms in time of war is the highest." Given the great hardships Flipper had suffered to win his commission, he probably would have preferred to have fallen dead to a hostile bullet in the untamed West rather than to bear the unanticipated and unwarranted court-martial charges, conviction, and lengthy disgrace that awaited him.

In early December 1880, Flipper was made acting assistant quartermaster and acting commissary of subsistence, staff duties usually filled for short periods by designated junior officers. Such administrative jobs are more tedious than complex, and the junior officers filling them are usually supported by sergeants subordinate to them but familiar with the routine. And above them, senior officers generally watch to make sure young officers avoid blunders. Flipper was to make youthful mistakes, but unhappily, he did not have the kindly oversight of a concerned superior officer to help him. Instead, most white officers wanted to get rid of him and would pounce eagerly on his first professional error. As the only black commissioned officer in the United States Army, Flipper held himself, and was held by others, to a higher than normal standard of conduct. That standard was of almost superhuman proportions. But because he was black, Flipper was unable to open himself in confidence with virtually any white officers, and he certainly could not seek their advice or counsel. Thus, truly alone in the army and somewhat innocent in administrative or financial matters, and with little more than animosity displayed toward him by most white officers, Flipper seemed destined to trip one day, sooner or later, and take a hard fall.

Flipper resumed his rides with Mollie Dwyer at Fort Davis in December 1880, but then a new lieutenant, Charles E. Nordstrom, arrived. In a few words from his frontier memoir, a rigidly correct Flipper only hints at what must have been his broken dreams, and the hell of Nordstrom's proximity, for even if his relationship with Mollie Dwyer was truly nothing more than a platonic friendship, he had precious few of those. Nordstrom, he says, came from the Civil War army. A Swede from Maine with no education, he was described by Flipper as a brute. He began taking Miss Dwyer out on buggy rides, and these gradually replaced horseback rides with Flipper. Sadly, this story only makes Flipper's efforts to defy longstanding tradition seem all the more foolhardy.

In the spring of 1881, Fort Davis changed dramatically. Until that time, the fort had been commanded by Major N. B. McLaughlen of the 10th Cavalry. During the months of March and April, all the cavalry units except A Troop were dispatched to other posts, and the headquarters of the 1st Infantry arrived, commanded by Colonel Rufus Shafter, who also took over command of Fort Davis.

Shafter's regimental adjutant, First Lieutenant Louis Wilhelmi, relieved the post adjutant, and his regimental quartermaster, Second Lieutenant Louis Strother, relieved Flipper as the post quartermaster. Shafter told Flipper that he would also be relieved as acting commissary of subsistence as soon as possible, in order for him to devote his time fully to his role as a cavalry officer, but that he would retain the position for an indeterminate period while personnel were shifted around. He ended up retaining the job until August 11, when he was replaced by Lieutenant Frank H. Edmunds. Meanwhile, Wilhelmi was a familiar face from Flipper's past.

Several years older than Flipper, Wilhelmi had started his military career as a cadet at West Point in 1872. He fell ill during his first year and started again in 1873, this time with Flipper's class. But the sickness returned, and he left West Point for good at the end of 1873. He recovered and was commissioned a second lieutenant in 1875, then was appointed regimental adjutant, a post for which he was promoted to first lieutenant in 1880. Thus, when he arrived at Fort Davis, although he outranked Flipper, the latter had the cachet of a West Point degree, and thus a far superior military education. This degree also gave him, at least in theory, vastly superior potential political power within the Army. That potential, however, as we shall see, was largely eliminated simply because Flipper was black.

In fact, there were at least five other West Point graduates at Fort Davis who were either Flipper's classmates or had graduated within a few years of him either way. Ordinarily, on a lonely frontier post, West Pointers would have been the fastest of friends, and they have historically maintained a sort of "insiders' club" that, coupled with their traditional dominance of the higher ranks in the Army, has long caused considerable bad feeling and resentment among officers who did not graduate from West Point. Though he did not graduate, his time at West Point probably would have allowed Wilhelmi access to this closed circle. But for Flipper, a freed black slave, this social world remained almost as closed in the Army as it had been at West Point.

The old "silence" from West Point days was back again—the institutional message, broadcast in the past to Flipper and all other black cadets by the white Corps of

Cadets: "We do not want you here, and despite the national governmental authorities that have appointed you a cadet, we refuse to recognize your presence and will do everything we can to force you to leave." And now some of his fellow officers on a remote western post were sending him the same message.

This initial impression of a young cadet was often lasting. For instance, in his testimony at Flipper's court-martial, Wilhelmi was asked if he knew Flipper (who had been his West Point classmate). He said that he did not know him, that he had never spoken to him, and that their only relations had been limited strictly to official business.

But this social shunning of Flipper was common. In his memoir of his life after he left the Army, *Negro Frontiersman*, Flipper described an occasion where he ran into a West Point classmate in a strange town. He says that when he went into the San Javier Hotel in Tucson one day for dinner, he saw Lieutenant R. D. Read from the 10th Cavalry already seated and eating. Read and he had been classmates at West Point, so Flipper went over and sat down to join him, which would ordinarily have been the most normal thing in the world. But as soon as he sat down, Flipper tells us, Read got up and left, abandoning his dinner rather than have to eat it in Flipper's company.

So the Army's racist mentality, to which Flipper had first been exposed at West Point, was not dead once he left that institution. At first, such slights must have been very hurtful indeed. But after four years of it at West Point, followed by nearly four years in the frontier army, it seems Flipper had come to expect such treatment.

Flipper, of course, was very popular among the African-American enlisted soldiers who filled the ranks of the 10th Cavalry. But the barrier of rank made an impenetrable wall between them socially: even had the disparity of education and experience not been enough to keep them apart, the rigid rules of the Army precluded social fraternization between officers and the enlisted ranks.

Flipper was largely alone socially, so far as other officers in the Army were concerned. In his small quarters, he kept a violin, an early typewriter (he had, after all, already written a book that was being commercially published and from which he was awaiting royalties), a "student's lamp," three albums, and seventy-nine books, so he clearly had developed ways to fill his frequent solitary moments.

But he also gravitated to the town that had sprung up outside Fort Davis, befriending many of the white, black, and Mexican civilians who lived there. His best friend was probably W. S. Chamberlain, a watchmaker, whom he apparently visited every day. They regularly went on rides and other social outings and ate meals together. He was also close to Joseph Sender, a merchant whose store, Sender & Seidenborn, was the largest in town.

Though his service as quartermaster had ended in March, Flipper continued to serve as the post commissary, with an office and a storehouse. Most of the details of buying and selling food for the soldiers and families at Fort Davis were taken care of by Commissary Sergeant Carl Ross, who recorded sales, prepared letters and receipts for Flipper's signature, and generally kept the books in order. Flipper's duties were primarily those of passing on instructions, taking responsibility for all funds received, and the efficient management of the commissary service.

All foodstuffs were purchased from the commissary by the soldiers at the post or their families. Officers were allowed credit, usually paying their accrued debt by check periodically, but soldiers were supposed to present cash at each transaction. Each week, the total amount of money on hand, in checks and specie—American and Mexican bills and coins—was tallied and approved by the post commander. Each Saturday, Sergeant Ross prepared these forms for Flipper's signature, and Colonel Shafter, in turn, signed them on Sunday morning. A copy of the Statement of Funds was sent to the chief commissary of subsistence for the Department of Texas in San Antonio, another to the commissary general in the War Department, Washington, D.C., while a third copy stayed in the post commissary office records. The funds themselves were to be sent to San Antonio as soon as practicable after the end of each month.

From March through May 1881, Flipper performed his duties as post commissary with no concerns. But then in May, he began to notice that he did not have as much money on hand, in the form of cash or checks, as he should have had. And here his problems began.

Until May 1881, Flipper's performance of his duties, even given the racist walls that surrounded him, had been truly professional and without the slightest fault. He had always taken the high moral ground and refused to allow himself to be angered by petty racial slurs or slights. And his record as an Indian- and outlaw-fighting cavalry officer had been superb.

But Flipper was especially sensitive to the plight presented by the accident of birth to other people of color who had not been so fortunate as himself. An obvious place where he could make their lives less difficult was in the purchase of foodstuffs from the commissary. Since he was an officer, he could buy on credit, while enlisted personnel had to pay cash. Though his pay as a second lieutenant was only $125 per month, Flipper made it a custom to allow enlisted men, laundresses, and others to buy from the commissary stores, drawing on his own credit for payment but keeping little or no record of such transactions. He eventually allowed others to spend on credit in "his" commissary an amount that, when combined with his own modest requirements, came close to consuming all his pay. He started with a commissary debt of $72.08 in December 1880, but by August 1881 it had ballooned to $1,121.71, with virtually no record of how much of Flipper's "credit" had been used, when it had been used, or by whom.

In May 1881, Flipper discovered that he did not have as much on hand in the form of cash and checks as he *should* have had. By the end of May, he was short some $800, and he began to alter his reports to his post commander to reflect the amount he actually had on hand rather than the amount he *should* have had, while he continued to list the larger amounts on reports to San Antonio and Washington, D.C. To him, this was easily justifiable: Lieutenant Flipper, 10th Cavalry, did not pay his commissary bills to Lieutenant Flipper, acting commissary officer, and as commissary officer, Lieutenant Flipper covered for the cavalry lieutenant Flipper who was trying to collect on bills owed him.

Another problem was caused by where the funds were kept. Flipper was told by his commander, Colonel Shafter, to simply keep the funds in his quarters rather than in one of the safes that were supposed to be used. Shafter assured him the funds would be safe there during the short time he was waiting to be replaced as commissary officer. But his quarters were never locked, and many civilians were commonly there when Flipper himself was not. He had given another key to his trunk, in which the commissary funds were kept, to his black female housekeeper, and it was often open in his absence.

In July 1881, Shafter ordered Flipper to send all the commissary monies he owed to higher headquarters.

Flipper later told him that he had done so, when in fact he had not. Some $1,440 was missing and unaccounted for, and to cover that debt, Flipper wrote a personal check in that amount and showed it to Colonel Shafter.

Some days later, Shafter saw Flipper's horse in town with empty saddlebags—saddlebags that were always on Flipper's horse, although Colonel Shafter later denied knowledge of this—and said that he suspected that Flipper was about to desert with the commissary funds. He therefore had him arrested and jailed in a small, cramped cell.

While Flipper was so held, Chamberlain and Sender and some of his other friends from town visited him. They were soon able to raise $2,300 to offset what was missing from the accounts. When Flipper was arrested and his possessions tabulated, after four days in jail, he was released.

As a result of this incident, Flipper later faced formal court-martial charges of 1) embezzlement, and 2) five counts of "conduct unbecoming an officer." These counts were 1) writing a fraudulent check for $1,440; 2), 3), and 4) sending three false reports to San Antonio saying that the money was in the mail, when in fact he had embezzled the money; and 5) telling Colonel Shafter that he had sent the money to San Antonio when in fact he had not.

Captain Merritt Barbour, his appointed Army defense lawyer, showed that he could not be found guilty of embezzlement since he had repaid the missing amount with money contributed by his friends. Since he could not be guilty of embezzlement, counts 2), 3), and 4) of the second charge, which included embezzlement, must also fail. Although Flipper had shown the check for $1,440 to Colonel Shafter, he had not "uttered" it, meaning caused it to enter the stream of commerce. It was therefore no more than a piece of paper, and was not a "fraudulent check."

And finally, Flipper admitted that he had lied to Colonel Shafter, but since he was the first and only black regular officer in the U.S. Army, he had to be especially careful, and he had lied only in order to buy time in which to make up the missing funds, which he had been able to do.

The court listened to these defense arguments, then withdrew and considered the charges in private. The verdict was "not guilty" on count one, and "guilty of all five specifications" on count two. The court sentenced him to be "dismissed from the service of the United States," with no further explanation.

The only appeal was to the president, and the judge advocate general of the army recommended leniency. But President Arthur, on June 14, 1882, signed a simple statement confirming Flipper's conviction.

After he left the Army, Flipper stayed in the Southwest and established quite a reputation as an engineer, as a linguist, and as an authority on Mexican land usage laws. By the end of the century, he had been hired by the U.S. secretary of the interior, where his work proved invaluable. He was thus able to use political friends to introduce legislation in both houses of Congress in an effort to correct his records.

But the institutional Army was ever his enemy, and all such legislation died in committee. As our nation went through the throes of Jim Crow laws and harsh segregation, Lieutenant Henry O. Flipper was unable to find a way to undo this terrible wrong. Fighting to the very end, he finally died in 1940 with that wrongful conviction still staining the record of the first black man to graduate from West Point.

In 1973, Henry Minton Francis, the eighth African-American West Point graduate (class of 1944), was appointed a deputy assistant secretary of defense. In 1977, he was awarded the Department of Defense Distinguished Civilian Service Medal, and he retired soon thereafter.

During his years inside the Pentagon, Mr. Francis heard details of the injustices done to Henry O. Flipper, the first African-American West Point graduate, at his court-martial. The Flipper family, led by the efforts of a white grade school teacher in Georgia named Ray McColl, was attempting to redeem the good name of Henry O. Flipper, but needed the help of someone inside the Department of Defense. Mr. Francis was the man who provided the help, and he was instrumental in getting administrative relief in Lieutenant Flipper's case.

The relief was carried out in 1976 by the army's Board for the Correction of Military Records. It formally upgraded his punitive dismissal, a court-martial sentence following conviction of a crime, into an honorable discharge.

Some years later, an article about Lieutenant Flipper appeared in the West Point alumni magazine, *Assembly*. Mr. Francis was then a trustee of the West Point Association of Graduates. At a trustee meeting, he and another trustee, federal judge Eugene R. Sullivan (West Point Class of 1964), discussed the article. Judge Sullivan praised Mr. Francis for his effective efforts in upgrading the discharge, and the two men discussed the issue of his court-martial in more detail. In that conversation, Judge Sullivan mentioned to Mr. Francis that, discharge upgrade notwithstanding, the status of Lieutenant Flipper remained, in the eyes of the law, that of a convicted felon. This was because the action of the Board for the Correction of Military Records, in the case of a judicial decision already handed down, could only affect appearances in some record systems. The underlying conviction could only be overcome by an act of court over-turning it or by a presidential pardon.

Mr. Francis was quite surprised, and he immediately asked Judge Sullivan if he could help in any way to change Lieutenant Flipper's status as a convicted felon. Judge Sullivan found himself in a delicate position. He informed Mr. Francis that, as a federal judge, he could neither give legal advice nor take any official action to change Lieutenant Flipper's legal status. Nevertheless, Judge Sullivan agreed, as a matter of historical and judicial interest to West Point, to try to acquire more information on the court-martial of Lieutenant Flipper.

Judge Sullivan found that the National Archives had a copy of all of Lieutenant Flipper's court-martial records, including the appeals. One of Judge Sullivan's secretaries, Ms. Barbara Burley, an African-American, had heard of Judge Sullivan's interest in Lieutenant Flipper and volunteered to help. Judge Sullivan sent her to the National Archives, where she obtained a copy of all the records in microfiche film format. She then went through the laborious process of placing the microfiches on a special format machine and turning each page on film into a page of printed paper.

The end result was a stack of historically rich paper some eight inches high. Judge Sullivan then asked his wife, Lis U. Sullivan, to go through the text and paper-clip the pages on which certain central issues—such as bias of the court, violations of due process, and key evidentiary rulings—were found. After his wife's work was completed, Judge Sullivan reviewed the documents himself. He was quite distressed by the many flaws he noted in the court's proceedings and was convinced that a grave injustice had been done to Lieutenant Flipper.

But at this point, Judge Sullivan found himself in a serious dilemma. He wanted to see that justice was done to Lieutenant Flipper. However, in his position as a federal judge, he could take no further action to help Flipper. In fact, he had decided that, if the Flipper case were to somehow be reborn and appealed to his court, he would choose to recuse himself because of personal prior knowledge.

His dilemma was solved when I went to see him in his chambers one day as just an old friend. A West Pointer and a lawyer myself, I had already been admitted to practice in Judge Sullivan's court. As it happened, at the time of that visit I was also in my first year of a Ph.D. program in American and military history at Princeton University. I mentioned that I was looking into writing my dissertation about African-American West Pointers in the nineteenth century, and Judge Sullivan was nothing short of delighted. He gave me the court-martial records, and I went right to work. Those materials are the primary source materials I used to write the chapter of my dissertation on Lieutenant Flipper's court-martial.

Once I had reviewed the materials, I was also convinced that Lieutenant Flipper had been done a terrible injustice. But what could I do? As a lawyer, I knew that the only real relief for Flipper would come from a voiding of his conviction by a federal court or a presidential pardon. The White House was far beyond my reach, but since I was admitted to the Bar of the U.S. Court of Appeals for the Armed Forces, I could present what is known as a "Petition for Extraordinary Relief" to that court and ask them to void Flipper's conviction. That seemed the only practical course for me, so I began work.

The legal brief at the heart of the petition came quickly, for I had already laid out the whole case in my Ph.D. dissertation: the factual story, the official records, and the compelling legal arguments that justified voiding the conviction. But it was clear that the U.S. government would oppose my petition in federal court, for convictions more than a century old had never yet been overturned. I could see that this was going to be a long and difficult legal fight, and it was just too risky and too important for me to pursue by myself. What I really needed was a major Washington, D.C., law firm, one that had both the resources and the will to accomplish this most worthy goal.

Fortunately for me, another close friend is Jeffrey R. Smith, a partner in such a major Washington, D.C., law firm. Mr. Smith was my classmate at West Point and also at the University of Michigan law school. I spoke to him about the Flipper case, and after some consultation with his partners, they agreed to take this cause on as a pro bono project of the firm. I gave them the draft brief and petition, relevant portions of my dissertation, and supporting documents, and they went to work.

This took several years, as the firm investigated the two options in some detail. They eventually concluded that, as a practical matter, the judicial review of such an old case would not get beyond numerous legal hurdles, including the fact that the appellant and all witnesses were long dead. The option of a presidential pardon appealed to them as both practical and attainable.

Finally, on February 19, 1999, in a White House ceremony, President Clinton awarded Lieutenant Henry O. Flipper a full pardon, the first posthumous pardon ever granted by a president of the United States. This was the final end to a long journey. Lieutenant Flipper's cause was championed by many along the way. The hues of their skins varied, but their resolution and belief in the value of doing the right thing did not. Some were West Point graduates, some were not. Together, they did make a difference. Justice, finally, was done.

Chapter 6:

World War I—George S. Patton, Jr., and Douglas MacArthur

GEORGE S. PATTON, JR., WAS BORN IN 1885 in an area that is now part of Pasadena, California. His mother was the daughter of a wealthy owner of vast vineyards and groves of orange and lemon trees, while his grandfather had commanded the Confederate "Patton Brigade" during the Civil War. Both his father and grandfather were graduates of the Virginia Military Institute, and the first Patton had immigrated to Virginia from Scotland in 1770.

George loved horses and the outdoors from childhood, and he decided as a teenager to become a professional soldier. Born to a wealthy family, he never had to struggle as many of his peers did. His family traditionally summered on Catalina Island, twenty-six miles offshore from Los Angeles, and in the summer of 1902, that's where George met Beatrice Ayer, the daughter of a wealthy Boston businessman. Then both returned to school, but from that summer onward, they were never much out of each other's minds.

George wanted to go to West Point after high school, but in June 1903, he failed to win a political appointment. He had been accepted by Princeton, but he and his father decided that VMI would be a better year of preparation for West Point or, if West Point was not to be, for a military career. So he spent a "rat" year at VMI, which was not much different from the hellacious difficulty experienced by a "plebe" in his first year at West Point. And after that year, Patton was appointed to West Point. At the end of his plebe year, however, the second consecutive difficult year as the subject of serious hazing, he failed mathematics and was "turned back," meaning he was required to repeat the entire first year of academics. His alternative was to leave West Point and enroll at a normal civilian college, but George badly wanted to win that West Point degree, so there was no hesitation from him. While the petty harassment was removed for such "turnbacks," it was still a very difficult repetition to ask of anyone.

George stuck it out, and in June 1909, after five years at West Point and one at VMI, he graduated and took his commission in—no surprise here—the cavalry. He married his beloved Beatrice in May 1910, and their first child, a daughter they named after her mother, was born in March 1911.

George had been rather a loner at West Point, with few friends. But as anyone who knew him there would have told you, he was bursting with ambition, and while he sometimes spoke to excess about what he could or would do, he often backed the talk up with action. For instance, in 1912, he was the only American to compete in the military pentathlon event of the Olympics.

While this competition was dropped later in the twentieth century, it was long considered an excellent test of a young military officer. It consisted of five events, usually held on consecutive days: pistol shooting, fencing, swimming three hundred meters, running four thousand meters, and riding a horse over a five-thousand-meter course that included jumping many obstacles. The Olympics were held in Sweden that summer of 1912, and out of forty-three contestants in military pentathlon, Patton finished in fifth place.

His next station, in September 1915, was to the 8th Cavalry at Fort Bliss, near El Paso, Texas. In March of the following year, Pancho Villa and a group of Mexican bandits made a raid into New Mexico in which eighteen Americans died, and General Pershing began forming a force to pursue them. When Patton learned that the 8th Cavalry would not be included, he made a personal plea to Pershing, whom he did not know, begging to be made a member of his staff. He was.

On March 25, President Wilson ordered Pershing to pursue Villa and his five hundred bandits into Mexico with a punitive expedition, but not to fight against the Mexican army. Pershing was a forceful, dominant leader, and the expedition ran like clockwork. Unfortunately, Villa knew the vast wilds of Mexico, and there was never any real hope that Pershing would catch him. They went some three hundred miles south into Mexico, and other than one brief gunfight in which thirty Villistas were killed by the U.S. 7th Cavalry, there was little contact.

While on an expedition to buy maize for the horses in May, however, Patton and four American soldiers took a detour to check out a ranch known to be a Villa refuge. There they surprised General Julio Cardenas, one of Villa's most trusted subordinates, and two of his men. Everything happened very quickly, but the Mexicans fired a volley of pistol shots at the Americans while trying to escape, two of them on horseback, one running across a field. Patton and his men, however, were not hit, and Patton drew his ivory-handled Colt .45 revolver and fired five shots at the horsemen. His fire and that of his men killed them both. Then they went around the house and saw the third bandito running, now perhaps two hundred yards away. Patton raised his rifle, as did two American soldiers, and together they killed him. The runner, they later learned, was General Cardenas. But that was to be the last spark in the campaign, and at the end of January 1917, the punitive expedition came back across the border into New Mexico.

But World War I, the bloodiest conflict up to that point in history, was underway, and by 1917, the indiscriminate sinking of Allied and neutral ships by German submarines finally drove Wilson to ask Congress for a declaration of war. And when Pershing left for Europe in May 1917 in command of the American Expeditionary Force, Patton was on his staff.

Within a few months, Patton had learned about some experimental tanks that the British had started to use in 1916, and also that an American tank school would be opened in Langres. He was able to get assigned there and established himself right away as an unbending man who enforced discipline and demanded the highest standards of performance. After a year of training, he was promoted to lieutenant colonel and given command of the 1st U.S. Tank Battalion. The baptism of fire was to take place in the Saint Mihiel offensive of early September 1918.

When the call came, Patton went forward with his reconnaissance officer. The plan was for an Allied armored force of over 550 tanks, supported by infantry, to make the attack. There would be one heavy U.S. brigade using 150 British Mark V tanks, three French brigades totaling 225 Renault tanks, and Patton's 1st Tank Brigade of 144 Renault tanks with 30 other heavy Allied tanks attached.

The Renault tank had a gas engine only capable of four to five miles per hour, and a two-man crew consisting of a driver and a tank commander, the latter also the gunner responsible for the 37-mm cannon. D-Day was put off until September 12, and at 1:00 A.M., a massive Allied artillery bombardment was accompanied by a hard, cold rain. Rain was the only thing Patton had feared, as he wasn't confident of his tanks in the mud. This was not as much of a problem as he had feared, although most of the German trenches proved to be so wide and muddy as to often become impassable to the tanks.

As Allied forces continued forward, they found most of the German infantry had been pulled back from their front-line positions. The main opposition they faced, then, was from German artillery fire, which was heavy. Allied tanks were not slowed by this, unless they took a direct hit, while Allied infantry had no protection and often were unable to keep up with the tanks that got past the trench lines. The advance was spotty, and at dawn, Patton was disheartened to see so many of his tanks hung up on muddy German trenches in front of him.

He watched the tanks continue forward; he was in somewhat of a dilemma. He was at the end of his telephone wire, and he had explicit orders from his boss, Colonel Rockenbach, not to go beyond telephone contact with headquarters. But at 7:00 A.M., the seduction was too strong. With a lieutenant and four enlisted runners, he moved forward onto the battlefield, following his tanks on foot.

They walked for many miles, passing through fields and several small towns. Finally, at around 10:00 A.M., they entered the village of Essey with American tanks as the Germans were leaving on the far side, in such haste that they left behind a battery of guns, the instruments and music of a brass band, and an officer's horse, saddled and waiting in a barn.

On the outskirts of town, Patton walked forward until

he could see, in a long row on either side of him, the men of the 84th Brigade of the 42nd Division (Rainbow), who were taking cover in shell holes where their drive forward seemed to have stalled. He walked along the line, and then saw their brigade commander, Brigadier General Douglas MacArthur, who was personally leading his men, standing on a small hill. Patton walked up and stood beside him, but there was very little talk. They both watched as a "creeping barrage" of German artillery fire moved toward them. When men yelled at them both to take cover, they ignored this unwanted advice. After the barrage had passed, Patton asked MacArthur for permission to cross a bridge out of Essey in front of MacArthur's men. When MacArthur approved the move, Patton ordered his tanks to move on toward the next village, named Pennes.

Once they had gotten clear of Essey, Patton was down to one runner and his lieutenant, and the three of them were moving with the lead platoon of five tanks. Two of these tanks ran out of gas, and while they waited for fuel trucks, Patton kept going with the three that were left and thirty-odd infantrymen. The road was littered with dead German soldiers and horses, and the destroyed remnants of what had obviously been another German artillery battery.

As they approached Pennes, two other tanks ran out of gas and were left waiting while Patton and the one remaining tank kept going. Then they drew rifle fire from town, and the infantry stopped. Patton leaped up on the back deck of the tank with his lieutenant and his last runner and assured the infantry in a loud voice that he would lead the way. But they were unconvinced, so he had the tank drive into the village. There were only a few cross streets, and at the first one, the lieutenant and the runner dismounted and used their pistols to capture some German soldiers who came out of a barn with their hands raised.

The tank kept going, and as it went beyond the last buildings of the village and back into the open, several German machine guns took it under fire from a tree line across a wide field. But the tank engine noise blotted out all other sound, and Patton only realized they were under fire when he glanced below his left hand, which was holding the top rim of the tank turret as he stood on the tank's body behind it. As he looked down, he saw pieces of paint disappearing on the side of the turret, only then suddenly realizing those were machine gun bullets bouncing off the armor.

Patton leaped off the open back and took cover in a shell hole, which the Germans sprayed with more machine gun fire. But as the fire shifted, he leaped up and raced back to the village. The American infantry had come through the village behind Patton and his tank, but they were not willing to move forward and support one tank by attacking those machine guns across an open field. This was long before radio contact was possible, and the only way to stop the tank was to catch it and bang on the hull to get the commander's attention.

So Patton ran back into the open and chased the tank, now some four hundred yards away and steadily churning forward with no infantry support to keep German soldiers from climbing on its back and killing its crew. He finally caught it and banged on the door with a stick. When the tank commander opened the door, Patton yelled at him to turn around and go back to the village, while German machine gun bullets kept smacking off the armor.

Once they got back to Pennes, the other four refueled tanks in this platoon arrived. That fresh firepower changed everything for the American infantrymen, and they eagerly accompanied them back out into the open fields toward the German machine guns. But in the face of all those American tanks coming across the field toward them, the German machine guns quietly withdrew.

Patton had trained his men in aggressiveness more than anything else. "Go forward," he had said repeatedly, "go forward! If your tank breaks down, go forward with the infantry! If you fail to do this, there will be no excuse for your failure in this, and I had better not find any tank officer behind the front line of infantry!" The result of this was that tanks many times got several kilometers out in front of the infantry, and when they broke down, their crews dismounted and advanced as infantry armed only with pistols, usually in support of other tanks.

When Colonel Rockenbach finally caught up with Patton, he gave him the tongue lashing of his life for going forward and out of telephone contact, thus cutting himself off from higher headquarters in direct disobedience of his orders. But Patton didn't care, for he had so strongly instilled aggressiveness in his men that his tank brigade was out in front of everyone, tearing through the Germans.

At noon on the fourteenth, Patton sent a reconnaissance patrol to the front, consisting of three tanks and five infantrymen under the command of Lieutenant Ted McClure. Near Jonville, they ran into a retreating infantry unit and an artillery battery. When the artillery pieces were unlimbered in an attempt to use them as a direct-fire weapon against the American tanks, they charged. The German infantry ran like deer before the tanks, and the Americans captured not only the artillery pieces, but a quantity of machine guns as well. But then German artillery fire started to fall, wounding McClure and two of his men. As they were moving back, two of his tanks broke down. Rather than abandon them, McClure had them linked together, with the one still running pulling the other two back toward friendly lines.

On September 16, Patton was able to report 131 tanks ready for action out of the 174 he had taken into the Saint Mihiel salient. Three had taken direct hits from artillery, while the others were out of action for various mechanical reasons or because they had become trapped in German trench works. But while the mechanics of the tanks may have proven fragile, the will of his soldiers had not. Patton was powerfully moved by McClure's exploit, which no doubt laid the seeds for the armored movement that would become his trademark in World War II, the deep penetration.

On September 25, Patton and 140 tanks were shipped by rail to the Meuse-Argonne front, and at 5:30 A.M. on September 26, they were part of a major Allied offensive. By ten in the morning, they were just south of the village of Cheppy. There, a prepared but unchastened Patton sent his first message to Rockenbach by carrier pigeon. It was to be his last.

In the morning fog, Patton and his command group had gotten more than a hundred yards out in front of his own tanks. And as the fog lifted, the Germans opened up. As at Saint Mihiel, Patton's tanks had gotten way out in front of the 35th Infantry Division, which was supposed to be moving with them. The few infantrymen among the tanks started to turn and head for the rear as the German machine guns in Cheppy opened up, but Patton started yelling at them, and then sergeants echoed. Most of the infantrymen stayed in place, but none came forward.

Patton and his group had found refuge behind a railroad embankment, and he sent three runners back to tell the tanks to come forward. Finally, he went himself, and he found the crews of two tanks trying to dig their way out of a trench that barred all movement, while other American infantrymen watched but did nothing. Patton blistered them, then picked up a shovel and hit one of the idle soldiers in the head with it, so hard he later said he thought he had killed him.

Patton acted harshly, but the conditions demanded it, for he was angry at stupid delays that might cost the lives of some of his men. While the name that later stuck to him, "Old Blood and Guts," implied that he was indifferent to the lives of his men, that is simply not accurate. In a letter to his wife, he spoke of walking across a battlefield the night after a bloody fight, where the dead soldiers lay in the moonlight and he had to look close to know whether they were German or American. He said they all looked the same—very young and dead. And as he walked, he couldn't help thinking about how this one had his nose wiped by his mother, how that one had his diapers changed, until finally it became unbearable. He consciously decided then that the only way he could make it through war as a commander was to think of the dead as numbers, not men. But his wife knew him well, and she knew he could never do that. To him, his soldiers were individual men, they were people, and their lives would always and forever be his responsibility.

They were under fire all this time, but Patton refused to take cover. They finally got five tanks across the trench, and Patton started them forward. As a result of his experience at Saint Mihiel, Patton had started carrying a walking stick, which he could use to bang on a tank door and get the commander's attention. He now waved the stick forward over his head and called out: *"Come on!"*

Then he turned and started forward between two tanks.

Behind him, about 150 American infantrymen raced to catch up with him. But as they moved up a rise, the German machine gun fire from the flanks became intense, and they all took cover. Patton admitted he was suddenly terrified; his mouth was dry and his palms were sweaty. But after a brief pause, the tanks went over the crest of the hill, and Patton stood up and raised his stick again: *"Let's go get them! Who's with me?"*

Then he started moving forward again with the tanks, with 150 men scrambling to catch up. As they passed over the rise, however, the German machine gun fire became intense from the front as well as the flanks, and the American infantrymen were either hit or began to drop out and take cover. Suddenly, there were only five men still moving forward with Patton, then two, then one. And as he walked next to a tank, he was struck by a machine gun bullet that went right through his upper thigh. He leaned against the tank for a moment, then started walking again. After about five or six steps, his legs stopped. A Private Angelo hurried over to him.

"Are you hit, sir?"

"Yes, I am, but I . . ."

The tank beside them stopped, and Private Angelo helped Patton into a nearby shell crater. He took out his knife, cut open his pants, and saw that the bullet had hit the front of his upper thigh and come out the back. He applied a bandage to stop the bleeding, and although Angelo knew he needed to be evacuated, there was just no way to do that at present.

When Patton went down, the attack ground to a halt, around 11:00 A.M. And as Patton lay there bleeding, the Germans began moving closer. But the tank that had been next to Patton stayed by his shell crater like a faithful dog and warded off all threats. As word got to the rear that Patton's attack had been stopped, two other tank companies moved out to the flanks and carried out their maneuvers as Patton had ordered. With infantry moving with them in the way Patton had taught them, they eventually took Cheppy around 1:30 and drove off the Germans and all their machine guns.

When the fire to the front ended, Patton was finally evacuated, and with a little over a month left before Armistice Day, this was the last fighting he would see for some time. The attack on Cheppy was probably the first use of a tank-infantry strike force that took a major enemy defensive position, an important event few men, even soldiers on the scene, understood. But Patton understood it fully. He had grasped the concept of tank-infantry as a decisive battlefield weapon, a concept he would use again on other fields of battle that still, in 1918, lay far in the future.

Douglas MacArthur

In 1862, President Lincoln offered an appointment to West Point to Arthur MacArthur of Wisconsin. After some hesitation, young Arthur did not accept the appointment and joined the Army to fight in the Civil War instead. Less than two years later, he picked up the flag of his volunteer regiment after its bearer was killed, then carried it and led them to the top of Missionary Ridge in a charge that broke the Confederate siege of Grant's troops at Chattanooga, Tennessee. He rose to colonel and eventually received the Medal of Honor for this act. After the war ended, he returned to the ranks as a lieutenant, and in 1875 married Mary Pinckney Hardy of Norfolk, Virginia. In 1880, a third son they named Douglas was born to Captain MacArthur and his wife, Pinky.

Douglas's oldest brother, Arthur, won an appointment to Annapolis, and his other brother, Malcolm, died of measles while still very young. Douglas was desperate to become a soldier like his father, and eventually won a competition for an appointment to West Point. When he arrived in the summer of 1899, his mother was with him. His father was fighting in the Philippines, and Arthur had graduated from Annapolis and was away on sea duty. The MacArthurs did not own a home, and her choices were a hotel in Washington, or the West Point Hotel, sited on Trophy Point and only a few hundred yards from cadet barracks. Almost every day over the next four years, Pinky and her son found a way to meet and talk.

By Douglas's second year, his father had been promoted to major general, and he was a much-storied hero throughout the army and even the nation. Douglas was five feet ten inches tall when he arrived, and he weighed only 140 pounds. Realizing he didn't have the bulk required, he didn't even try out for the football team. But he was not a bad baseball player and was on the varsity team for his three upper-class years. Before his senior year, he had been named first captain, the highest-ranking cadet officer in the entire Corps. And he was also very bright. He was ranked first in his class academically at graduation, and he took his commission in the prestigious Corps of Engineers.

After graduation, Douglas was able to get assigned right away to the Philippines. His father commanded the entire Pacific area from San Francisco, and he spent a few months with his family, which delighted him. His older brother Arthur was in command of a destroyer that had just returned from Japan, and when Douglas was leaving for Manila, Arthur met him on the dock. They hadn't seen each other for ten years, since Arthur had left for Annapolis. But they had been very close as children, and their meeting on the dock was very emotional for both.

Once he arrived in the Philippines, Douglas was kept busy with engineering work that included the construction of piers and wharves. It was not particularly exciting or colorful, perhaps, and it was not quite like leading an infantry regiment in a charge up Missionary Ridge. But it was the sort of engineering work at which he excelled. He later told the story of having been surprised and shot at by two rebels one day in November 1903, with one bullet supposedly going through his hat. He said that he had then drawn his pistol and shot them both dead. It is impossible to confirm or deny that story, and it could well be true. But even if it was inflated, it helps us realize the enormous pressure he must have felt as a young lieutenant. How could he live up to the image set by his older brother, then commanding an American warship on the high seas, let alone that of the Medal of Honor–holding general who was his father?

After a year in the Philippines, marked mostly by the fact that he contracted a bad case of malaria, Lieutenant MacArthur was assigned to the District Engineer's Office in San Francisco. In February 1904, the Russo-Japanese War broke out, and General MacArthur asked to be assigned as an observer from the Japanese side. By the time his request was granted, Port Arthur had fallen, so he was made a temporary attaché in Tokyo. He arrived in Tokyo with Pinky, and he was able to spend a lot of time in China. In September 1905, his military aide returned to the United States, and his replacement was Lieutenant MacArthur. General MacArthur set off on an eight-month tour with his wife and son in November 1905. They started with Japanese military bases, then went to the great British post at Singapore, followed by the Dutch East Indies (today's Indonesia), Burma, India, Siam (today's Thailand), China, then back to Japan.

Douglas would later say that this trip was one of the most important experiences of his life. He drew from it an awareness that European colonialism had provided for the reliable rule of law, and in so doing had helped stabilize government of the people in many locations. But it also meant the enduring subjugation of great masses of those people, and it seemed to preclude the education and growth that would allow the standard of living for whole nations to rise steadily. He also understood his father's feelings about the future importance of Asia to Americans, and he agreed with him that, one day, Asia with its enormous populations would be more important to the United States than would the Europe to which most Americans traced their origins.

Upon his return to the States, Douglas embarked on a normal routine of schooling and various Army posts. In 1912, his father died, a blow to all. Then in 1913, a political crisis erupted in Mexico. U.S. Marines had been captured in Vera Cruz, and eight thousand American soldiers and Marines were sent there by ship. War seemed inevitable, and the U.S. commander proposed to repeat Winfield Scott's 1848 march from Vera Cruz to Mexico City. Captain Douglas MacArthur arrived in Vera Cruz on May 1, 1913, under orders to "obtain through reconnaissance and other means . . . all possible information which would be of value in connection with possible operations" by the American army expected to arrive there soon. He also knew that the Americans would have great problems with transportation because, while there were countless boxcars in Vera Cruz, there were almost no locomotives. Because American railroads operated on a different track gauge than did Mexico's, it would be pointless to ship any down from the United States.

So MacArthur decided to try to resolve both problems

with one deep penetration behind Mexican lines, gathering information and hoping to find and bring back Mexican locomotives. He started by bribing a handful of Mexican railroad workers to sneak him through the lines on a hand-car to Alvarado, forty miles down the track. They went on a moonless night, and sure enough, they found three big locomotives there. In his official report, MacArthur report-ed all sorts of gunfire aimed at him by different bands of Mexicans, all of which were narrow misses, and next morning, he returned safely with the three locomotives.

It is not entirely clear that there was as much hostile gunfire as MacArthur claimed, but that really doesn't mat-ter. The important thing for the U.S. expedition was that he returned with the three locomotives. He was later nomi-nated for a Medal of Honor, which he clearly wanted in the worst way. But there were no American eyewitnesses, only three Mexicans who had accepted bribes to betray their country. Eventually, the Army decorations board rejected the nomination. MacArthur was furious, and he even com-plained in writing to the new Army chief of staff, Major General Hugh Scott, condemning the board's "rigid nar-row-mindedness and lack of imagination."

When the United States entered World War I, Douglas was promoted to colonel of infantry, and he became the chief of staff of the 42nd, or "Rainbow" Division. MacArthur went to France in October 1917, and the Rainbow Division was one of the first four American infantry divisions to arrive. They were assigned to the French VII Corps area, covering the mountains and forests of northeastern France. They spent the first few months of 1918 trying to learn from the French how the infantry and the artillery should work together as a team. But besides teaching the Americans, the French were also conducting raids into German lines, hoping to capture prisoners and bring them back for interrogation.

MacArthur, of course, wanted to go on such raids. On February 20, he learned that the *Chasseurs Alpins*, elite French mountain troops, were going on a raid. He insisted on going along, and after painting his face black, he refused the offer of a trench knife, but carried a swagger stick in one hand, wire cutters in the other. The raiding party went over the top and slithered through the mud between the lines, then carefully cut their way through the German wire. When they were on the edge of the trench, a few grenades were thrown in. After their explosion, the raiders jumped into the German trench and began slashing with their knives, herding prisoners into one section while fighting and killing those who resisted. A German colonel came out of a dugout bunker into the trench line, and MacArthur stuck the end of his swagger stick into his back. The German immediately raised his hands. He was herded over with the other prisoners, and soon enough they were driven through the openings that had been cut in the German wire and back to French lines.

MacArthur would receive the Croix de Guerre from the French for his part in this raid, and he would eventually receive a Silver Star from his American commander. On March 6, he went on another such raid, and was cited for "advancing coolly under fire of the enemy, in order to follow at close range the movements of our troops." Then on March 9, he went "over the top" with a battalion from the 168th Infantry. He later commented on this:

> You never really know about men until a time like that. You never really know what's inside them. I thought I knew what was inside our men, but after all, they were not really professional. They had

been National Guardsmen. They had never been under fire. And then, there we were—ready to go. When the time arrived, I climbed out and started forward, and for a dozen terrible seconds, as I went forward, I felt they weren't following me. But then, without turning around, I knew how wrong I was to doubt even for an instant. In a moment, they were all around me, some even ahead of me. I'll never forget that.

This raid knocked out a key salient covered by German machine guns, and MacArthur would receive the Distinguished Service Cross. In June, he was promoted to brigadier general, the youngest in the Army at the age of thirty-eight, and he took over command of the Rainbow Division's 84th Infantry Brigade.

On September 12, MacArthur led his infantry brigade personally in the Saint Mihiel attack. The afternoon of that first day, he was standing on the east side of a small village they had just taken. His men were exhausted, and they had all taken cover in shell craters while MacArthur stood alone on a small hill and looked across the open fields to his front, beyond which German forces waited. A man came up behind him and stood next to him. It was Colonel George Patton, who had just arrived with his tank brigade. They both stood silently as they watched a German rolling barrage approach them. Neither moved while the lesser human beings they commanded cowered in shell holes behind them. The barrage missed, and Patton spoke.

"General, I would like your permission to take my tank brigade across the small bridge to the south and then order them to advance northeast on the right of your men."

"That will be fine, Colonel, we will not interfere with your movement."

The Saint Mihiel offensive was an enormous American success, and it was over by the sixteenth. But the Meuse-Argonne offensive in October was far more demanding, and it almost cost MacArthur his life.

American success depended on their taking the Romagne Heights, where the Germans were strong. The key to Romagne was a low hill mass known as Côte de Chatillon, and it was heavily fortified by the Germans. The 84th was scheduled to attack it, along with the rest of the 42nd Rainbow Division and the American 32nd Division on the fourteenth of October. During the evening of October 13, the corps commander, Major General Summerall, visited MacArthur to emphasize the importance of his attack.

On the next morning, the 84th met heavy resistance, but MacArthur led from the front, urging his men forward. The 83rd Brigade on their left faded, then stopped, leaving their left flank open as they advanced. The 32nd Division on their right was stopped by a German counterattack, so now MacArthur's right flank was open as well. The farther forward they went, the more vulnerable were their flanks. As darkness fell, one of MacArthur's regiments got to the crest of one of the hills in the Côte, but its hold was quite tenuous.

On the fifteenth, the attacks resumed, but the American troops could make no headway at all. The Germans had vast fields of barbed wire secured across the slopes of the Côte, covered by 230 machine gun emplacements on the Côte de Chatillon, most of them heavily bunkered positions with overhead cover. After a day of bloody assaults that were uniformly repulsed, MacArthur returned to find a raging General Summerall waiting for him in his headquarters. He had just relieved the commander of the 32nd Division, as well as other regimental and brigade commanders. He didn't want to hear any excuses. All he wanted was results. He ordered MacArthur to take the Côte on the sixteenth, the next day.

As soon as he left, MacArthur organized a reconnaissance patrol. Reports from aviators and other patrols were that on one flank, the German wire field might be much narrower, so narrow that it would only take a few wire cutters to open a wide path. MacArthur wanted to investigate this and see what the possibilities were with his own eyes. They crawled through the mud of "no man's land" between the opposing lines for what seemed like hours. And then, sure enough, there was a narrow place in the mat of tangled wire that was usually ten meters wide or more. A few men could quickly cut an opening here with wire cutters and an infantry force could then pour through this open door into the German rear.

As they started to crawl back across no man's land, the patrol was hit by one of those random artillery barrages both sides threw out to discourage any enemy troop movement through no man's land. Everyone knew what to do, and they all scrambled for cover, most crawling into their own shell craters to wait it out. But when the barrage lifted a few minutes later, MacArthur didn't understand why no one reappeared. He started crawling from crater to crater, checking each individual soldier that had come on this reconnaissance run with him.

They were all dead, every one of them killed by that artillery barrage.

Except MacArthur. He later said God had led him by the hand the way he led Joshua.

When he got back to his headquarters, his planning was

swift. At dawn, most of his brigade resumed the frontal attack of the day before, but swinging as far to the right side of the hill as possible. This time, however, MacArthur told them to maintain as heavy a rate of fire as possible so as to keep the Germans both busy and distracted. One battalion, meanwhile, had the special mission to move off to the left side of the hill and wait until the fire on the right had built up. They were then to get forward to the thin area in the wire as quickly as possible and cut their way into the German rear.

On the next morning, everything went as planned. The infantry brigade got through the wire in late morning and began attacking the Germans from the rear. All of a sudden, the German trenches began to empty as they either withdrew or, in surprising numbers, simply surrendered. The 84th moved forward nearly a mile before stopping, but other American forces flooded past them. By nightfall, the entire German defensive system in the Romagne area had begun to fall apart.

The very next day, General Pershing, the commander of the American Expeditionary Force, telegraphed Washington that MacArthur should be promoted to major general. And within a few weeks, MacArthur took over as commander of the 42nd Division. They stayed in place until November, and by then, the war was all but over.

MacArthur's daring and success had really impressed, even staggered, other American commanders, and he was seen by many as the best American field commander in World War I. But when the men in his division recommended him for the Medal of Honor, the only general so recommended and a man who had already received two Distinguished Service Crosses, Pershing refused to approve the recommendation. MacArthur would have to wait for another world war for that.

Chapter 7:

The World War II Era—
Benjamin O. Davis, Jr., and
Russell P. Reeder, Jr.

Ben Davis

During the nineteenth century, after the end of the Civil War, a total of twenty-seven African-Americans, many of whom had been born as slaves, received political appointments to West Point. Of this number, only three ever graduated and received the much-coveted diploma. Charles Young graduated in 1889, but after him, the arrival of Jim Crow and a widespread sense of racist distaste among white Americans slammed the West Point door, as well as most other doors leading to any social prestige, shut against African-Americans for a long time to come.

As a smart young man from a good, well-educated family, Benjamin O. Davis tried hard to win such an appointment. But after it was made abundantly clear that his race would bar his appointment, he joined the U.S. Army as a private in 1899 and was assigned to Troop I, 9th Cavalry, stationed at Fort Duchesne, Utah. This was one of four regiments in the Army at the time whose soldiers were all black, but they were led by white officers. Davis was far superior to most other enlisted soldiers in the 9th Cavalry, the bulk of whom were illiterate. But Davis was a well-educated young man, so it was not a complete surprise when he won a commission as a second lieutenant a year after he first joined up. There had been other black officers before him, although most who served with front-line combat troops had been West Point graduates. But Davis shone brightly, and as his career progressed, he became a splendid success.

The primary problem he faced, however, was being an officer in an army that was rigidly segregated by race. As a junior officer, he could be placed in command of soldiers in one of those four all-black regiments. But the moment he had white officers below him, even if the enlisted men were all black, there was political trouble in store. Consequently, the Army ended up shuttling Davis between service with black cavalry units in the Far West or in the Philippines and assignment to one of two large all-black colleges—Tuskegee Institute in Alabama and Wilberforce University in Ohio—that had Junior Reserve Officer Training Commands. While Davis was assigned to Fort Russell, Wyoming, in 1912, his pregnant wife made the long trip back to Washington, D.C., so that their second child would be born in the family home of the father. There, on December 18, 1912, Benjamin O. Davis, Jr., was born.

With an older and a younger sister, Ben had a happy childhood, one in which his parents were able to protect him from many of the most harmful aspects of the rigid segregation in which much of this country was gripped. One vivid memory he retained, however, was of a Ku Klux Klan march in 1924 that went right in front of his home. The KKK was a powerful political force in the South at the time, and it struck fear into the hearts of many. This was an era when the lynching of blacks who might have done little more than appear to forget their low station was not uncommon in Alabama and Mississippi.

The Davis family lived in a house amid others occupied by Tuskegee faculty and staff. On the night of the march— in protest of proposed employment of a black staff to run a new Veterans' Administration hospital devoted to the treatment of black veterans—all lights were out in other houses in this black neighborhood. But the Davis family, neatly dressed, sat on their front porch, their father wearing his white dress uniform, as the marchers went by in their white robes, masks, and hoods. The only lights in sight were the Davis porch light and the torches carried by the marchers. Nothing happened to the Davis family that night, and perhaps that's the point: Benjamin O. Davis, Sr., had stood up to the Klan with his family.

In 1926, when young Ben was only thirteen, his father took him to Bolling Field in Washington, D.C., where for the then-princely sum of five dollars, a barnstormer took the young man up for his first ride in an airplane. It was love at first rush, and from that moment on, young Ben knew that he wanted to do one thing more than anything else when he grew up, and that was to fly airplanes.

As a senior at Central High School in Cleveland, Ben was elected president of the student council and graduated at the top of his class in June 1929. Having skipped a grade earlier, he was only sixteen, but went straight into Western Reserve University, where he intended to major in mathematics. But after finishing his first year, Ben learned that his father had been in contact with the only black congressman, Oscar De Priest, a Republican from Illinois. It became clear that if Ben could satisfy residency requirements by living in Illinois, Mr. De Priest might be willing to make him his appointee to West Point.

In the fall of 1930, young Ben enrolled at the University of Chicago, where he was to earn straight As. In February 1931, he received Mr. De Priest's principal appointment to West Point, but failed to prepare adequately for the entrance exams and was surprised to be tested in English and European history, areas where he knew little. He failed in these two areas and was humiliated to learn that meant he was not admitted to West Point. He went to the University of Chicago the following fall, but dropped out after the fall term ended and worked exclusively on preparation for the West Point entrance exams. He took them in May 1932, and this time he passed.

He was sworn in as a cadet in July 1932, and immediately went through a most difficult Beast Barracks. All was not to be roses and lollipops. In addition to the normal strain felt by all cadets, Ben was to feel an added measure based on race alone.

In 1925, the Army War College produced a study entitled "The Use of Negro Manpower in War," a study it said was the product of "several years' study by the faculty and the student body of the Army War College." As Benjamin O. Davis, Jr., has noted in his splendid autobiography, *American*:

> The study concluded that the intelligence of black people was decidedly inferior to that of white people, that blacks lacked courage, that they were superstitious, and were dominated by moral and character weaknesses. It also stated that the "social inequality" of blacks made the close association of whites and blacks in military organizations "inimical to harmony and efficiency." The Army had approved this "study" and used it as the basis for its discrimination against blacks.

But this wasn't the first such study. During the Civil War period, the work of abolitionists was all too often more than offset through the reinforcement of prejudices by supposed scientific studies that were less accurate than they pretended to be. For instance, the United States Sanitary Commission, a semiofficial organization dedicated to the improvement of the physical and moral condition of Union soldiers, assembled massive data and published it in 1869 as "Investigations in the Military and Anthropological Statistics of American Soldiers." The data had been compiled from some 16,000 soldiers and sailors, of whom over 2,000 were classified as "full blooded" Africans and 863 as "mulattoes." The results, assembled by individuals with no training, were predictable: By every measure, blacks were inferior to whites, and the mixture of white blood did nothing to ameliorate their innately inferior status. Five years later, the Provost Marshal General's Office released another massive study corroborating that of the Sanitary Commission. But the most powerful destruction was probably done by a Union physician's report to the Sanitary Commission that appeared in two scientific journals shortly after the war.

In that report, Dr. Sanford B. Hunt drew on his own personal experiences and more than 400 autopsies, mostly those of black soldiers. A number of his comments had to do with such unimportant issues as the bone structure of African-American feet, which might affect the way they would march, the discipline of slavery, which might allow them to endure hunger and other privations, and so on. But the most damaging part of his report dealt with the data he provided on brains. He said that the size of the brain has much to do with mental power, and he found the brains of white Americans to be 10 percent larger, and five ounces heavier, than those of black Americans.

With this mass of data available to them, physicians and scientists who had opposed emancipation, particularly in the South, leaped into the fray. Using flawed census data, they presented evidence that freed slaves were dying as a race. In the Union army, they showed that black deaths from disease had occurred at a rate three times as high as that of whites—as clear a sign as possible that freedom was injurious to blacks. There were defenders, black and white, who tried to correct the record, but they were fighting the tide. Overall, these early reports of inferiority had simply confirmed the disparaging stereotypes of African-Americans, long held even if only subconsciously, by most white Americans as a function of centuries of slavery.

But for Ben Davis, the reality of his day-to-day life at West Point was to be harshly conditioned by this officially perceived racial inferiority. At first, his other classmates were quite curious about him and happy to talk with him. But after a few days, he accidentally walked up on a meeting of all cadets that was being held in the basement of the barracks in his New Cadet Company. And as he approached, he heard a cadet ask the rhetorical question of the group, "What are we going to do about the nigger?" Realizing that the meeting was about him and that his presence was not desired, he went back to his room. Thereafter, it seems clear that the official policy promulgated to cadets was that Ben was to be subjected to the old "silence" in an effort to drive him away—no other cadet would speak to him except on official business, under pain of being subjected to the silence themselves. But they did not understand his resolute character:

> I was silenced solely because cadets did not want blacks at West Point. Their only purpose was to freeze me out. What they did not realize was that

I was stubborn enough to put up with their treatment to reach the goal I had come to attain.

After that, he spoke briefly to a few cadets who wished him well. He tried to find refuge in his books, but without any social company at all during the week, and on weekends only that of friends who made the long trip to West Point just to see him for a few hours, those must have been some long, lonely winters. Unless someone was angry at him, as far as all other cadets were concerned, he was, he says, an "invisible man." But worse than being ignored, he was actively shunned. He correctly calls into question the nature of West Point's commitment to virtuous behavior on the part of cadets and graduates:

New cadets were presented with a little volume entitled *Bugle Notes 1933 United States Corps of Cadets*, which we were required to study. We even had to memorize parts of it. . . .

I was struck in particular by the hypocrisy of one section of *Bugle Notes*, "Advice from the First Captain: Everyone [at West Point] begins on the same basis for there is no distinction except merit. Money is nothing; character, conduct, and capacity everything. In this respect West Point is truly the greatest democratic institution in existence." In my idealism I respected these principles and believed they were worth striving for, even though they apparently did not extend to blacks.

Also included was a section on honor, in which the "Guiding Principles" of the West Point honor system were enumerated. For the most part, besides familiarizing myself with these principles, I followed the dictates of my own conscience. The kind of honor spelled out in the "Guiding Principles" referred to a legal system with which every cadet was required to comply. In practice, it was painfully apparent that the system overlooked another and more basic kind of honor: the simple respect of one human being for another. Throughout my career at West Point, and beyond, it was often difficult to reconcile the principles of Duty, Honor, and Country with the Army's inhuman and unjust treatment of individuals on the basis of race.

Ben did very well academically, finishing his plebe year ranked twelfth in his class. But life at West Point was quite tedious until, during Christmas leave of his sophomore year, he met Agatha Scott from New Haven. Both were smitten, and she soon began to come to West Point every weekend. This, he knew early, was the woman he would marry.

In the fall of his senior year, Ben applied to be commissioned in the Army Air Corps. Somewhat later, the superintendent, General Connor, called him into his office and showed him the letter from Washington denying his request because no black units were to be included in the Air Corps. He said that there would be many more blocks put before him in the Army because of race alone, and then he proposed an alternative route for Ben. He recommended that Ben consider an assignment that would allow him to study law. But Ben had decided that he wanted to fly, and this first refusal did nothing to deter him.

After graduation, Ben and Agatha were married, and his parents hosted an enormous reception for them at Tuskegee, a reception attended by such luminaries as George Washington Carver. In 1936, Second Lieutenant

Benjamin O. Davis, Jr., and his father, Colonel Benjamin O. Davis, Sr., were the only two African-Americans serving as regular Army commissioned officers. It was a bright and welcome homecoming.

Ben had been commissioned in the infantry and was to serve first with the all-black 24th Infantry Regiment at Fort Benning, Georgia. Segregation at Fort Benning was complete and absolute, but because Ben was an officer, their quarters were not in an all-black area, but rather in the all-white officers' area. Their neighbors, however, other young officers and their wives, ignored them or shunned them. Despite the fact that he was a West Point graduate, he and Agatha were not allowed to join the Officers' Club. It was a bitter pill.

Ben then was assigned early to go through the course at the Infantry School, also at Fort Benning. But at the end of that period, he found that he was assigned to Tuskegee Institute to teach military science and tactics, the job his father had only recently left to command an all-black National Guard regiment in New York City. He was depressed, for his "job" would consist of giving three forty-five-minute lectures each week between September and May, nothing more. He was depressed, but Agatha did her best to console him. In September 1940, he was promoted to captain, and he held on. He was far from fulfilled professionally, but he was also very much aware of his importance as a door-opener for other black men who might follow in his wake. He stayed loyal to his commitments and responsibilities and he held on to his dreams. You never knew what lay around the next bend in the river:

Despite his resolve, Ben Davis soon found himself mired teaching military science and tactics at Tuskegee

Institute. Because of the lack of challenge, or even the opportunity for a normal military career that involved steadily increasing authority and responsibility, he felt enormous frustration. It was increasingly apparent that, because of race and the rigid segregation policies then in force within all branches of the American military, he was locked in the cycle that had captured his father before him: regular and repetitive assignment to small, all-black educational institutions, with only the dream, really, of ever returning to lead troops in the field. But in the fall of 1940, his father, Colonel Benjamin O. Davis, Sr., was nominated for promotion by President Franklin D. Roosevelt to the rank of brigadier general. He would thus become the first African-American general in American history. This seemed a nakedly political act by Roosevelt, seeking black votes. It is important to remember that in 1932, Ben Davis had been appointed to West Point by Oscar De Priest, the only black member of Congress and a strong Republican. It was Republican president Abraham Lincoln, after all, who had freed the slaves, and most blacks able to vote remained loyal Republican partisans until the brink of World War II.

General Davis was assigned to command the 4th Cavalry Brigade—the 9th and 10th cavalry regiments, all of whose soldiers were black and whose officers were white—at Fort Riley, Kansas. And he requested that his son be made his aide de camp.

Generals normally were given such courtesies, and the request was granted. So young Ben and his wife Agatha arrived at Fort Riley in February 1941. This was a time when the entire U.S. Army, as a reflection of attitudes widely shared by most white Americans, thought all blacks were vastly inferior to all whites, and there was no hope blacks could ever deliver a satisfactory performance of any important military mission. But a few people at the top of the Roosevelt administration apparently did not share this attitude.

A few weeks after young Ben arrived at Fort Riley, his father received a letter from the office of the chief of the Air Corps, which recommended that his son be released for pilot training. This was the result of a directive from the White House to the War Department, telling them to form an all-black flying unit.

Such was the response by the administration to increasing pressure for greater black participation in military mobilization plans. The Army Air Corps was then all-white, but this new policy was to result in the creation of the all-black 99th Pursuit Squadron, and once he had satisfactorily completed pilot training, Ben Davis, Jr., would command it.

And this, finally, was all Ben had been waiting for: an opportunity to learn and then apply military skills where the ultimate arbiter would not be able to show or feel prejudice based on race. This time, he and other blacks in uniform would not have their performance judged by some flawed human being who saw and assessed things as he thought they should be, not as they were, and thus repeated and reinforced old prejudices. No, this time they would be judged by the indifferent hand of the enemy: Their success or failure would be assessed simply by how well they fought, relative to other similar all-white units, against the Germans. For the first time, young Ben's dreams of a career beyond instructing military science and tactics at an all-black college began to take form.

In the late spring of 1941, Ben was to report to what would become the Tuskegee Army Air Field as a member of the first black pilot-training program. There, selected black candidates would be given thirty weeks of flight training under white instructors. The training of black pilots in heavily segregated Alabama in 1941 presented myriad administrative problems, not the least of which would be the cultural prejudice against the abilities of their students that would be held by many white instructors. But the ultimate question was whether blacks could be trained to fly airplanes to the standards required by the Army Air Corps, a question that only black pilots could answer with their actions.

As the first all-black class began their training at TAAF, many Americans felt that our nation's involvement in the war then raging across Europe was all but inevitable. Despite the great harm that could come from such a war, Davis also knew that it could force open the door of prejudice long enough to allow proof of black professional competence through demonstrated achievement in many fields. And if black fighter pilots could rise into the sky alone on winged stallions, do battle with the Teutonic Knights of Germany and at least hold their own, well, what white American, after such a demonstrated feat, would dare to try, ever again, to close that door of prejudice against them?

In August 1941, they started flying, and for Davis, as he later said himself, this was "complete, unadulterated joy." In September he soloed, meaning took off, flew, and landed alone. Over the next seven months, he immersed himself in what he called "the miracle of flight." After graduation, he continued to fly, and moved up to the P-40, which was to be the aircraft flown in combat by the 99th. By the summer of 1942, the 99th was at full strength in all personnel specialties required, ranging from pilots to mechanics, and ready for deployment.

Under the rules of the time, of course, all members of the 99th were black. And while many airmen at all levels were unhappy with segregation, they were at least comforted by the fact that they would be allowed to fight for their country. Their enemy would have no way of knowing the skin color of the pilot of a fast-moving American fighter plane. So at last fate would offer them a field on which to prove their mettle in battle and in life, a field on which success would be judged purely on the basis of performance, on fighter pilot competence alone.

Despite their preparations, however, the political aspects of deploying the first all-black fighter squadron slowed things down. Their unity grew across the squadron while they waited, but as first weeks, then months flew by, time hung heavy on their hands. The one thing they could do, which only added to their preparation for war, was fly. And they flew, and they flew, and they flew.

Finally, their orders came down. They left Alabama on April 12, 1943, sailed to Casablanca, and arrived at their new base at Oued N'ja, near Fez, Morocco, on May 1. It was not much more than a dirt strip, really, but they got twenty-seven brand-new P-40L aircraft and began to fly them. Within weeks, they felt they were ready, and on June 2 they flew their first strafing run, against the German-held island of Pantelleria. It wasn't until June 9 that they had their first contact with enemy aircraft.

Twelve P-40s were escorting twelve A-20 bombers on a mission when they were attacked by four German ME-109 fighters. The ME-109s had more power and speed than the P-40s, but every dog has his day, and such advantages do not always spell victory. On June 9, eight of the P-40s stayed with the A-20s and herded them home while the other four turned into the ME-109s. An American shot up one of the German planes and even blew big chunks out of the fuselage. But it wasn't shot down, and it even managed to get away as the other three ME-109s cut off American pursuit.

Combat flying, the pilots of the 99th quickly learned, was much more stressful than training, where there was no one out there trying to kill you. In order to become good at this game, it was very important that all members of a particular flight work together as a team, with their heads on a constant swivel watching for enemy planes attacking them. The German planes they faced, ME-109s and FW-190s, could fly higher and faster than the P-40s, and this advantage meant that the Germans could usually choose when and if to attack an American flight. When they did, they usually attacked in a dive out of the sun. And while their main targets in such attacks were the bombers that the 99th was escorting, any American airplane was a legitimate target, and they loved to take on our fighters.

On July 2, Davis led twelve P-40s in an escort of 12 B-25s in a raid on Sicily. That day, they were attacked by both FW-190s and ME-109s. They lost two P-40s to enemy fire, but they also brought down one FW-190, the first German aircraft shot down by a black pilot. And while it was great to bring down enemy fighters, the loss of every plane from the close-knit 99th was like a family loss. They grieved, and they kept going, even though they had no information outside their small unit on the overall conduct of the war. And they would not receive any, for they were flying in combat and might be shot down, captured, and interrogated. So they were given as little information as possible and told just to fly and fight. And they did.

On July 21, the 99th left Africa and moved to a forward base in Sicily. From there, they flew every day on fighter sweeps, patrol, strafing, and escort missions. But in September 1943, Davis got orders to return to the United States and assume command of the new 332nd Fighter Group, an all-black unit activated in October 1942. He was to prepare it for combat, then lead it back to fight in the European Theater of Operations. But a nasty report on the operations of the 99th in combat had been submitted to Washington by a white colonel, calling into question the discipline, teamwork, and aggressiveness of black pilots. The main recommendation of the report was that the 99th, and all future black-piloted units, be removed from combat duty and kept busy on coastal patrols with little or no risk of enemy contact. This report and its recommendations were endorsed all the way up the chain of command and ultimately to the desk of George C. Marshall, chief of staff of the U.S. Army.

This report had been written behind Ben's back, and when he learned of it, he was furious. But when called to the Pentagon to comment before the McCloy Commission on this report, he maintained his composure and relied on facts. His testimony was long and deliberate, and he used hard data drawn from results attributable to the performance of the 99th and other American fighter squadrons in their area to support his contentions.

He first established that the 99th had performed as well as or better than any other new squadron in similar circumstances. He then used their escort mission on July 2, when they were hit for the first time by enemy aircraft, as an example. Despite the fact that they were all having their first exposure to combat, they responded by the book and as they had trained: Eight P-40s stayed with the bombers and got them out of trouble while the other four P-40s turned on the enemy and fought with everything they had.

Eventually, they drove the ME-109s away, thus validating their role as competent bomber escorts. But over time, and as their experience grew, Ben assured the commission, they had become at least as good at their job as any other American fighter squadron then serving in the Mediterranean basin.

This testimony resulted in a formal Operations Office study of the role of blacks in combat, and its opening sentence tells the story:

> An examination of the record of the 99th Fighter Squadron reveals no significant general difference between this squadron and the balance of the P-40 squadrons in the Mediterranean Theater of Operations.

So Ben's testimony before the McCloy Commission had essentially drawn the fangs from the negative report, and plans for the deployment of the 332nd Fighter Group continued apace. But all critics of the 99th were silenced by two days in January 1944. On the twenty-seventh, the 99th shot down eight enemy fighters over the American beachhead at Anzio, Italy, and on the twenty-eighth, they shot down four more.

Ben took command of the 332nd Fighter Group, which was composed of the 100th, the 301st, and the 302nd fighter squadrons. He established a tough regimen of training, and set the very highest standard in every conceivable aspect of their operations. The men immediately felt the strain, but Davis told them they were not only going off to war for their country, but also were embarking on a mission. And this mission was almost sacred, for if they served it well, it could dramatically change the image and the future not only of black airmen, but also of blacks as American citizens across the country. They heard him, and caught with the fervor of true pioneers, they worked hard to improve their performance in every field.

The 332nd left for Italy on January 3, and as soon as they landed, they heard of the triumphant days of the 99th over Anzio. They were flying P-39s, and while these were not the best American fighters, Davis stilled all criticism by telling his men they were what they had, and they would make the best of them.

But he was quite distressed by the mission of the 332nd. It consisted of convoy escort, harbor protection, scrambles, point patrol, reconnaissance, and strafing. They were not, in other words, being thrown right into the teeth of the war and German fighter pilots. But after a few months, his men began to get acclimated, and although they rarely fired at or were fired upon by enemy aircraft, they were slowly but surely learning to play the game.

Then in early March 1944, Davis was called in by General Ira Eaker, commander of the Mediterranean Allied Air Force. He was quite concerned about losses to his fleets of B-17 and B-24 bombers, and he felt the 332nd could help him. Having lost 114 planes the previous month, he wanted to have the 332nd equipped with better fighters, the P-47 Thunderbolt, and then have them escort his bombers on their missions into enemy territory. And he assured Davis that the 99th would be reassigned so as to become part of the 332nd.

In June, the 332nd established itself at Ramitelli, a farming area on the Adriatic, and flew from an airstrip covered with pierced steel planking. The group soon started flying the P-47, a big, rugged airplane armed with eight .50-caliber machine guns and an enormous engine. It flew higher and faster than most of the pilots in the 332nd had dreamed possible, and with external fuel tanks, it could stay with bombers on flights deep into enemy territory.

Davis made it a habit to lead the 332nd on almost all their missions, and that is how they started. Their first two missions were flown against German forces inside northern Italy on the seventh and eighth of June, and there were no enemy aircraft around. But the third mission they flew, on June 9, was escorting B-17s and B-24s in a deep bombing raid against a heavily defended industrial complex near Munich. The B-17s usually flew at a higher altitude than the B-24s, and the fighter group had to position itself so as to be able to protect the entire flight. This included the ability to have fighters drop back and escort bombers that, hit by flak or enemy fighter fire, were unable to maintain airspeed.

On that mission, the 332nd destroyed a total of five German fighters and badly damaged a sixth. No American bombers were lost, and when they got back, Davis received a message from one of the bomber wing commanders that said: "Your formation flying and escort work is the best we have ever seen."

For the rest of June, they saw no enemy aircraft, though they flew escort most days. The dry spell lasted until July 12, when they shot down four FW-190s attacking their formation of B-24s. And once again, no American bombers were lost to enemy fire.

Early in July, the 332nd turned in their P-47s and got P-51 Mustangs, which had a longer range and were far better at the high altitudes where they flew with the B-17s. And they really began to rack up the enemy fighter count. On July 16, they brought down two Macchi 205s near Vienna, and on July 17 shot down three ME-109s while escorting bombers deep into occupied France. The best day that month was the nineteenth, when the entire four-squadron group flew escort for B-17s attacking the Memmingen airport. They shot down two FW-190s over Memmingen, and another nine ME-109s above Udine and Treviso. During the last ten days of July, pilots from the 332nd shot down nineteen enemy fighters, making a total of thirty-nine aerial victories between July 12 and 30.

August and September were busy months as well, but increasingly, there were fewer enemy fighters in the air as they escorted bombing raids. During August, they flew on twenty-eight missions, some in preparation for the invasion of southern France, others escorting long bombing raids against oil refineries in Ploesti, Rumania. They also destroyed twenty-two German fighters on the ground in one raid deep into Germany, twenty-three in another. In September, bad weather limited them to sixteen missions, but a strafing run against the airport at Ilandza, Yugoslavia, left thirty enemy airplanes burning on the ground.

Morale was high, and the 332nd was building quite a name for itself. Because of the color its P-51 tails were painted, they became widely renowned as the "Red Tails," and no American fighter group carried a higher reputation. Black reporters were always there on the ground at Ramitelli, eager to tell all the details of their exploits in black publications back in the States. But with some exceptions, mainstream white publications made little mention of what was undeniably a conceptual-blockbusting reality for white Americans: that black fighter pilots were doing a splendid job in taking the fight to an all-white German opponent.

During October 1944, the 332nd was to suffer the loss of fifteen planes and pilots. Some of these were shot down by German aircraft, some by flak, and others were just plain unlucky enough to roll those dice once too often and run out of luck. Such was the case of Lieutenant Fred Hutchison. Davis was watching as he strafed an enemy position from a very low level. When his fire hit an enemy ammunition dump, the resulting explosion seemed to just blow his airplane from the sky. Davis was stunned when he returned unhurt only a few days later, and a few other pilots from among the fifteen that had gone down somehow managed to get back to friendly lines. The only good day that month for the Red Tails was the twelfth, when Davis led a raid on Budapest and Vienna during which they destroyed nine German aircraft in the air, twenty-six on the ground, and quite a bit of military materiel.

In November, the Red Tails lost seven aircraft, and their only victories that month came when three of their pilots were escorting a crippled bomber back from Germany. Pounced on by eight ME-109s, Captain Luke Weathers shot down two of them, and he and the other two American pilots warded off the rest until the bomber got safely back to base. In December, January, and February, bad weather cut sharply into operations, but the Red Tails had their first encounters with ME-262 jet fighters, and it was clear that they had a major advantage over the propeller-driven American fighters.

Early in March, the 302nd Fighter Squadron was inactivated, and missions were stepped up as the weather cleared. On March 24, the 332nd escorted B-17s all the way to Berlin, a sixteen-hundred-mile round-trip mission and the longest flown during the war by the Fifteenth Air Force. Near the target, they were attacked by thirty ME-262 and ME-163 jet fighters, but the Red Tails were not surprised. They shot down three ME-262s, and probably got two more ME-262s and one ME-163. And on March

31, Davis led a fighter attack on Munich. They surprised seventeen German aircraft and hit them all, destroying thirteen, probably destroying three, and damaging one, their best count on any one day in the war. But during that month of March, they also lost eleven pilots. And during the month of April, they destroyed seventeen enemy airplanes while losing only three.

Berlin fell on May 2, and the war in Europe was over. The Red Tails had truly shown their skill, for from the time they began to escort bombers in early June 1944 until the end of the war, they never allowed an American bomber under their care to be shot down by enemy fighters. This is a claim no other American fighter group from World War II can make.

Despite their heroic and selfless actions at war, however, when they finally got back to the States, it must have been most disheartening for men of the 332nd to see the rigid lines of segregation enduring in so many places, including the U.S. Armed Forces. President Harry Truman issued an executive order in July 1948 calling on the Armed Forces to provide equal treatment and opportunity for black servicemen. The Air Force was first to implement this order, starting in May 1949, followed by the Army and the Navy. But the elimination of all-black units and the acceptance and absorption of blacks into all ranks without barriers would not be complete for many years to come. And without Benjamin O. Davis, Jr., and the Tuskegee airmen he led so skillfully, we might never have come as far as we did during the middle years of the twentieth century.

Russell P. Reeder

After graduating in 1926, Russell P. "Red" Reeder had served more than fifteen years in the peacetime Army before World War II broke out. He then worked on the personal staff of the commander of the U.S. Army, General George Marshall, and was sent to Guadalcanal in 1942 to report on the war. He spent several months there, interviewing Marine and Army combat veterans as well as traveling around and observing the situation, then returned to Washington and delivered his report to General Marshall. It was entitled "Fighting on Guadalcanal," and it contained lessons learned by American forces on Guadalcanal, primarily in areas of leadership and weapons use, but it also detailed such arcane issues as how to reduce Japanese pillboxes. Marshall liked it so much that he turned it into a sixty-nine-page pamphlet and had two million copies printed, then made sure that every American soldier and airman in uniform had access to a copy.

The specific details on Red's combat experiences came from several extended interviews I conducted with him in the last few years of his life, supplemented by geographic and mental facts drawn from other sources, including Red's wife, Dort, and his autobiography, *Born at Reveille*.

Guadalcanal, November 1942: Red rode in the front seat of a jeep as it bounced along a bumpy red clay road. To his left was the turquoise Pacific Ocean, and only a few hundred yards away white surf exploded on yellow sand. The sky was a dazzling, clear blue. Then they turned and entered the a dark green jungle, still following the red clay road. Red was cooler now, and they drove for perhaps another half hour. To his front, the *whump!* of incoming artillery rounds impacting grew ever nearer, balanced by the sharper explosions of answering American guns somewhere off to their right. Then Red saw Marines run by, bent over, carrying rifles and other gear. For the first time, he could make out distant machine gun fire. Then they stopped in front of an open-sided tent surrounded by a waist-high wall of sandbags. Inside, Red saw a few men behind desks, one of them hammering on a typewriter.

Red got out of the jeep as it stopped, and a bare-headed Marine in dirty fatigues came toward him. The small silver oak leaves of a lieutenant colonel were pinned to his collar, and his shirt was unbuttoned all the way down, exposing a bare, hairy chest wet with sweat. He extended his hand as he grew near.

"I'm Lieutenant Colonel Lou Puller, the commander of 1st Battalion, 7th Marines. We've been expecting you."

The two men shook hands. Both squeezed hard.

"Pleased to meet you, Colonel, I'm Lieutenant Colonel Red Reeder, and I hope you'll call me Red. I've been sent here by General Marshall to try to see if I can gather up some information on combat in Guadalcanal. We're going to try use the lessons you and your men have been learning here to upgrade our training back in the States."

"We've heard all about you, Red. Call me Chesty. We've got some good men picked to talk to you, all have seen plenty of combat, but we didn't know when you'd get here, so they're still down with their units."

A jeep pulled up and stopped and a major got out and walked toward them.

"Red, this is Major Lou Walt, he's the commander of 2nd Battalion, 5th Marines. Major Walt, this is Lieutenant Colonel Red Reeder, the man from General Marshall's office we've all been waiting for."

The two men shook hands.

"Pleased to meet you, sir."

"It's my pleasure, Major. General Marshall wants me to gather up as many lessons as I can that you men have learned from your combat against the Japanese so we can use them to train new recruits back in the States, so I'm here to learn from you."

Puller continued.

"Y'see, Red, Major Walt and I and another battalion, we have our companies deployed in a sort of horseshoe around a sizable Japanese unit that crossed the river a couple of days ago. The Japs have still got their backs to the river, but on this side they're pretty well surrounded. They've tried to break out a couple of times now, but so far we've held them, and we want to keep them boxed in while we try to crush them with air and artillery or at least push them back over the river. Now I can send for these guys if you want, or else we can go down to their positions and you can interview them there, whaddya say?"

Red shrugged. "Let's go, Chesty."

"All right, we'll start you in Lima Company in my battalion. They got hit two days ago, and I guarantee they won't get hit again, so you should be safe there. We have some good sign the Japs are going to hit Major Walt's battalion, either tonight or early tomorrow, way up by the river, and we've got a surprise ready if that happens. But everything should stay calm in the Lima Company part of the line, so you'll be able to get some good interviews."

Reeder turned to the Marine major.

"What about you, Major Walt?

"Well, my battalion, we're right next to Lima Company on their left, so I can give both of you a ride down to L Company, then Colonel Puller is coming over to my position to coordinate some things for that expected attack on my left flank, right sir?"

"That's right, so we can all ride down to the line together if you don't mind and we can talk as we go. We'll drop you off at L Company, Red, I'll get back to pick you up later, okay?"

The two men nodded, then Puller turned and shouted an order.

"Sergeant Fox, call down to Lima Company and tell them to have Master Gunnery Sergeant Fowle waiting for us at the reserve platoon position. See who else is down there who's supposed to be interviewed by Colonel Reeder."

Walt climbed back in front with the driver, while Puller and Reeder hopped in back. As the jeep pulled out, Red opened his notebook and started scribbling furiously. Walt was the first to speak.

"In combat, the training the men have been through counts most, so make sure they go through some hard stuff: don't get enough to eat, no time to sleep, and then change their orders a lot so they learn to react, especially the commanders. Now here in the jungle, silent movement is all-important, especially in the thick stuff. And an individual soldier is often only in contact with a few of his buddies, so he's really got to know what he's doing, and as much as possible, he needs to know what's going on."

Puller chimed in: "Yeah, that's where good sergeants come in, and they're worth their weight in gold. It's best to get rid of the bad ones fast, because they can get people killed if they don't know what they're doing. Now another thing is the big reputation these Japs have got as mighty warriors. But that's blown way up—they're human, too, they've just got more experience fighting in the jungle, that's all."

Walt had more: "And the Jap is not an individual fighter. He won't fight with the bayonet unless he's backed up by another dozen Japs, but that's the way they attack, a dozen of 'em shoulder to shoulder, screamin' as they run at you."

Back to Puller: "Now, once our boys get broken in, we're tougher than they are, and we've got better sergeants than the Japs do, too. Their officers give all the orders, and you can usually pick them out right away because they are the ones who carry big two-handed swords. Once you kill the guys who are swinging them, then the Jap units they command usually just fall apart."

Red scribbled notes as Puller spoke again: "That's true. But we need better communication. The 'walkie-talkie' the Japs have operates—why can't we have a similar one? To *hell* with telephone wire with advancing troops. We can't carry enough wire. We received an order, 'The advance will stop until the wire gets in.' *This is backwards!*"

"Yeah, and the men have got to learn the value of hand grenades, they don't like to carry them because they're so heavy, but they really do a job on the Japs, and our men need practice using them in heavily wooded country."

"I agree. I consider it *imperative* that the Army and Marines be equipped with knee mortars and only carry one type grenade. Have the hand grenade fit in the knee mortar and be of use as a hand grenade and also as a rifle grenade. You need a rifle grenadier in each squad for use against enemy machine gun nests."

As they moved closer, scattered gunfire got louder. Then they came into an area of high trees, relatively open on the ground, with sandbagged defenses going off a hundred yards on either side. They left the jeep and walked up to a group of sandbagged bunkers, inside which the reserve platoon was huddled. They stopped at the entrance of one bunker and Walt continued to talk.

"Here is something I know the Army teaches, sir, but I

would like to say it, as we really believe it here, and that is, don't put troops in a skirmish line until physical contact is made. Keep 'em in squad columns, with two scouts in front of each squad. As in the Basic Field Manual, each man should know the objective. I make my platoon leader designate an objective every hundred yards in the jungle, and they work to it and reorganize. They don't push off for the next objective until they get word from the company commander. This method, we have found, ensures control, and I control my companies the same way: I set up an objective for each company; when they reach that they report, reorganize if that's needed, then we go ahead. And in the attack, I keep the reserves up close so they can be committed immediately."

Puller weighed in: "That's the right way to do it. But this jungle really restricts movement and reconnaissance, to say nothing of communication, so in handling my companies, I take the company commander's word for what is going on. You have to do this to get anywhere. In order to get a true picture of what is going on in this heavy country, I make my staff get up where the fighting is. This command post business will ruin the American Army and Marines if it isn't watched. Hell, our platoons and squads would like to be in the command post during the attack if they aren't watched! As soon as you set up a command post, all forward movement stops.

"Okay, Red, here we are at Lima Company's reserve platoon. The other three platoons are on a line right up there, you can see the back of their trenches and strong points from here. Platoon leader is Lieutenant Cragg, here, platoon sergeant is Sergeant Dorland. Company commander is Captain Borden, but he's up forward on the line right now, and here comes Master Gunnery Sergeant Fowles, your first subject. I'm going over to Major Walt's area to work out some things, but I'll be back in an hour or so, we'll see what you want to do then."

After they parted, Reeder sat down and wrote as Sergeant Fowles spoke: "Sir, you gotta teach young fellows to look over the ground and look in the trees. The Japs will be in the toughest places and naturally on the best ground . . ."

When Red finally got back to the Pentagon, he started assembling his notes into the book Marshall wanted. His wife, Dort, and their four kids were happy to have him home, although he wanted desperately to take part in the impending invasion of Europe. He knew his family would be frightened when he left them to take command of an infantry regiment, and that was a bridge he would cross when he came to it. But he wanted command of a regiment almost desperately, and he knew the only way to ensure that would be to do a bang-up job on this book.

In his mind, those Marines on Guadalcanal were still as real as if they were right outside his office door. And they were soldiers fighting the war, while he was sitting behind a desk. But he could fix that, he knew, if this book turned out all right. He ran his hands through his thinning red hair as he read his notes and converted them into text on the blank sheet of paper:

"Your men have to be rugged and rough, sir, and to win they must disregard politeness and kill."

"Teach your soldiers, sir, that when a man is hit in the assault to leave him there. Too many of our men suddenly become first-aid men."

"We learned not to fire unless we had something to shoot at. Doing otherwise gives away your position and wastes ammunition."

"You have to *kill* to put these Japs out of action!"

"At night, sir, if the numbers on the mortar sight were luminous, with a luminous strip on the stick, we wouldn't have to use a flashlight. This flashlight business is dangerous."

"Our rifle grenades have been effective against hidden machine gun positions. You have to *kill* these Japs before they will leave. Just turning a large volume of fire in his direction will not make him leave."

"The big problem, which we have not solved completely yet, is maintaining contact in the attack between units in this jungle."

"We learned the hard way to move quietly in this jungle. I have been shot at by snipers many times and haven't seen one yet."

"On the Matanikau River, we got firing at each other because of careless leadership by our junior officers. We are curing ourselves of promiscuous firing, but I should think new units would get training to make the men careful."

"Men get killed rushing to help a wounded man. You gotta be very careful."

"Be mean and kill 'em. Kill 'em dead."

"It's okay to say that an outfit cannot be surprised, but it is bound to happen in this sort of warfare, so the men must know what to do when they're ambushed."

Some weeks later, Red was asked to report to General Marshall's office. It didn't take him long to get there, and he was ushered right in to the front to General Marshall's desk. Marshall looked up wearily as Red came in, then smiled.

"Oh, Reeder, good to see you. Listen, I read that report of yours from Guadalcanal with the utmost interest, and it's splendid, truly splendid. It reminded me of a time when I was on General Pershing's staff in France in 1918, I wrote a report in my own style and an officer above me suppressed it. I like particularly the thoughts you brought back from Guadalcanal on leadership and weapons."

Marshall stood up and came around his desk to shake Reeder's hand.

"Well done, Red."

"Thank you, sir."

"Now look, I'm going to have quite a few copies of your 'Fighting on Guadalcanal' report printed up in booklet form, and I'm going to have it studied widely. I want you to go around and help out with this, speak at our Infantry School, and then at different training sites around the country. We've *got* to get our men trained properly before we throw them into combat, and this report is key. Now, do you think you can help me with that?"

Reeder shrugged.

"Yes, sir."

Marshall continued to glare at him.

"You don't sound too happy, Colonel."

Another shrug.

"No, sir, I'll do whatever you say . . ."

"What is it?"

"Nothing, sir, it's just . . . well, I've been in the Army almost twenty years now, sir, and finally my country is at war, and I could be out there leading men, but instead, I'm back in Washington . . ."

"At ease, Reeder. I can't spare you now, I need you. Understand?"

Red's answer was barely audible.

"Yessir."

"What does your wife think about you wanting to go off and fight?"

"She wants me to stay here, sir . . ."

"Well, she'll get her wish for now. You pack a bag and get going, there are a lot of training commands that need to hear you."

When he got back to the Pentagon after his training trip, news of Colonel Reeder's success had preceded him. General Marshall held a small ceremony in his office, where he pinned a medal on Red's chest.

"Well, Red, I'm very proud of you. I can't say enough about the effect you and your Guadalcanal trip have had on preparing our soldiers for combat. You have truly earned this Legion of Merit."

They shook hands.

"And you've earned my sincere thanks, too, Red. As you know, we've had some two million copies of your booklet printed up and distributed to the troops, and the instruction you've given in person has been superb. Your new colonel's eagles fit you well, and you have become a real asset to my staff."

"Thank you sir. I just . . . I . . ."

"What is it Red?"

"Well, sir, I mean . . . well, with all this troop buildup going on in England for the invasion, and since you asked me once what I wanted to do, well, I thought maybe you could spare me . . ."

"Oh, we're back on that combat thing again, are we?"

"Well, yes, sir, I mean . . ."

"All right. You know, it seems like every other colonel in the United States Army is trying to use some kind of influence to get a command for this invasion, so no promises. But let me look into it."

Reeder's smile was suddenly beaming.

"Thank you, sir."

"Well, you've done good work for me, and I could still use you here."

"Sir, if it's all the same to you . . ."

"All right, Reeder, I understand. All commands are long taken, but maybe something will open up."

A few days later, Red was called into the office of his immediate boss, Major General Brown.

"You wanted to see me, sir?"

"Ah, Reeder. Come on in, Red. The Old Man asked me to tell you you're bigoted now."

"I am?"

Brown laughed.

"Yes, you are. That means that you will know the dates of the invasion because of your work for General Marshall, and when you get to England, you're not to breathe a word to anyone, understand?"

"England?"

"Yeah, that's the other thing General Marshall asked me to tell you. In a few days, you're to take over command of the 12th Infantry Regiment, 4th Division. On D-Day, you land on Utah Beach."

"Really? Why that's *wonderful!*"

Brown smiled.

"Well, Red, that's one way to look at it, but as your commander and your friend and your West Point brother, let me give you another look. You're going over to replace a guy who just had a heart attack, and they've got colonels ten deep over there grasping for this command. But General Marshall is the boss, so the command goes to you."

"Yes sir, and I'm very grateful to General Marshall."

"Well, Red, he really does need you here, you know. And so do I. Look, Red, you're one of my key planners, there's not another colonel like you in the whole Army, I *need* you right here!"

"Well, thank you sir, but . . . if I'm good, isn't that all the more reason why I should command a regiment?"

Brown stood up, exasperated, and began to pace.

"No, Red, it isn't. Look, let's be honest for once. It doesn't take any brains to fight, anyone can do that. But military planning for war fighting, why, that takes many long years of study and hard work and learning, and you've got those things in spades! Now look, I won't take anything away from your leadership abilities, but in a major war, the influence of one particular regimental commander on the ability of his men to perform their missions and survive is not nearly as important as the abilities of an operations and planning officer who knows what he's doing. This is what West Point trained us for: to plan warfare and guide armies to victory, not to die like sheep among some brawling mass of blood-lusting brutes. You risk dying like that and you risk everything West Point and our nation tried to build in you, brains rather than brute brawn."

"Sir, I understand your concern, but I don't agree with you. We owe it to our men to give them the best-trained and motivated leaders possible, and with all due respect, that's where I think I'll shine!"

"Red, what about our top commanders, General Marshall and General Eisenhower? They're not combat leaders, and they've never pretended to be! But they're great generals because they see the big picture and they know what to do!"

"Sir, that may all be true, but I'm not a general, and the nation has invested a lot in me. I am the one who should be responsible for both the welfare of the soldiers in that regiment and the accomplishment of our mission, whatever it might be. I feel that commanding troops in war is my duty, it's what I've trained for all these years . . ."

"Red, look at me. I've been a general for almost a year, just got my second star. Now I'm telling you, if you stay here on General Marshall's staff working for me, you'll be promoted to brigadier general within six months, probably have your second star within a year. You go off to fight and there are no such guarantees. You could even die, Red. You really could die!"

"Sir . . . thank you, sir, but I just don't feel . . . you know, you were talking about our days as cadets at West Point, and I just can't stop a line from the Cadet Prayer from running through my mind . . ."

"Which one is that, Red?"

"Lord, help me always to choose the harder right instead of the easier wrong."

"Oh, you think I'm doing wrong to stay here and be loyal to General Marshall instead of going out and trying to get killed so that whatever abilities I may have acquired over the years go up in smoke?"

"No, sir, I didn't say that."

"You came awfully damned close, Reeder! Tell me, are you trying to make your wife a widow?"

"No, sir, of course not. I guess Robert E. Lee said it best: 'A call to serve one's country is a high call; a call to serve her under arms in time of war is the highest.'"

"Well, Red, I am almost embarrassed to say this, but I'm afraid you really are the fool some people have always accused you of being. General Marshall got you what you wanted, a regimental command for the invasion of Normandy, and you really seem stubborn about it, so there's nothing more I can say. I gave you an opportunity to serve your nation with your brains instead of your brawn, in a position where promotion to general and a key role in developing our war-fighting strategy are assured, and you have spurned me. So go on off to war and find your destiny, Reeder. I wash my hands of you."

On a rainy morning in February 1944, an Army staff car met Red at the airport, and he rode for several hours. Finally, they drove through a gate in a high stone wall and pulled up to the front of a large mansion that was being used as the 4th Infantry Division headquarters. Red was to report to the division commander, Major General Raymond O. Barton, class of 1913 at West Point. Red remembered Barton, who had been a tactical officer at West Point during Red's last two years as a cadet, but he was sure there was no way Barton would remember him. Red walked into his office, locked his heels together, and saluted.

"Sir, Colonel Reeder reports to General Barton for duty."

Barton stood and returned Reeder's salute, then extended his hand.

"Well, well, well. Colonel Red Reeder! Welcome to the 4th Infantry Division, Red. I still remember watching you steal home against Navy in 1926 to win the game. What a great day for Army that was!"

Red was pleasantly surprised, and he couldn't smother his smile.

"Well, thank you, sir, but my stealing home only tied the game, we didn't win it until Buck Thompson, the next batter, hit a home run."

"Oh, all right, but you still saved the game. Two outs in the bottom of the ninth inning when you stole home, weren't there?"

"Yes, sir, and two strikes on the hitter, Charley Gibson, and he just couldn't hit that Navy pitcher."

"Well, Red, I'm just delighted to get you. We've all read your 'Fighting on Guadalcanal,' and let me tell you, it's very good, and even though we have no jungle and we're going against the Germans rather than the Japanese, it's just the sort of thing our men needed to learn before going into combat."

"Well, thank you, sir, but I'm the first to acknowledge that there's a big difference between serving on a high-ranking general's staff writing books and commanding troops in the field."

"Don't be too modest, Red. I remember you well from West Point, and you're just the sort of leader that we need, a hard fighter who will never give up."

"Thank you, sir. I hope my ability to command troops will meet with your approval."

"I'm sure it will, Red. I'm giving you command of the 12th Infantry Regiment."

Barton gestured to his other staff officers to leave. After the last one left, the door closed, and he and Red were alone.

"Sit down, Red. Relax. I want to give you some inside information, but please keep it to yourself."

Barton sat back down behind his desk as Red pulled a chair in close on the other side and listened attentively.

"The 12th, until a few weeks ago, was commanded by Colonel Crimp, who, just between us, was a real problem. He was quite a few years older than you, almost my own age, and he had no real gumption at all. He refused to push his regiment hard, and it only barely got the job done. He had established himself as a very fatherly sort with his men, and they really loved him. But he was way too soft on them, especially on the eve of our invasion of Europe. The result was that I made the other regiments, the 8th and the 22nd, the maneuver elements, while I've kept the 12th back with me, where I could control things a bit, push Crimp when I had to. He was the wrong guy, but I didn't have much choice, it was awfully late in the game to try to bring in a new regimental commander. But then he had a heart attack a few weeks ago, and that's how I got you, and I couldn't be happier."

Barton paused to light his pipe, then resumed his talk.

"Anyway, Crimp's heart attack really depressed his whole regiment. His executive officer, a Lieutenant Colonel Luckett, took over, and he has been fine, I suppose. But these young men need some fire put in their bellies before we land in France, they really need some spirited leadership to get them ready for combat. Think you can handle that, Red?"

"I think I can, sir. Do I have a free rein with them?"

"Sure, Red. And let me say that, as long as you don't intentionally kill anyone, I want you to do whatever you think is necessary to get your men ready for combat, because I want to be able to use the 12th as a full-fledged maneuver element I can throw into the fray and depend on, understand?"

Reeder stood up and saluted.

"Sir, it shall be done."

"Good, good. We have a five-day exercise scheduled to start tomorrow up on the moors. I know you must be exhausted from your flight over here, so if you want to observe for a few days while you catch up on your sleep and try to get the lay of the land, why, you can just stay up here on division staff as my special assistant, what do you think of that?"

"Sir, if it's all the same with you, I can catch up on my sleep later, but time is short, and every moment of training before the invasion is important, so I'd like to take over command right now."

"I was hoping you'd say that, Red. Good for you!"

An hour later, Red walked into the 12th Regiment headquarters, located in a large manorial house behind hedges. Lieutenant Colonel James Luckett called the room to attention, and a half-dozen men spring to their feet.

"Good morning, sir. We got a call from Division that you were on your way down here. We've tried to clean the headquarters up a little bit for you, and we're certainly glad to see you. I'm Lieutenant Colonel James Luckett, your executive officer. I've been the acting regimental commander since Colonel Crimp entered the hospital two weeks ago, but I've moved my stuff out of your office and it's all yours now, sir."

"That's fine, Colonel. I care about function more than appearance. As long as things work, there's no reason to shine them up for me. I understand from General Barton that we're going out on the moor for a five-day training exercise tomorrow, is that right?"

"Yes sir, our gear is all loaded on trucks, we've been out in this area twice before. Let me show you on the map in your office, sir."

Luckett led the way into an internal office, and Red closed the door behind them

"Okay, Colonel, I want you to round up my staff. I want to spend half an hour with my operations officer first, then I want three hours with the intelligence officer, the operations officer, and you. See if you can arrange for us to get something to eat as we start that. After that, I want you to schedule about half an hour with the supply officer, then at five o'clock, I want to see all my battalion commanders and their own battalion staffs—executive officers, operations officers, intelligence officers, supply officers. Can we get that many men into my office at once?"

"I . . . I don't know, sir, it might be a little crowded, but we can try."

"Okay. Where are we quartered?"

"Sir, the regimental staff has complete use of this house, and we have plenty of room. We eat in the dining room, and as the regimental commander, you would get the owner's main bedroom upstairs, we've already got fresh linen on the bed for you."

"Well, as the new commander, I intend to establish my own mark on things. We'll go over that later. Right now, send my operations officer in with the maps for tomorrow's operation. If I've not called you in half an hour, I want you and my intel man to join us, we've got a lot to do."

Later that day, about twenty men were tightly packed into Red's office.

"All right, please let me have your attention. I'm Colonel Red Reeder, your new regimental commander. I already know some of you from staff work in Washington, but we are now in a most important position. As you know, we are preparing for invasion of Europe, to close with and destroy the forces of Nazi Germany. Now the German soldiers are not ten feet tall, they're no better fighters than any of our men. The most important distinction is that many of them have already seen quite a bit of combat in Russia. The only way we can make up for that, of course, is through training, and the training has to be as realistic as possible. After this exercise is over, I will come down to your battalions and try to spend some time getting to know you and your men personally, just so you have a better idea of what kind of man I am. Most people think I am a nice guy, and I always try to be that way. However, as we prepare to go to war, the most important thing I can do or any of you can do is help get our men ready to fight and win. Now unless I specifically tell you otherwise—and there are a few things that *must* stay between us, at least for now—I want everything I say here tonight to be passed on down the chain of command so that every soldier assigned to this regiment hears it, understood?"

There was a chorus of subdued "Yessirs."

"All right, now first of all, we've got to be ready for some of the harsher aspects of war, and the first thing that means is that from now on, everyone under my command will sleep under canvas. No more sleeping in houses or in beds. You can sleep on Army cots for now, but that may change so that everyone, myself included, will be required to sleep on the ground. We'll see. At any rate, I have already instructed my regimental supply officer to see that the word goes out tonight, tents go up for all soldiers, including staff officers. From now on, that's where we will all sleep."

A chorus of groans went up, but Reeder spoke over it.

"And as of this moment, we will always be ready to go to war. That means every night from now on, we will all sleep in our field uniforms, remove boots and web gear for sleeping, but that's it. We will continue to wash and shave every day, bathe when schedule breaks permit. But the soft times are *over!* From this moment, we prepare on a full-time schedule to go to *war!* While we are eating breakfast tomorrow, the tents will be taken down and loaded on trucks for use on this training exercise. And tonight, everyone out of the houses. Another adjustment the staff is going to have to make is that, from now on, whatever the enlisted soldiers eat, that's what we'll eat. No more fresh game or other special treats will be prepared for officers in the kitchens of these big houses we've been occupying."

There was another wave of groans from the back of the room.

"Now you may not be happy about this, but we are going to war, and we *must* be prepared. A small sacrifice like those I now mention will pay big benefits in lives saved and missions performed in the long run, believe me."

A voice spoke out from a muscular blond major with distinctively rugged looks.

"Sir, we all know that we're going off to war, and when that happens, we may well have to sleep on the ground after the invasion, and—"

"What's your name, Major, and what do you do?"

"I, I . . . my name is Major Lyons, sir, and I'm your liaison officer with the Army Air Corps."

"All right, continue, Major Lyons."

"Sir, we're only getting *ready* to fight, we're not actually fighting yet, we all know that. What possible difference does it make if we sleep in nice beds inside nice houses now?"

"It makes a difference because I *say* it does, Major. We *must* do everything we can to simulate the realities of war, and if we don't expect to sleep in comfortable beds inside comfortable houses after the invasion—and we do *not* expect that, Major!—then we will no longer do that now, while we prepare for the invasion and fighting. Do I make myself clear, Major?"

"Yes, sir."

"All right. Now on this exercise, I've been over it in some detail with my own staff, I've gotten a fair picture of what these exercises have been like, and I think I understand what will happen. As we operate, we will be simulating action along with the rest of our division and other divisions in our corps. We will constantly be told by control at corps level what happens to our organization, the realities of war that we will simulate occurring. They will be taking certain forces out of action and so on, you all know how this exercise works. Well, one difference between me and your former commander will be that I will have no fixed command post. I will always be in radio contact with my subordinate commanders, but I will be mobile, up near the front where I can see what is going on and react. And I want the very best contact maintained in this regiment, I want constant communication between our neighboring battalions. That has been a major problem for the Marines in the Pacific, and I imagine we can expect problems there as well. Now in addition, I am going to put some added constraints on the problem, and this will be the information I said must be held in strictest secrecy. No one in this room is to mention the things I will now tell you to *anyone* until they unfold. Is that understood?"

There was a soft chorus of "Yessirs."

"Right. On day one, that's tomorrow, we will begin the operation as scheduled. During the night of day one, all our field messing facilities will be packed up and returned to base, and at dawn of day two, the men will be told that all our kitchen and messing facilities have been taken out by German air. There will be no resupply of food until day four, when each man will receive two K rations, one for each day. At nightfall of day four, I will coordinate this with Division, we will simulate being thrown back ten miles from whatever position we have reached, and will then countermarch that same ten miles back to our positions before dawn. I want *every man* in this regiment to share in this 'surprise' hunger that will be brought on by the vicissitudes of war, and also to be on that final night march, with no exceptions. And this order specifically includes all staff officers and NCOs at all levels in the regiment except for emergency medical personnel, who will follow a slightly different protocol to be spelled out by Lieutenant Colonel Luckett. Do I make myself clear?"

A hoarse grumbling of "Yessirs" brought a louder response from Red.

"I said, 'Do I make myself *clear?*'"

They were surprised but loud in their response.

"Yes, sir!"

"Now, you may not like my training methods right away, but I *assure you*, they will keep men alive! And there is to be no squirreling away of extra rations for the benefit of those in the know. What's good enough for the men is good enough for their leaders, and I will be hell on anyone I catch in violation of that concept. Colonel Luckett, anything else?"

"Sir, only that I want to meet with all the battalion supply officers right after this to make sure we have the K ration requirement met, and then I want all the medical commanders at the battalion and lower levels to report to me right here in half an hour."

"Thank you, Colonel. All right, men, now you know what I have in mind, and again, I remind you to keep all this in the strictest confidence. This will be a more demanding exercise, I think, than any you've been on so far. But we're about to see what kind of men we have in the 12th Infantry Regiment, and I will be watching you as you watch those below you. This isn't combat, but it's pressure, and we may see who can handle the pressures of combat and who can't. Watch closely, for later on, lives will depend on leadership abilities we are about to test. Dismissed."

Over the next few months, Red was able to reshape the performance of the men in his regiment, and their attitudes, from doing only the bare minimum it took to get by to aggressive engagement in a conscious effort to, when the moment came, close with and kill enemy soldiers. The training was tough, and the extra road marches at first brought howls of protest. But within a few months, while his men weren't happy to be doing an extra ten miles on the road while the soldiers from other regiments were drinking beer in local pubs, they were grudgingly grateful. They knew the extra work might be what it took to keep them alive.

Finally the orders came down, and the men packed their duffel bags and were ferried to the port of Penzance in Army trucks. Then, as the sun was setting, troops from his regiment crowded around Red's jeep as they prepared to board ship. Standing on the hood, Red spoke, his voice loud: "All right, men, this is it. You've trained hard, and you've shown how tough you are. When I first got here, I gotta tell you, I wasn't sure. But I drove you hard, and you've earned my highest respect. I've seen a lot of fighting men in my day, and I will now stand here and tell you there are no tougher troops than you men anywhere in the world!"

A huge roar erupted from the men. Red held up his hands and they were quiet again.

"When we land in France tomorrow morning, we expect to be opposed by some of the best troops in the German army. They'll be heavily supported by tanks and artillery. Our first concern is to get off the beach, and our intelligence says the Germans have flooded the fields behind the beach. But you've trained getting through deep water here in England and you know what to do, so I don't think we'll even be slowed down by that. All I can say is that I'm glad I'm going to be with the 12th Infantry tomorrow and not the Germans. May God have mercy on them, for we will have none!"

As they landed, the 12th Infantry took quite a bit of

small-arms fire. But they were ready for this, and they were quickly off the beach. Red was everywhere at once, directing traffic, urging men forward, yelling at incompetence that might get people killed, forging ahead, personally leading the way toward the beach wall through enemy fire.

Once beyond the beach, they came to the flooded fields they expected. Red urged his men forward, telling non-swimmers to hook up with swimmers, amid constant incoming artillery and small-arms fire.

A few hours later, soaked soldiers from the 12th Infantry were reaching dry ground on the far side of flooded fields. Red needed a radio but was told there were none functioning. He then asked for a runner, and after a few yells, a sergeant appeared with a tall, lanky soldier.

"Sir, this is Private Smith, he was a champion distance runner in high school in Iowa."

"Okay, Smitty, I want you to get back to Colonel Luckett on the beach and tell him that it's just what we suspected. We landed about a mile down the beach from where we should be, so I'm moving the 2nd Battalion out in front, we're going to head toward the village of Saint Martin. Tell him I want the 1st Battalion to follow us, and then he is to follow in line with the 3rd Battalion. And tell him I want Major Lyons, our Air Corps liaison, up here with me. Say that back to me."

"Sir, I am to find Colonel Luckett and tell him that we landed a mile too far down the beach, and you are going to move toward the village of Saint Martin with 2nd Battalion, the 1st Battalion will follow you, and Colonel Luckett is to follow them with the 3rd Battalion. And he is to send Major Lyons, the Air Corps liaison officer, up here with you."

"You got it! Now don't go back through the water, there's

a road on a dike over there, but it's plugged up with vehicles coming off the beach, you'll have to work your way around them. Tell Colonel Luckett I need a radio, and if he can't send me one I'm gonna have to use runners! Go!"

Smitty ran off as Red turned and moved through woods with a handful of staff officers and NCOs.

After Smitty delivered his message, Colonel Luckett had his own for Red.

"Okay, now you get back to Colonel Reeder and tell him I already sent the only spare radio forward to him, that was the only one I had left. Intelligence just told us there is a major German troop concentration behind Saint Martin, artillery as well as infantry, tell him we might do better if we try to go around the village to the east before we attack. If he goes right through the village they'll be waiting for us. And tell him Major Lyons was just killed by German artillery fire, so we don't have any liaison with Air, but I've sent for a replacement. Say that back to me."

"Sir, I am to tell Colonel Reeder that you already sent your only spare radio forward for him, and that there is a major German troop concentration in Saint Martin, and that he should try to go around it to the east or else—"

"No, no, not *in* Saint Martin, they're *behind* Saint Martin, at least that's what *intelligence* said, and they said the Germans have infantry *and* artillery waiting for us there, say that back to me."

"Sir, the Germans . . . intelligence said that the Germans have infantry *and* artillery waiting *behind* Saint Martin, we might be better off going around the village to the east before attacking, because if we go right through it they'll be waiting for us. And Major Lyons was killed but you have sent for a replacement."

Smitty ran like a deer, but he had a long way to go, and

he kept getting waved farther to the front. Eventually, he was moving along a row of trees when he saw a group of men crouched behind a small wooden farm hut some hundred yards to his front and very close to a village of chipping ochre houses. That must be the village of Saint Martin, he thought, and he had to get to Colonel Reeder and tell him that Colonel Luckett had warned him not to go into that village before he walked into a trap. Smitty bent over and ran like the wind, holding his helmet on with his left hand while he prayed half-aloud that the Germans wouldn't see him and kill him. He arrived unscathed and slid behind the hut next to Red.

"Sir, Colonel Luckett said to tell you there's a large German . . . I mean, he said to tell you *intelligence* said there's a big German force of infantry *and* artillery behind the village, maybe it would be better to go around the village to the east before you attack, because if you go through the village, then the Germans will just be back there waiting for you . . ."

Red turned to Smitty as he spoke and gave him a wry smile.

"Smitty, that's what intelligence says, and paratroopers were supposed to come through here ahead of us and clean Saint Martin out. But even if they did, the Germans are back, and they're in Saint Martin and it looks like they are at least using the steeple of that church as a fire direction center to hammer American troops, so we can't really go around it if—"

"Sir . . . I'm not through, sir, he also said to tell you Major Lyons was killed by enemy artillery fire, but he has sent for a replacement . . ."

"Major Lyons is dead?"

"Yes sir, that's what Colonel Luckett—"

"Damn! All right . . . now, look at this map, there's an

important road intersection behind Saint Martin that we're going to try to take and control, whether there's a German troop and artillery concentration there or not, but first we've *got* to go through the village. The 22nd Infantry is coming up on our right, while the 8th is off to our left. After we're through here, I'm gonna send you back to Colonel Luckett, but stay with me for a while to see how things develop."

Red, still crouching, moved out from behind one corner of the hut and pointed.

"Now, everybody see that church steeple with a big opening near the top?"

The rest of his staff moved around behind him so they could see, and they all nodded.

"Okay, some of you guys get back out of sight, because they're up there looking for us, I'm sure of it. And one of the guys in that steeple looks like he's a forward observer for the German artillery, he's adjusting their artillery fire from there and he's pounding our units as they move up as well as hitting our units that are still on the beach. If you watch that opening, you can see his head and shoulders and you can see the sunlight glint off his binoculars when he raises 'em . . . there, see that? He's no more than two hundred yards away from us right now."

The half-dozen men around Reeder nodded and grunted agreement.

"Okay, I don't think the Germans know we got this close, and we've got about five or six rifles. I want everybody to get into an open area where you can shoot, and put your sights on that opening on the steeple, I'd say it's two hundred yards away. All right, good, good. Smitty, can you fire a rifle?"

"Yes sir, I've been a dead shot since I was ten years old."

"Good. Sergeant Curtis, you're from Philadelphia, give Smitty your rifle. Now, the next time he raises his binoculars, we'll fire together on my command, one of us ought to be able to hit him."

All six men, including Reeder, raised their rifles.

"Okay, ready . . . ready . . . *fire!*"

There was a crash of gunfire, and Reeder jerked out of the wisps of gunsmoke to see clearer.

"Well, I think we got him, either that or scared hell out of him! Second Battalion should be ready to make their assault into the village any time now, shouldn't they?"

A wave of small-arms and machine gun fire, accompanied by roars and shouts, was his answer. Reeder stood up and raised his binoculars to his eyes.

"The Germans are pulling out. Come on, we've got to get control of that intersection, then move northwest up to Boozeville, maybe hook up with some of the units from the paratroops that jumped into the area around Sainte-Mère-Église last night, make us that much stronger by nightfall."

As he moved forward, another runner caught him.

"Sir . . . Colonel Luckett says please, wait, that the 1st and 3rd battalions are not able to move as fast as the 2nd, he says he is concerned we are getting too far out in front and too strung out, he suggests you look for a defensive position for the night."

Red was angry and frustrated.

"Okay, you go back and tell Colonel Luckett we can't wait for anything, to get those two battalions moving as fast as he can. Tell him I expect to get to Boozeville tonight, he is to come through Saint Martin, that's the village with the church steeple, and get up here as fast as possible. There are still American paratroopers scattered out in front of us, we have to link up with them or rescue them, Colonel Luckett knows that! Say that back to me."

"Sir, Colonel Luckett is to move those two battalions up

here as fast as possible, he is to follow the 2nd Battalion through Saint Martin with the church steeple, and you want to try to reach Boozeville tonight, and there are still American paratroopers out in front waiting for us."

"Go! Smitty, I want you to stay with me, I'm gonna need you."

Red's troops quickly swept through the village of Saint Martin and met only light resistance at the crossroads behind it, then the Germans pulled back.

"Okay, Smitty, I want you to tell Colonel Luckett we've taken the crossroads, now moving northwest toward Boozeville, tell him to get the 3rd Battalion up here on the double, I want them to come up on the 2nd Battalion's left flank as we move through these hedgerows, we expect lots of resistance. Now there's the ruins of an old Norman castle short of Boozeville, here on the map, see that? I'll write the map coordinates down on a piece of paper, here. Now . . . take this back to Luckett, tell him that if our troops get to Boozeville today, that I'll meet him there before dark. I want to use that castle as regimental headquarters, we'll keep the 3rd Battalion there as regimental reserve. Say that back to me."

"Sir, you have taken Saint Martin and the road intersection behind it, you are moving on Boozeville with the 2nd Battalion, you want the 1st Battalion to come up on their left flank, and if our troops get to Boozeville today, you want to use the old Norman castle at these coordinates as regimental headquarters and keep the 3rd Battalion there as regimental reserve, you'll meet Colonel Luckett there before dark."

"Go! And tell Luckett I still haven't got a radio, if he can't get me one he is to keep sending you and that other guy, what's his name?"

"Private Jones, sir."

"Okay, you and Jonesy, you will go back and forth as

our regimental runners; when you're too tired he'll have to find other men."

"Sir, I ran cross-country in high school, and Jonesy ran the mile, we can run forever!"

"Okay, Smitty, go get 'em! And be careful, I don't want you to get hit!"

"I'll be fine, sir!"

Hours later, Red, with Jonesy and a few other riflemen, walked into a large, tumbledown courtyard. There were piles of hay along the walls, some chickens, goats and cows, and jeeps and ambulances were parked everywhere. American soldiers in combat gear bustled around carrying papers and radios and other gear. Red walked up the wide steps and through huge open doors into the expansive hallway of a Norman castle left over from long ago. Lieutenant Colonel Luckett came around a corner and nearly ran into him. They both went into a room filled with staff officers, clerks, and orderlies, all hustling around, talking on telephone or radio and trying to manage the administration of an infantry regiment in combat.

"Glad to see you, sir! I wasn't sure we were going to take Boozeville, but I hustled up here. We didn't find any Germans, just an old French farmer and some of his animals, and he was happy to see us!"

"Well, looks like you're all set up. Do we have commo with division headquarters?"

"Yes sir. We got the last land line laid about twenty minutes ago, the division commander wants you to call him."

"Where's the phone?"

Luckett gestured to a chair behind a big antique wooden table. Red sat down and picked up the phone. As he talked to Division, Luckett was talking to Jonesy and Smitty.

"You boys were both great as runners, but we've got two radios for Colonel Reeder now, so you can return to your companies."

"Thank you, sir."

"Sir . . . sir, I don't know about Jonesy, but I kinda like helpin' Colonel Reeder, any chance we could, you know, carry his radios or help with other stuff, 'cause you never know when those radios will go bust and you'll need us as runners again."

"Yeah, that's right, sir, you might need us again . . ."

"Well . . . you're probably right, hang around for now. Sergeant Wallace! I want these two men who have been regimental runners to stay on the staff. Keep them close in case we need them again!"

The next day, the hedgerow fighting had gotten intense. Red, with a half-dozen members of his staff beside him, came out of a hedgerow and into an open field where more than a hundred riflemen were sitting or lying down.

"What are you men doing here?"

A taken-aback captain was startled.

"Sir, we're A Company, 2nd of the 8th, we were told to come up as your reserve for—"

"Well you're too far forward and too bunched up! You'll draw fire! Spread out and get back!"

The captain was still startled as German artillery hit a few hundred yards behind them, but Red never hesitated, yelling at the men as he ran into the field.

"Up on your feet, all of you! Now move out, double time!"

More German artillery hits, now off to the side, and Red was livid.

"The Germans are ranging in on you! Run like hell! Spread out and take cover!"

The formerly quiet group of soldiers was spurred to life, and Red and his staff ran with them as they spread. They had gotten a few hundred yards away and passed through two hedgerows. Red and about twenty other American soldiers burst through a third hedgerow and into another open field. But on the other side of the field, no more than forty yards away, they saw an equal number of Germans tumble out of the hedgerow, coming toward them. Both groups were drop-jaw amazed by seeing their enemies bursting through the hedgerow into the same field, and as individual soldiers on both sides began to clamber back into their own hedgerows, Red leaped to his feet and charged the Germans, firing his pistol at them and yelling to his men as he moved:

"Let's go men! Follow me! Let's *kill* those bastards!"

The American troops quickly recovered and followed Red, firing as they moved. A handful of Germans went down in the field, dead or wounded, and others had their hands up and were trying to surrender. Red and his men reached the hedgerow into which the Germans had disappeared, and his troops followed them, roaring and shooting. Red stopped and shouted orders after them not to enter the next field. Then Luckett came up to Reeder, panting, his hands trembling.

"Colonel Reeder, that's . . . that's the closest to combat I've ever come . . ."

Red's sunburned face was now beaming.

"What do you mean 'closest,' Jim? That *was* combat, and you were *great!*"

"I don't know about that, sir, I mean . . . I just followed your lead, you were . . . I mean, where did you ever learn that?"

Red's grin was infectious as he carefully reholstered his .45 automatic pistol.

"What, how to fire a .45 while I'm running? Listen, firing is key to any attack in combat, whether you hit anything or not, and that's because you want both to frighten the enemy and to get our own men going too, makes it easier for them to join in and then keep up the attack, you understand?"

"Yes, sir, I do. But that's not what I was asking about. I mean, where did you ever learn that, in a surprise like that, when the Germans and us, we sort of stumbled into each other and we were all just surprised and scared, Germans too, and you just jumped up and started to run at the enemy, shooting and yelling for us to join you, and next thing you know, we did! And the Germans, why they just turned and ran, and every one of them we didn't kill or capture is probably still running! I mean, we're all a little bit in shock, but we won, and we could very easily have lost! What made you do that?"

"I'll tell you, Jim, during the summer almost twenty years ago, we were learning cavalry tactics back on the dirt roads across the Hudson from West Point. Now I know horses can't make it in the world of modern weapons, but some of the principles stay the same. They taught us that in a meeting engagement, like this, which is almost always a surprise to both sides, the side that acts first wins. It's just as simple as that. And, as you can see, we acted first, and we won!"

Red smiled broadly as he patted Luckett on the shoulder.

"Make sure that A Company's commander drops back a couple hundred yards and gets his men concealed in the hedgerows. I'm going back up front with the 1st Battalion, we've got a lot of fighting in front of us. The Germans will soon be cut off, and we've got to push them all the way to Cherbourg at the end of the peninsula, where they will either surrender or die."

Several days later, Red and his staff came out of another hedgerow, and he paused and asked for the regimental engineer to come forward. He was looking at his map while he waited, and riflemen emerged from the hedgerow on either side of him and moved forward. A dozen riflemen were almost across the field when a German 88-mm field gun concealed in the hedgerow down at the other end of the field, a hundred yards from Red's position, fired one shot. It hit right next to Red's left foot and exploded.

Inside Walter Reed Hospital, Red was lying in bed, surrounded by his elated (that he was home alive) but subdued family. In walked General Brown, now a lieutenant general with three stars on his shoulders. He had only strong praise for Red's heroism as he ceremoniously pinned a Distinguished Service Cross, second only as a decoration for personal valor to the Medal of Honor, and a Purple Heart on Red's chest. Flashbulbs popped, and as the two shook hands, Red forced a smile.

"Well, Red, I'm very proud of you for your actions in Normandy, and so is General Marshall. He asked me to extend his best to you, he's sorry he can't be here, but the war goes on and all that, you know . . ."

"I know, sir. I really do want to go back and fight, but now that my leg is gone . . . I mean, I know the Army doesn't have room for amputees in the field, but I can still do a lot, and I remember once you offered me a shot at staying under your command and planning the war. Is there any chance I could . . ."

General Brown was smiling as his words hissed out through his steel teeth:

"Gee, Red, I'm sorry, but a lot of eager men filled my command after you left. But don't worry, I'm sure they'll find something for you to do back up at West Point . . ."

Chapter 8:

Korean War—Joe Clemons

JOE CLEMONS WAS BORN IN CLEVELAND, but grew up on a farm in central Florida and moved to Baltimore in 1940. He enlisted in the Army Air Corps out of high school in February 1946, and was serving in the Philippines when he was selected to go to the Army's West Point prep school. Sworn in as a cadet in July 1947, he graduated in 1951, was commissioned in the infantry and assigned to the 82nd Airborne Division at Fort Bragg, North Carolina.

Joe married Cecil Russell, the sister of a West Point classmate, Walt Russell, in September 1952 and went to Korea in October 1952. He went to the 31st Infantry at Kumhwha, and the whole division was pulled back for retraining in the wake of the heavy losses they suffered on the twin hills they called Jane Russell after the buxom movie star. On Christmas Eve, Joe was an infantry platoon leader with Able Company, 1st Battalion of the 31st. In those days, companies were generally called by the phonetic word used for their letter of the alphabet. Able Company was really A Company, but everyone knew it as Able.

Able was sent to an outpost about one thousand meters forward of their main line of resistance (MLR), atop a hill known as "T-Bone" because of its shape from the air. From there, Joe was kept busy mainly with patrolling, and his unit was not in any major firefights. In February, Joe was reassigned as the new company commander of King Company. They were in battalion reserve, dug in at the south base of Hill 347 and close to the MLR. From that position, Old Baldy, now occupied by the Chinese, was six or eight hundred meters off to the left front, while T-Bone was off to the right and much farther out. Between those hills was the steep-sided hill known as Pork Chop Hill.

In April 1953, Pork Chop was occupied by Easy Company of the 31st, commanded by Lieutenant Tom Harrold. It was a relatively small hill, shaped much like a pork chop, roughly circular with some concave indentations in the wire and trench lines to conform roughly with topography. Its crest was covered by a half-dozen connected and overlapping loops of trenches and bunkers that had been laid out by Lieutenant Paul Gorman only months before, when American troops first occupied it. The position was compact, and Easy Company's hundred men seemed to be just the right-sized garrison to occupy and hold it.

At this time in the war, the lines of the two adversaries had become relatively stable while fruitless political negotiations were carried on at Panmunjom. American and South Korean troops heavily dug into defensive positions on the south confronted their Chinese and North Korean counterparts to the north. Most combat came only when patrols from the two sides accidentally collided with each other in the no man's land between their lines.

Pork Chop was in that no man's land, but it was of no particular value to either side, save only as an outpost from which the Americans could glare more closely at the Chinese from behind barbed wire and stout defenses. The

Chinese on Old Baldy, for their part, could watch the rear of Pork Chop, from which a primitive road used for supply runs reached back to American lines. But that was the only thing even remotely unsettling to most of the men in Easy Company, for they were on top of a steep hill with no cover, surrounded by many coils of concertina barbed wire, and they had massive American artillery defensive fire support on call, day or night. The hundred well-armed American riflemen huddled in Pork Chop's defenses felt quite secure in what seemed to them a pretty impregnable position. None of them ever dreamed the Chinese would launch an attack against them, and that may have been a fatal assumption.

On the night of April 16, Pork Chop Hill was overrun by Chinese forces, and King Company was alerted at 2:00 A.M. on April 17 for a possible counterattack. Clemons passed the word and made sure everyone got a full meal in them. Then he made sure that everyone carried plenty of extra ammunition for their weapons. Lieutenant Harrold had recommended that each platoon also bring a flamethrower and a heavy rocket launcher, and Clemons made sure those were secured and distributed.

At 3:30 A.M., Clemons was told to move King up to an attack position on Hill 200 near the base of Pork Chop. As the men in King moved, they all saw that the crest was being hammered by American artillery. Once they got to 200, Clemons was met there by Lieutenant Colonel Davis, his battalion commander. Davis told Clemons that two platoons from Love Company would be joining his attack from the right, although they would not make contact before the attack was launched. Davis told Clemons to call him on the radio when they started the attack, and he would lift the artillery. He also reminded Clemons that there was what they called a "chow bunker" just outside the wire and near the road up into Pork Chop Hill. Bulk food was stored there and drawn on regularly by the garrison. He suggested that King use that as its staging point for casualties, as vehicles or litter bearers could find it easily and transportation would be easiest from such a central point. Then he disappeared.

But Clemons didn't really understand whether or not there were still any survivors from Easy Company alive on Pork Chop. Davis sort of skipped over that, so Clemons assumed the worst, that by this time they were all dead or captured.

Clemons had 135 men in King Company, and he deployed them with two platoons up front to make the attack side by side, 1st Platoon on the left and 2nd Platoon on the right. He held the 3rd Platoon back in reserve. When the men had been spread out into their attack formations, Clemons called Davis and asked him to lift the artillery. Clemons moved with the 2nd Platoon on the right, and at 4:30 A.M., they started forward.

The Chinese had no idea they were coming, and when the American artillery barrage ended, they suspected nothing. They had no illumination, and King would not be fired on by Chinese soldiers during their whole climb. When they started their climb, they were only about 170 meters from the first bunkers along the trench line held at the crest by the Chinese. But the slope was steep, and it would take them a full half hour in the pitch black before the first men from King were to reach the crest.

Clemons and the 2nd Platoon got to the chow bunker just outside the wire and found no enemy soldiers there. Finally, they came to the huge coils of concertina barbed wire outside the perimeter of Pork Chop. In front of the 1st

Platoon to the left, artillery had cut openings that the men used to bypass this last obstruction. Clemons and the 2nd Platoon weren't so lucky, but they were still not under fire, so men began to throw their bodies down on the wire, and others walked across the wire on the backs of the first men.

Clemons was now near the center of the southern defenses of Pork Chop Hill, and the command post bunker was ahead and off to the left. Love Company was supposed to be coming up on their right flank, but no one had seen or heard anything from that direction. Clemons was a little bit worried about them, hoping that they were not already on top, thus risking an unfortunate exchange of gunfire between American troops. But as his men approached the crest and climbed over it into the first trench line, he forgot about Love Company completely and went forward with the rush of his men.

It was still dark, and the first trench line was empty. Clemons told some men to move over the trench line and fan out, setting up their machine guns and watching for enemy movement all around. Others he ordered to walk inside the trench and kill any enemy they found.

Clemons had passed the word before they started that there were only Chinese soldiers up here, and he and his men believed that and acted on it. As they moved forward, they fired intense bursts of BAR or machine gun fire at bunker doors, fire that shattered them and was followed by hand grenades thrown through the jagged openings they had just made. But soon Chinese soldiers poured out of bunkers farther away and into the trench network. They ran toward the men of King Company, spraying fire from their submachine guns as they came. And suddenly the Chinese seemed all around Clemons, firing their weapons and heaving "potato masher" hand grenades at Americans who were taking cover behind bunkers or in the trenches or down the hill. Then machine gun fire was pouring down the slope at those still climbing, followed by a rain of Chinese hand grenades. Clemons cringed at the explosions and the sheets of tracers gouging the hillside, hoping desperately that all his men had gotten up over the crest and into Pork Chop trenches. He glanced down several trench lines as he moved slowly forward with his men, and saw long stretches where artillery fire from both sides had collapsed sandbags or cratered the trench line. Dead and wounded, also from both sides, made those obstructions all the worse. The noise from gunfire and grenades was becoming a constant now, and he only flinched when something came very near.

Then Clemons and some men from the 2nd Platoon were at the command post bunker. Someone fired a burst through the door, and they were stunned by a voice from within:

"Hold your fire! We're Americans!"

Clemons was right by the door as it opened and a heavily bandaged Lieutenant Jack Attridge from Easy Company peered out. Relief washed across the men from King, who had thought there would be no Easy survivors. Men on both sides of the bunker door had been prepared to hurl grenades at each other, believing they faced enemy soldiers. Instead, Clemons rescued six men who had passed a very bad night: Besides Lieutenant Attridge, Lieutenant Tom Harrold, the Easy Company commander, was inside the CP bunker with four other American soldiers, one of whom had lost a leg. Clemons's men helped them down to the chow bunker for treatment and evacuation back to American lines.

But the Chinese troops seemed to be everywhere,

throwing grenades and spraying gunfire at the Americans, then disappearing. There seemed to be few safe places on top of Pork Chop, and King Company was hemorrhaging dead and wounded men that seemed to flow down that road in a steady stream.

The heavy weapons platoon from King Company had been sent off somewhere else by Battalion a few days earlier, and Clemons wished he had their firepower with him now. Three medium tanks had been assigned to his left flank below Pork Chop, and they were covering the low ground to the west with their main guns and machine guns. But as the sun was just coming above the horizon, he was unhappy to hear the radio calls in which they requested permission from higher headquarters to pull back inside American lines. He was unhappier still to hear that request granted. He knew the tanks would be sitting ducks once they were seen by Chinese artillery spotters, and that it was no doubt reasonable for them to pull back. But their withdrawal also cost the ever-shrinking manpower of King one more way of warding off death and defeat.

Then a rifleman sent word to Clemons that he could see "many Chinese" heading toward Pork Chop from a hill off to the west that the Americans called Princeton. Clemons called for artillery on Princeton, and he got it almost immediately. But as he was trying to determine its effect, they were subjected to a storm of gunfire from downhill to their right.

Clemons knew immediately this fire came from the two platoons of Love Company that had not yet appeared. His men stayed down, and the Love fusillade eventually died out. They had no radio contact, but a runner from Clemons finally looped around and came up behind Love to tell them they were firing on King.

But even after the "friendly fire" was straightened out, Clemons knew he was in a difficult position. He thought the Chinese held well over half of the trench lines, and they were still inside most of the bunkers. He didn't have enough unwounded men left to launch an all-out attack that could wrest control of the hill from the Chinese, but his company was still too strong to consider giving up what they had won so far. His men were still moving forward, but they had slowed dramatically. Flamethrowers and rocket launchers were brought to the front and used on bunkers thought to contain Chinese. Some of these bunkers were destroyed, some were consumed in flames, but Chinese hand grenades were taking a heavy toll.

It was 7:30 A.M. now, and Clemons was worried. As best he could tell, he had lost about half the men from the 1st and 2nd platoons, mostly to hand grenades. And he feared they had used up much of their ammunition. He had received no supplies from the rear as yet, no ammunition, no grenades, no food, no water, and after two hours of heavy fighting, the men who had come up the hill as part of the assaulting force now seemed exhausted. He decided it was time to throw in his reserve, the 3rd Platoon. But he had no contact with higher headquarters, as his telephone line had been cut, and five radios had been knocked out along with three radio operators. His contact with other platoons depended on runners, and he was wondering if Battalion understood their plight. He realized that the more of Pork Chop he took, the more he risked overextending his steadily thinning ranks. He sent out word for the men from 1st and 2nd platoons to hold in place while they waited for fresh American troops to arrive.

Around 8:00 A.M., the first reinforcements arrived, but they were far from fresh. A dozen men, they were all that was left of the two platoons from Love Company that had started up the hill on Clemons's right, now under the command of Lieutenant Arthur Marshall. Sixty-two men from Love had started forward under Lieutenant Forrest Crittenden, but they had been under heavy Chinese fire all the way up. Crittenden had been hit, as was his replacement, Lieutenant Homer Bechtel, who gave way to Lieutenant Marshall. This Love detachment had taken fifty casualties on the way up, and the few who finally made it were far less of a boost to Clemons than he had hoped to receive.

Then at 8:30, more riflemen started to trickle in. They were the men of George Company, 17th Infantry, and their company commander was none other than Joe Clemons's West Point classmate and brother-in-law, Lieutenant Walt Russell. Despite their dire straits, Joe and Walt had a brief reunion of hugs and smiles. Walt told Joe the mission of George Company was to "assist Clemons in the mop-up," then withdraw from Pork Chop Hill as soon as possible.

Clemons was shaken by this news. It seemed that the commanders in the rear really had no idea what was going on out here. He was down to about thirty-five men from King, another ten newly arrived from Love—two more Love men had been hit by submachine gun fire before they could even move forward into the trenches—and perhaps a dozen from Easy they had rescued from various bunkers who were not seriously wounded. Not yet, that is. How could their commanders have been so oblivious to their situation as to have sent George forward to "assist in the mop-up"? By this time, an armored personnel carrier ferrying casualties from the chow bunker to Hill 200 was always on the move. Battalion must realize this, they must know that King was hemorrhaging men. Why did they send George forward for just a "mop-up"?

Clemons decided to pull his stretched forces back into a tighter perimeter, with the fresh men of George giving them bulk. But this was a mistake, for a fresh Chinese company had just arrived, and as the men of King pulled back, these new troops followed closely, renewing their automatic-weapons fire and the hail of potato masher grenades.

By 11:00 A.M., water and C rations got to the chow bunker, but the intensity of the gunfire on top of the hill made it impossible to get it moved forward. And more supplies, all carried by Korean bearers, began to pile up in the chow bunker or at the bottom of the hill. There was no one to order the Koreans to take their supplies forward, and it looked far too dangerous to them, so they just abandoned the supplies by the road and left.

At noon, a messenger handed Clemons a note from Colonel Davis, ordering him to send all survivors of Easy and Love companies to the rear now, and to release George Company at 3:00 P.M. Clemons told the messenger to return to Battalion and tell them he had very few men left, all exhausted, that George Company was down to fifty-five men, and that if they left it was not reasonable to expect King to be able to hold Pork Chop Hill. He still assumed that Davis knew how small King Company had gotten just from the number of casualties that must be flowing past him at battalion headquarters.

But such an assumption by Clemons was probably a function of his youth or his exhaustion or both, for Davis had no idea of King's perilous situation. He, too, believed they were carrying out some kind of "mop-up" of the last remnants of far outnumbered Chinese forces, and that King Company was still a powerful fighting force in control of Pork Chop. The enormous and steady stream of casualties was simply unknown to him. Apparently no one from the medical staging area had thought to tell him what was happening, for they were too busy trying to handle the flow. So when the messenger told Davis what Clemons had said to him, he simply acknowledged it, but did not change his orders. Clemons later heard from a runner that his message to Davis was acknowledged, but nothing more. The orders for withdrawal of Easy and Love and George, he was stunned to realize, therefore remained in force.

At about 2:45, in what must have seemed like some sort of cruel joke, Lieutenant Jim Barrows, the division public relations officer, arrived on Pork Chop with two photographers in tow. He found Clemons and told him they wanted to get some photos of what they thought was a successful American action. But this made Clemons suddenly realize that they had no idea in the rear how bad things were on Pork Chop, and how dire King's situation would be if the men of Easy, Love, and George were withdrawn. Clemons told Barrows to forget the photos, but he could perform a much more important service by taking a message to Battalion. Then Joe wrote a brief note: "We must have help or we can't hold the hill."

Barrows took it right to Battalion, and they acknowledged its receipt. But they did nothing.

Precisely at 3:30, Walt Russell led his weary men from George Company down off the hill, a force shrunk to half the number that had gone up the hill six hours earlier. Clemons was left with twenty-five men, including Love survivors and Lieutenant Marshall, and it was clear they could no longer try to occupy a front across Pork Chop. As George Company was leaving, Clemons moved this small force to the top of the highest point on the left side of Pork Chop Hill, where they settled into a small perimeter, taking cover in craters and a few broken-down small bunkers.

Then Joe returned to the CP bunker with his radioman and two riflemen/runners. The one radio they had left must be protected at all costs.

Clemons made radio contact with Battalion at about 4:30, and he told them that he was down to about twenty men who had not yet been hit, but that they were completely spent and there was no fight left in them. If they could not be reinforced, he said, he recommended that they be withdrawn.

But by that time, Clemons was unable to get back to the twenty men he had left on the hilltop, for Chinese soldiers had followed him and surrounded the CP. Having no choice, Clemons and the three enlisted men with him began firing their rifles through holes that had been blown through the bunker door and walls in one last, final, desperate effort to keep the enemy at bay until a rescue force could arrive. But would Battalion send a rescue force? That was the final question whose answer Clemons just didn't know.

As soon as Battalion heard that message from Clemons, however, they realized for the first time how bad things had become for King. A scratch force of fifty-six men was thrown together under Lieutenant Earle Denton, and they were ordered up the hill to rescue King. These men arrived around 6:30, the long-awaited rescue force, and they set up in a hasty perimeter that covered only part of Pork Chop. Then, around 9:30, the much larger force of Fox Company of the 17th started arriving from the south, although they didn't get up to Clemons's position until almost midnight. Fox was followed in the early morning hours by Easy Company of the 17th from the east. These fresh troops washed steadily over the entire outpost position, and by

2:30 in the morning, they reported that they controlled all of Pork Chop Hill.

Joe Clemons finally left the hill after the men of Fox Company had arrived. As he moved away from Pork Chop, unexpected waves of built-up exhaustion rolled over him.

He was completely drained. But he was also still alive.

Pork Chop Hill had become well known to the American public back home. The fight for it was far from over, and it would be a bloody bone of contention between the two armies for some time to come. But this day of April 17, a day in which King Company had come very close to being completely wiped out, would be remembered. A best-selling book entitled simply *Pork Chop Hill*, by S. L. A. Marshall, published in 1956, tells the story, and a movie starring Gregory Peck as Lieutenant Joe Clemons became a box-office smash.

Joe later read the book and saw the movie. They were fine, and he was even surprised that the Hollywood version came so close to what had really happened. It was always hard for him to explain the harsh realities of that day, especially to civilians. That day on Pork Chop Hill had been a world unto itself, and unless you had been there, you could never fully understand it. You just could not understand . . .

Chapter 9:

The Cold War—Nicholas S. H. Krawciw

NICHOLAS S. KRAWCIW WAS BORN IN LVOV, Ukraine, in 1935 to Ukrainian parents. After World War I, Ukraine had been partitioned, and the section where Nick was born had been given to Poland. Nick's father was a Ukrainian nationalist opposed to Polish occupation of the Ukraine, and he got into a lot of trouble for that. He was a newspaperman, but he was also a writer of popular tracts, and he wrote quite a bit about the famine in eastern Ukraine in the thirties, in a part of the Ukraine that was occupied by the Soviets. That was when Stalin murdered many millions by starvation. Hitler invaded Poland from the west in 1939. He had made a secret agreement with Stalin, and Soviet troops invaded from the east. So when German forces came into the Polish town where Nick's family was then living, they were all to stay put, because the Soviets were going to come in within the next few weeks and take over administration of that part of Poland.

But Nick's father knew he would be on all the Soviet lists, so they headed west. They finally got to the river Sian, which they knew would be the border between German and Soviet control. Nick was four, and he got quite sick with flu. But his father knew he would be at very great risk when the Russians got there, that they would arrest him and probably shoot him. So he went over the river, and Nick's mother and his two-year-old sister stayed with him in a little village on the eastern side of the river. By the time he got well, the first Soviet troops had arrived.

Nick's father, by this time, was waiting for his wife and children in Krakow, Poland. Then late one night a Ukrainian underground fighter came and got Nick and his mother and sister, and they slipped down to the riverbank. There were about twenty people waiting to get across, but since Nick's mother was the only woman, they let her go first with her children. The plan was for the boat to come back and ferry the others across. But just as the boat was approaching the far shore, a bright light was suddenly shined on them and loud voices ordered them to return to the eastern bank.

At the worst possible time, a Russian patrol had seen people on the riverbank and had investigated. They caught the refugees waiting for the boat to come back, and they ordered the Krawciws to come back too. But the two men rowing the boat just ignored the Russian order and pulled all the harder. The Russians opened up on the small rowboat with submachine gun fire, but by that time, they had reached shallow water. The two men jumped out and took off, never to be seen again. Nick's mother jumped out with his sister too, but Nick just froze in the boat, watching all those flashing lights. So his mother had to put Nick's sister behind a mound on the bank and come back to the boat for her son. His mother often joked with him later that the first time he was in combat and being shot at by communist soldiers, he froze under fire. And that, after all, was true enough.

Nick's father sent word that he was going into Czechoslovakia, so his family followed him there. They eventually found him, but the Germans made them register. And once they found out Nick's mother was Ukrainian, they told her Ukrainians were part of their labor force. So they sent her, with Nick and his sister, to a castle in Austria, where many wounded German soldiers from the Balkans were being sent. Nick's mother worked hard there, but Nick and his sister had fun playing around the castle.

Meanwhile, his father was sent to Berlin where he had to publish German propaganda material for the Ukrainians in the forced labor brigades. He and other Ukrainian nationalist leaders used this opportunity to also smuggle Ukrainian literature to these laborers. Nick's mother kept filing petitions to be sent to Berlin: She said she'd do anything, she just wanted to rejoin her husband. And finally, the Germans let her go to Berlin in 1941. The family was finally reunited in the small apartment the father lived in near the city center.

But the British bombing of Berlin started that year, and the United States entered the war after Pearl Harbor. By 1943, the bombing had gotten pretty heavy, with the British bombing at night and the Americans bombing during the day. One of the most frightening of Nick's memories is of an American bombing raid. He first heard this enormous rumbling in the sky. They lived on the second floor, and his mother raced toward the basement bomb shelter with Nick and his sister. But on the way, he stole a glance at the sky, which was black with an enormous array of American bombers.

They were in the bomb shelter before the bombs got close, but the shaking became so violent that Nick was sure he would be crushed. Eventually, it ended, and they came out of the shelter. Their apartment building had been heavily damaged, and half of Nick's kitchen had disappeared, with one wall gone and a huge crater below.

The Germans had already become worried by the bombing, and they had already started sending their wives and children off to the east, to East Prussia. But by 1943, the German army in Russia was on the defensive and was slowly being driven back to the west. Nick's parents knew that the Russians would eventually be coming through East Prussia, and they did not want to go that way. So Nick's mother volunteered to be a farmhand, and in March 1944, she was sent to Bavaria, down in the southwestern section of Germany. His father had to stay behind in Berlin.

The farmer to whom Nick's mother was assigned was Herr Poehlmann, and he turned out to be a very kind and decent man. When he found out she was a schoolteacher, he told her that, out of respect for teachers, he couldn't have her doing farm work. So he gave her a little plot of land, and she planted vegetables that they later ate. For the three of them, the final year of the war really wasn't bad at all.

When the war was finally in its last stages, part of General Patton's XII Corps came through their village. They had tanks and trucks and halftracks rolling through town for two days, and Nick thought it was the entire U.S. Army. And, of course, American GIs gave him chewing gum and chocolate and rations. He thought they were just gods.

After the war was over, Nick and his family heard nothing from their father. After a few months with no leads, his mother began to resign herself to the fact that, like so many other married women caught in Germany's wartime labor force, she had become a widow. But then one day in the fall of 1945, Nick's father walked in the door.

As it happened, Nick's father's uncle was the Ukrainian Catholic archbishop in Philadelphia. Eventually, he would sponsor their immigration to the United States. The first task was reestablishing contact, and that took a year or so. But even after that had taken place, the next step was screening by U.S. counterintelligence. Given the tortuous political experiences of Nick's father, that took several more years. Nick's first schooling had taken place in a German school, and he had learned to speak German quite fluently. By 1946, Nick's family was placed in a displaced persons camp, and Nick went to fifth, sixth, and seventh grades there, in a special Ukrainian-language school. Then, in 1949, the family finally got on a boat, and Nick went to eighth grade at Saint Henry's Catholic School in Philadelphia. The next year, he started at Northeast Catholic High School. But something still gnawed at him.

When he was in the displaced persons camp in Germany, in 1946, 1947, 1948, one of the U.S. Army corporals serving in the American Constabulary had set up a Boy Scout troop for the Ukrainian boys. Nick and the others were just learning to speak English, and they already thought America was a land of miracles. They had no Boy Scout uniforms, of course, but there was all sorts of U.S. Army gear available, so the corporal very easily got them helmet liners and web belts with canteens and so on. When they had regular meetings, or especially on Boy Scout troop outings, they all wore the same sort of semi-uniform and felt like they were Americans. The corporal was also able to get them free railroad tickets, which they used to travel all over Germany. And while they were on those trips, the corporal used to tell them all about great American leaders and where they had gone to school—West Point. So Nick decided, if he ever got to America, that he would try to go to West Point.

By the time he had started high school, Nick's English was nearly flawless. Since arriving in the United States,

Nick had easily found materials on West Point in the local public library. He had read a lot about it, and the early vision he had built in his mind's eye began to take on both shape and detail. And the more he learned about the United States Military Academy, the more he wanted to go there.

While still in eighth grade, he had gone down to Philadelphia City Hall and asked around about how he could apply to West Point. But he was obviously too young, and after being sent to different offices, he was politely but firmly given the brush-off by some bureaucrat.

But rejection only gave him focus. His next step was to write to Valley Forge Military Academy, but he never heard back from them. Undeterred, he took the next step.

He had heard about a small high-school military academy in Trenton, New Jersey. One day when he had no school, he got on the public bus, paid the driver his quarter, and rode to the Bordentown Military Institute.

Nick walked in what seemed to be the main headquarters building and told the woman behind the counter that he needed to speak to Dr. Harold Morrison Smith, the headmaster. A young man his age arriving without either parent and asking to speak to the president was unusual enough, but somehow, after a short wait, Nick was ushered into his office. Nick knew what he wanted, however, and he was not the slightest bit hesitant: He told Dr. Smith that he wanted to go to West Point one day and needed to get ready for that by going to this military school, Bordentown Military Institute.

Dr. Smith was intrigued by this brash young man who had come by himself, and he asked Nick how he would pay for tuition, uniforms, and other expenses. Nick answered that his parents were war refugees who were working hard and not making much money, but that if he would let Nick in on credit, he promised he would repay him the entire cost after he graduated from West Point.

Dr. Smith was very impressed, and he decided to give Nick the opportunity he sought: He went to Bordentown Military Institute on "credit." And from that moment, "Only in America" became an enduring truth for Nick, a truth he knew was real, and that he would never forget. Nick graduated from Bordentown as the salutatorian, won an appointment to West Point, and graduated in 1959. And the best part of the story is that, after graduation, most of Nick's classmates were paying for their new cars, but he was paying for his high-school education!

But before he went to West Point, Nick was to make the most important discovery and decision of his life. It happened the summer he was sixteen, when he went off to upstate New York where he would work as a counselor at a Ukrainian Boy Scout summer camp. One of the first days he was there, he was introduced to Christina, a fourteen-year-old counselor of Ukrainian Brownies, who were in a different part of the camp. Christina had a story very similar to Nick's. They were both refugees from Ukraine, and meeting her was the most amazing experience of his life. They had been formally introduced, although they didn't talk much at all. But he saw a light in her eyes that he had never seen before. And later that day, he took her hand. It was soft as a lily, but she held Nick's hand firmly, and he thought he might melt. When she had duty in the kitchen, Nick heard about it, so he volunteered to help her. And their first time alone together in the kitchen was the stuff of songs: Christina would look at Nick, then blush and look away, then turn back to him, still red but smiling. Nick was stunned and smitten. He had never believed in love at first sight, but after that day, he changed his mind completely. From then on, Nick was "taken," and he never even dated another girl.

Compared to his West Point classmates, Nick had a somewhat unusual and demanding childhood. And when he finally got to West Point, it was a dream come true, a dream he had been fighting for through military school and childhood deprivation for quite some time.

West Point's purpose, of course, is the production each year of a cohort of physically and morally strong young military professionals who will lead the American Army in war and peace. To reach that end, West Point has gradually developed a four-year program that both educates cadets academically and trains them militarily. But it does these central things in what has always seemed to outsiders to be a rather rigorous environment. In their first year, they are caused to experience a sense of personal insignificance and even failure. Over the three ensuing years, they are then gradually built back up, constantly tested and hardened. This is all done in the hope that the finished product will be a strong character reliably able to adhere to principled behavior in the face of myriad and unpredictable external pressures.

The West Point experience, therefore, has traditionally been quite demanding, something that most cadets, in looking back, would say they "endured" more than "enjoyed." But not Nick: He felt as if this were something he had fought for his whole life, and from the moment he first put on that cadet gray in Beast Barracks, he loved every minute he was there.

During Beast Barracks, Nick was in the 3rd New Cadet Company. His first company commander was named Bob Sorley, and he was a giant in Nick's eyes. So was another New Cadet Company commander, Jack Nicholson. Once the academic year started again, Jack was to rise to become a regimental commander. Nick lived downstairs from him as a plebe, and ended up acting as his "runner," carrying messages to and from other cadet rooms or the offices of the Tactical Department. While he was doing that, he got a close look at Jack, and he discovered that there wasn't the slightest bit of phoniness about him, that he really was the straight-arrow cadet he seemed to be. He quickly became Nick's role model, one of the greatest leaders he was ever to meet.

Nick was well-liked by his peers and well-respected by anyone and everyone who saw him in action. At the end of his junior year, he learned that he had been named to be the company commander of 2nd New Cadet Company for the first month of a two-month period of training during the summer before his senior year. This meant that and he had done quite well in terms of cadet rank, probably to be included among the top thirty or so men in his class of five hundred.

There were eight of these companies, each consisting of about one hundred "New Cadets," or freshmen, commonly referred to as plebes. These *innocenti* would be managed by some twenty juniors and seniors in each company through the two-month hell known as "Basic Cadet Training" or "BCT." While this summer is more commonly referred to as "Beast Barracks," this name no doubt comes from the slurring of the initials "BCT" into "Beast" rather than as a designation of the way New Cadets are treated. But few of the individuals who have experienced this special, focused attention would see it that way.

The upper-class cadre of a New Cadet Company instructs, disciplines, and controls New Cadets as they learn the rudiments of cadet life—uniforms, marching, appearance, cleanliness, many other details, all under time constraints of too much to do in too little time. Add to this the constraint that plebes were required to "brace"—assume an exaggerated, rigid, and painful position of attention—whenever they were out of their rooms but within the Area of Barracks, and you have the ingredients for an extremely difficult introductory experience.

To an outsider passing by in the 1950s, the most obvious aspect of Beast Barracks in those days was the horrendous noise that reverberated out of the Area of Barracks, where outsiders were forbidden. The pressure on plebes was enormous. It was the unspoken goal of all upperclassmen to frighten and distress all New Cadets whenever possible, for knocking them off-balance was a key aspect of Beast Barracks: Before you could teach them anything, you had to break down whatever ego security these young men had built up, to get them to operate as much as possible out of fear. And yelling was a key fear-instilling factor. Only gradually, the revealed wisdom said, would this fear begin to scar over. During that first plebe year, it was believed, plebes who did not wash out would develop coping mechanisms, which, in turn, would help them deal in the future with sudden frightening pressures.

But this tradition of loud, harsh treatment had not been discovered in a human behavior laboratory somewhere. Rather, it had just grown up as a function of hazing of freshmen in the nineteenth century—common in almost all American boarding schools and colleges—and obvious reluctance to challenge a tradition that had seemed to work for many U.S. Army officers who were sequentially in charge of cadet military training at West Point.

But Nick wouldn't allow anyone on the upper-class detail in 2nd Company to raise his voice. He told them that if they wanted to chew out a plebe, they had to get up close and whisper. Everyone understood that there was to be no yelling in Silent 2nd, or even any raised voices at all. They were to be disciplined and professional. Yelling was a sign of loss of control of emotions, and a good leader never lost control of his emotions.

As things worked out, they had very good spirit, they worked as a team, and it was really a great experience for all: The plebes learned about West Point and earned their places as team players, while the upperclassmen learned a great deal about true military leadership rather than how to effectively instill fear. But most important, the strong response of the plebes resulted in Silent 2nd winning all the awards that were given by the officers who worked for the commandant of cadets and who were in charge of BCT. And this was really just a lesson in true leadership, provided by Nick to the older and supposedly wiser officers at West Point, who, for the time being, outranked him.

This, of course, was a dramatic change from past experiences. It would not be until the middle 1970s, still another twenty years in the future, that upperclassmen on BCT details were formally forbidden to yell at plebes. Rather than trying to instill fear, they were instructed to focus on the plebe's ability to perform a given task under certain time constraints. But twenty years from the time the ice of a given military tradition is cracked until it crumbles completely is not bad. The fact that it took a young cadet who wasn't intimidated by the weight of tradition and simply thought things through to overturn a counterproductive ritualized custom is only more credit to his innovative thought.

The cadres rolled over into a new set of upperclassmen after one month, and Nick went on thirty days' leave. When he came back on Labor Day, he found that Silent 2nd had so impressed the officers that he had been jumped over perhaps a dozen or so classmates and been named as commander of the 1st Regiment, one of the two regiments making up the brigade.

This meant that he was the second-highest-ranking cadet in his class, outranked only by the brigade commander, Pete Dawkins. But Dawkins was also their class president, captain of the football team and an All-America halfback who was to win the Heisman Trophy in 1959. Pete was ranked number ten in his class academically and would win a Rhodes Scholarship after graduation. So all in all, Nick had done very well indeed.

Nick played soccer, and during his senior year, they beat Navy, the key game of the season. Their team record that year was 9–1–1, which was almost as good a record as that of the undefeated football team. But Nick played the whole game against Navy, and he was deliriously happy that they won.

Three days after graduation, Nick and Christina were married in the Cadet Catholic Chapel at West Point. Then it was off to the Army, and Nick went to Airborne and Ranger schools, then he took the Armor Basic Course at Fort Knox, Kentucky. This last course had the normal Army school mix of reading assignments that aren't too tough, classroom lectures that range from interesting to deadly boring, and field exercises that were, to these new lieutenants, just plain fun.

One field exercise in particular caught Nick's attention. For these exercises, the lieutenant students would take turns playing platoon leader and squad leaders. They set up in a night defensive perimeter, and Nick, as the acting platoon leader was supposed to, sent out individuals as listening posts or LPs. Their job was literally to go out to a specified position and wait, watching (difficult at night) but mostly listening for approaching enemy. When they were aware of this enemy, they were to alert the platoon leader.

This "enemy" consisted of "Aggressors," which meant troops assigned to the school whose job was to go out every few months with a new set of lieutenants and play that role. Naturally, since they lived here and were in charge of maintaining the ranges and so forth, they knew just where the weak points were in every "problem" of every exercise. The LPs were always placed in the same locations, and they knew just how to slip up on them and capture them, usually to their great embarrassment. The result was that they were almost never surprised by some daring move by a new lieutenant. In fact, the more cynical of the Aggressors were absolutely convinced that the new lieutenants they faced were uniformly dumb, incompetent, and incapable of an original or creative military thought.

But one of the LPs Nick sent out was his West Point classmate and good friend, Lieutenant Rocky Versace. After he was placed in his position, he had been told to stay in that position and listen. But Rocky thought he was in a bad position, and the fact that the school rules called for him to stay in that one poorly placed spot was not important to him. His job was to be a listening post and be prepared to detect enemy approaching. So he moved. In fact, he moved around quite a bit.

Over the space of about three hours, Rocky brought in two Aggressors as prisoners, men he had simply slipped up on and captured as they prepared to attack those "dumb lieutenants." When the second Aggressor was brought in, he was angry and demanded to be released, and he started to get loud:

"That lieutenant who was supposed to be on that LP

wasn't there! You guys aren't playing fair! Only reason I got caught by this man is 'cause he . . ."

Nick had his hands tied behind his back and told him he would be gagged if he didn't stop talking. Then Rocky went back out into the dark woods. An hour or so later, that "dumb lieutenant" brought in a third very bright Aggressor.

When the course finally ended, Nick was off to his first assignment as a platoon leader with the 14th Armored Cavalry in the Fulda Gap in Bad Hersfeld, Germany. Their daughter Maria Alexandra (she goes by Alex) was born there, and when the Berlin Wall went up in 1961, the Cold War suddenly got warmer. Nick's unit was constantly on the border, but in February 1962, President Kennedy made his call for volunteers to serve in Vietnam.

Despite his love for his wife and his angel daughter, Nick could not hold back. He volunteered to be part of that first group, and by the summer of 1962, he was on his way. He went to the second course ever given at the Special Warfare School in Fort Bragg, North Carolina, called MATA II, for Military Advisory Training and Assistance. And then he was on a plane for The Republic of Vietnam.

In September 1962, Nick arrived in Saigon, processed in, and went to his assignment. There were as yet very few American soldiers serving in Vietnam, counted in the low thousands, and most of them were officers and senior NCOs trying to help the South Vietnamese Army in their fight against small bands of guerrillas in the countryside. Nick was to fill such a role as an advisor to the South Vietnamese 2nd Armored Cavalry Regiment that had just been organized.

As a first lieutenant, Nick would be the only American operating with a particular armored cavalry troop that had just gotten American M-113 armored personnel carriers. A troop, of course, is the organizational name used in armored cavalry units for what would normally be called a company in other units, made up of three or four platoons. But all American armored cavalry units have long been proud of their nomenclature, and they have maintained use of names and nomenclature that were in use in the old horse cavalry days. Given the source of South Vietnamese vehicles, arms, ammunition, equipment, supplies, and money for operation, of course, this tradition was very readily and easily transferred to South Vietnamese armored cavalry units.

The senior advisor Nick worked under at that time was Lieutenant Colonel John Vann. On his first mission, he was to leave Saigon and take his troop down to the tip of the southernmost Camau Peninsula for counterguerrilla operations. He was equipped with GRC-3 radios, which had a range of about four or five miles, and he was going about two hundred miles away. As he was about to leave in his jeep, John Vann came up behind him and slapped him on the shoulder. They smiled and waved, but for Nick, Vann's parting comment, thrown out almost like an afterthought, was puzzling.

"Stay in touch, Nick!"

As he drove away, Nick couldn't help but reflect on that for a minute, but he just couldn't figure out what Vann might have meant. From where he was going, they would be far out of radio range, and the only possible way for him to "stay in touch" would be by courier, which could take days. Heading south on primitive roads into the vast green expanse of the Mekong Delta, Nick sobered as he realized that now he was fully on his own.

On this operation, Nick's squadron was only engaged in

brief firefights. They drew a certain amount of sniper fire, but whenever their armored vehicles were able to confront communist forces, these invariably fired brief bursts of small-arms fire and quickly disappeared.

After several weeks, they returned to My Tho, a large city in the Mekong Delta some fifty miles south of Saigon. Here, Nick took part in operations with bigger South Vietnamese units. On these occasions, there were always some other American advisors around, although Nick had never felt in any particular danger when he had been alone with just one South Vietnamese cavalry troop. The men were reasonably well trained, the officers seemed competent, and even under fire, Nick was quite pleased to see that they seemed quite dedicated, even loyal. He was encouraged.

The next major operation for Nick's unit took place in December 1962, a joint operation with several South Vietnamese Ranger battalions in the Seven Mountains region on the Cambodian border. Seven Mountains was a name given to an area a few miles square where seven huge and steep-sided stone hills erupted incongruously out of the flat, fertile, heavily inundated Mekong River Delta right on the Cambodian border.

From the days of French dominion throughout all of Indochina, the Seven Mountains, a vast expanse of rough ground covered with thick underbrush and honeycombed with tunnels, had been a haven for communist guerrillas. Now Nick was to participate in a most unusual South Vietnamese Army effort to attack the enemy on his home ground.

The operation started off slowly, but as they approached the Seven Mountains, resistance stiffened. Then on Christmas Day, Nick survived an ambush only by jumping from his M-113 when it was under heavy fire and using up all his "grease gun" ammo in about five minutes. A grease gun is a short-barreled automatic weapon with no recoil-absorbing spring that could perhaps be most accurately described by saying it "sprays" rather than "fires" .45-caliber ammunition. This was a reminder of stark reality for Nick, and he was lucky to get through it unscratched. But that was just for warmups.

About one week later, the armored cavalry troop Nick advised was trying to break through a Viet Cong encirclement and rescue a South Vietnamese Ranger company. Some time earlier, the Viet Cong forces they were fighting had taken some bombs from an American bomber that had crash-landed near the Seven Mountains, and they had set some of these up as booby traps right along the trail Nick's unit was using in their attempt to break through and rescue the Rangers. The VC blew three of these, and two of them did no damage to Nick's unit at all. But the third one went off right under the right rear track of the M-113 in which Nick was riding and blew right through its steel carapace. This explosion killed a South Vietnamese battalion commander standing right behind Nick, and it also killed four other South Vietnamese soldiers nearby. In fact, Nick was the only person riding in the passenger compartment who wasn't killed by it. He was hit by shrapnel all down his back and his legs, and the ring finger on his left hand was thoroughly smashed, although he would not even be aware of that or other wounds until much later.

After the Viet Cong had set off the bomb and blown up the back end of the APC, they weren't sure if any occupants had survived. They wanted to kill all the men in the vehicle before anyone could come up and rescue them, so a heavy storm of small-arms fire quickly assailed the burning vehicle from all directions.

Nick knew he had been hit, but he didn't have time to

think about that. His grease gun had been blown away, but his actions now were all about survival, so he picked up an M-1 and started shooting back. His body was still protected by the steel front and sides of the APC, but he was leaning his head, arms, and shoulders over the forward slope of the vehicle as he fired his rifle. He was bracing the barrel against the antenna guard that came up out of the thick armored plate, and he had reloaded several times and was maintaining a brisk rate of fire that kept VC soldiers from getting close to the burning wreck in which he huddled. Then an enemy round went through the base of the antenna guard and slashed open the side of his cheek. To Nick, it felt as if he had just taken the hardest punch in the jaw any man had ever thrown, and he fell back, stunned. Had the bullet been an inch to the side, he simply would not have survived. But instead, Nick picked up another M-1, leaned forward over the shattered antenna mount, and began to fire once again.

Soon enough, another M-113 drove up behind Nick's burning vehicle, quickly followed by another to his left. The only thing he was aware of was that friendly machine gun fire was sweeping the area to his front. Only when they laid him down inside another APC and started to move did he realize that his legs felt as if they were on fire. The pain in his ankle was becoming intense, so he reached his left hand down to try adjust his leg. But somehow he couldn't seem to grab anything with his fingers. He was amazed and raised this hand that suddenly wouldn't work to look at it. He was stunned to see a red pulp of broken fingers. Then he could feel the blood pumping out of his jagged cheek, and he dropped his hand on his chest, confused. He closed his eyes, saw Chris and Alex smiling at him, and began to pray.

Nick was evacuated by H-34 helicopter, and was taken to the first Mobile Army Surgical Hospital (MASH) in Vietnam that had just been set up at Cam Ranh Bay. His back and the backs of his legs had been badly ripped open by the explosion. He had several breaks in several smashed fingers, had suffered four breaks in his ankle, and his heel was only attached by a tendon.

Once he had been evacuated, he received the very best care available for traumatic injuries. Two weeks later, he was medically evacuated to Valley Forge Hospital, Pennsylvania, near his family home in Philadelphia.

After he came home, Nick had to log about four months in the hospital before he was considered fit for duty. As soon as he measured up, he went to the Career Course at Fort Knox, Kentucky, where his son Andy was born, then on to Fort Hood, where Nick served as a troop commander for a few years. After that came a three-year tour as a tactical officer at West Point, which was a wonderful family environment. For his family, this was far better than his previous command slot, for they knew they could count on him coming home virtually every night.

But then it was back to Vietnam. A new major, Nick was the operations officer of a cav squadron up on the Demilitarized Zone, or DMZ, a buffer zone along the border between North and South Vietnam. The North Vietnamese threw fresh regiments at Nick's unit every few weeks, and they did a lot of fighting that year. Although Nick's helicopter was hit often, he came home after a year without a scratch.

Within a year, he was working in the Pentagon in the Politico-Military Division of the NATO office, but he was pulled out of that slot to accompany top Army leadership on extended trips around the Mediterranean basin. When the Palestinian uprisings occurred in Jordan, Nick was named the chief operation officer in the UN Truce Supervision Organization (UNTSO), the headquarters of which has been in Jerusalem since 1949.

In May 1972, Nick was promoted to lieutenant colonel and assumed his new duties. He then had people on all the cease-fire lines around Israel, on the Golan Heights, along the Suez Canal, and in southern Lebanon. When the Yom Kippur War broke out in October 1973, he had about one hundred men deployed and about two hundred back in reserve. The Arabs attacked across the Suez Canal and into the Golan Heights. The Egyptians placed Nick's boss, Finnish major general Ensio Siilasvuo, in house arrest in Cairo, and Nick ended up running the UNTSO mission until he returned some six days later.

After first reporting the major cease-fire violations, Nick went out to the Golan Heights, and he had to rescue some of his men who were caught between the lines. Then later, he went down to the Canal and followed General Adan's Israeli division. Three of his men were killed and quite a few wounded or captured because the Arabs couldn't distinguish between UN troops and Israelis. They wore no helmets, only berets, and, as observers, they were unarmed, so it was pretty dangerous for them.

When the war ended, General Abrams, the chief of staff of the U.S. Army, had Nick come back to Washington for a few days and debrief him and the Army staff on all the tank battles that had taken place. He returned to Jerusalem and finished his tour, and then was assigned straight to battalion command. In May 1974, he took over command of the 1st Squadron, 2nd Cavalry Regiment, in Bayreuth, Germany, which was right next to the village where he had lived as a kid during World War II. He went back to visit the family of Herr Poehlmann, the farmer who had taken care of Nick, his mother, and his sister, but he and his wife had died. He was warmly greeted by his son Georg, whom Nick remembered as a wounded German Wehrmacht soldier, and who was then running the farm.

This was the time when the Army was trying to recover from the doldrums it had been in because of Vietnam and its fallout, and Nick was part of the group of professional officers that was basically trying to rebuild the Army. But the going was hard, and while they earnestly believed they were making progress, it was a very long haul indeed. After his years of command ended, Nick was scheduled to attend the National War College. But before he returned to the United States, he was to accompany Lieutenant General Hollingsworth on a two-month inspection of all elements of the U.S. Army in Europe (USAREUR). That resulted in some fifty U.S. Army recommendations to the office of the secretary of defense for organizational and technical improvements in USAREUR because of depletions in stock due to Vietnam and the Yom Kippur War. Nick learned a lot in those two months.

When he came back to the United States to attend the War College, however, Nick was given a last-minute opportunity to go to the Hoover Institute at Stanford and serve as a fellow while still getting credit for the War College. So he chose the Hoover Institute, and when they asked him why, he said that he wanted to learn what combat developments and force structuring was all about, and that he thought he could do that at the Army Combat Developments Experimentation Command at nearby Fort Ord, California. Also, General Gorman had just written a famous letter saying that we needed a national training center and should look at Fort Irwin, California, for this.

So Nick went to Hoover, and while most of the others in these fellowships were pursuing their Ph.D.s, he was working on an assessment of how the operations of the national training center could be refined through the use of newly developed instrumentation. He had to look at the work of the Combat Developments Command at Fort Ord, at Fort Hood, Texas where they had an organization that was already testing some battalions for the Army's Training and Doctrine Command (TRADOC), and at other efforts underway at Nellis Air Force Base where the U.S. Air Force was monitoring simulated combat known as "Red Flag." At the same time, he had a wonderful year at Stanford. He and Chris had a lovely little house in Palo Alto, and they could often play tennis with the kids or take the whole family for rides to lovely parts of California. And at 3:15 every weekday that he was in town, he could meet and interact with people like Professors Ed Teller and Milton Friedman, and some of the other great scholars of American academia.

After that year, Nick was about to make colonel, and he went to TRADOC at Fort Monroe as the director of concepts and doctrine in combat developments. In 1977 they started working on the "Division '86" project, looking eight or nine years into the future. It was exciting because Nick could put to work the things he had just learned about combat developments. But more important, at Fort Monroe, his son Paul was born. Since Chris and Nick were older, they appreciated him more and he started his life being loved as a very special baby by his parents and his older sister and brother.

After two years at Fort Monroe, Nick's name came out on the brigade command list in 1979, and he took over the command of the largest combat brigade in Europe, the 1st

Brigade of the 3rd Armored Division, which had three battalions of tanks and two battalions of mechanized infantry.

The Army, meanwhile, had been slowly but steadily improving—you could see that everywhere you looked. Nick ran his brigade like an armored cav brigade, and there was a lot of esprit in their units. After a year and a half of command, the chief of staff of the Army, General Shy Meyer, nominated Nick to go to the Senior Seminar at the State Department as a senior fellow.

Nick didn't want this, and he started to resist, but soon learned he had no choice. He really didn't know what to expect, and thought he would be little more than a paperpusher. But he was to get a major surprise.

There were only about twenty-five people in the seminar, and some of them were to become ambassadors right after the seminar year. But the year consisted of traveling around the United States and taking a close look at various life experiences. One month, Nick would find himself living on a corn and dairy farm in Minnesota, getting up to do the milking at the crack of dawn, or even before. The next month, he would be with cops in different precincts in Chicago. The concept was that you had to really know your own country before you could represent it abroad, and it turned out to be an enormously rewarding experience, one of the genuine high points of his life.

Nick went up to the Pacific Northwest with Weyerhauser, the big lumber company, and watched them try to clean up from the Mount St. Helens volcano eruptions. Then he went down to Puerto Rico with other fellows, where they were the guests of the governor. They were able to talk with the governor and other key Puerto Rican leaders about the different options before them: remaining a commonwealth, seeking statehood, or going their own way as an independent country. It was an eye- and mind-opening experience. Then they went to Florida and worked with the Coast Guard and DEA, watching their interdiction efforts and all the immigration problems they also confront as part of their jobs.

When that wonderful year was over, Nick went back to the Pentagon, where he was the military assistant to the deputy secretary of defense. Colin Powell was a major general at that time, and he was the military assistant to Secretary of Defense Caspar Weinberger. These two coordinated many actions and shared the morning meetings chaired by the secretary of defense. Nick was promoted to brigadier general while in that post, and he left almost immediately after he pinned on his star to become the assistant division commander in the 3rd Infantry Division (Mechanized) in Europe.

This division was already equipped with and using M-1 tanks and Bradley fighting vehicles. They trained to be capable of being a counterattack force in case of all-out war with the Soviet Bloc in Europe. And this was also the time when the U.S. Army finally won the Canadian Arms Trophy for the first time.

Every two years, the Canadian Army hosts a competition for tank units on a specially prepared course. A team of tanks goes down the course, engages infantrymen, other tanks, and other targets, avoids firing on "friendly forces," that sort of thing. Each nation sends a team through the course and receives a score, and at the end of the competition, the scores are tabulated and the national teams are ranked. These competitions had been going on since the early 1970s, and the American teams continually came in dead last.

When the new Abrams tank was deployed in 1980, the

Americans thought they finally had a winner. But that was not to be, and they kept finishing dead last. What was wrong?

The basic problem is the way the U.S. Army is structured. In the Army, normal tours of duty at any geographical station for an individual soldier are two to three years. The direct result of that is that every unit in the U.S. Army experiences between a 30 percent and a 60 percent personnel turnover every year. For units in so-called "hardship" areas, such as Korea, tours only last one year, in which case the unit experiences a 100 percent personnel turnover or worse each year. This means that, in a constant state of flux and turnover, Army units very rarely get beyond the "crawl" stage to "walk," and are simply incapable of getting to "run."

If you want to have an effective set of tank crews that work smoothly together, of course, nothing can replace personal familiarity. The other NATO teams the U.S. Army was competing against have all long been structured on some variation of the regimental system. This means that individual soldiers in those armies stay in the same unit performing the same job for virtually their entire military careers. They provide opportunities for advance and promotion within that unit, of course, but unit cohesion, reliability, and predictable competence in performance of mission are the unit goals. The units are well-oiled, with carefully nurtured esprit de corps, and these goals are routinely attained. But not in the maddeningly confused American Army, a band of strangers temporarily aligned with other strangers for reasons no one fully understands.

Finally, in order to win the Canadian Arms Trophy, the 3rd Infantry Division simply froze the personnel who would be competing for two years—nobody would come in, nobody would go out, with the end result that the crews that finally competed had been training together for two years. And it worked. For the first time, we won the Canadian Arms Trophy in 1984.

(The personnel system of the U.S. Army deserves a small side comment by the author here. The personnel freeze that finally allowed this American victory in the Canadian Arms Trophy competition was something barely tolerated by the self-licking ice-cream cone known as the Army personnel system, and that only under great pressure from Army leadership, and only for the great prestige they were assured would attach to victory by the U.S. Army. For less important things, such as preparing to fight a war, the Army personnel system continues to keep all soldiers steadily on the move, routinely moving in and out of various assignments where they work with virtual strangers. But these "strangers" are other soldiers, and on their coordinated performance of their mission under great pressure many lives will depend, certainly including their own. Isn't it time someone told the Emperor of Constantly Changing Personnel in All Units that he has no clothes? Wouldn't it seem reasonable to take a look at the stability and superior performance of mission readily available with a regimental system, some version of which is in use by every other army of significance in the world?)

Nick next held a high staff job in USAREUR for a year, then was promoted to major general and assigned back to command the 3rd Infantry Division. Many of the people in the 3rd Division when he took over had been there when he had been the assistant division commander just a year or so earlier, so it was a little bit of "Old Home Week" when he got back. He was to be the commander of that very powerful division for two years, during which they got the even newer M-1A1 tanks, newer Bradleys, and other modernized equipment, all as had been envisioned in the "Division '86" process.

After his division command, he went back to the Pentagon in 1990 and was working for Secretary of Defense Cheney as the director of NATO policy. He was deeply involved in actions with Spain as they tried to help that country get ready to join NATO, and Nick was also working with Norway on some unfinished Cold War business. But by that time, he was having another problem that had apparently been there all his life.

He had a very high cholesterol and triglyceride count, to the point that doctors had told him earlier that his life was in danger. In fact, he had undergone elective bypass surgery in 1986, before he took over command of the 3rd Infantry Division, in the hope that would clear things up. It worked for a while, and he got his "profile 1" back. But then, back at the Pentagon, he had a physical. His cholesterol was in the five hundreds and his triglycerides were up over two thousand. So he was advised to retire. And after considerable discussion with doctors and others, that's what he did.

Most of Nick's friends were floored. He was a guy, they knew, who always kept a cool head, no matter what was going on. But it was true.

As part of his physical, the doctors had always asked Nick if he ever got excited. He told them that he almost never got excited, but medically, the doctors said, there's just no such thing. Some people's palms sweat, some people get a headache, and some people apparently pump enormous amounts of cholesterol and triglycerides into their bloodstream. And this was no doubt what had happened with Nick.

Perhaps without realizing it, he really was under quite a bit of pressure. In the month of March 1990, for instance, he had flown over the Atlantic Ocean eight times. A few months after he retired, however, his cholesterol and triglyceride count had dropped by about half.

So Nick retired from the Army in the summer of 1990.
By this time, his oldest son, Andy, had graduated from the
Air Force Academy, and he flew an A-10 over northern
Iraq during the 1991 "Desert Storm" war. That was also the
year when Ukraine won its freedom. And since Nick not
only spoke Ukrainian but had even started life there, a lot of
people who knew that were advising him to get involved in
helping Ukraine establish political freedom and a marketplace economy. Undersecretary of Defense Paul Wolfowitz
was among the strongest voices, and he was well connected.

Some months later, Nick was contacted by two
Ukrainian officials who invited him to meet them in
Switzerland. He checked with the government, where he
found great support, so he went to Switzerland. The two
Ukrainians then asked Nick to come to Ukraine in January
1992 to help them set up a nonprofit, nongovernmental
political science institute. All that spring and summer, Nick
worked with Jack Nicholson, an old friend from West Point
days. They incorporated themselves in Virginia as NKI
(Nicholson Krawciw, Inc.), applied for nonprofit status, and
got modest funding that enabled them to set up such an
institute, which in turn was to incorporate in Ukraine.

In March 1993, Nick was in Ukraine, still working with
the Institute on Global and Regional Security, the nongovernmental organization he had helped Ukraine set up.
He felt they needed a bright young American scholar in residence. So he sponsored Ian Brzenski, who then spent two
and one-half years working in Kiev and assisting in the
nuclear missile debate campaign. During that time, Ukraine
was setting up governmental institutions, and Ian wrote a
paper on how they should set up their National Security
Council. Eventually, they followed his plan fairly closely.

In 1992, Ukraine had eighteen hundred ICBMs and was

the third-largest nuclear power, so one of the first priorities of the institute was to get them to turn in their nuclear missiles. NKI played a central role in getting people from the institute on the air and in print in Ukraine to make the argument that it makes no sense for a country without an adequate command and control system to own nuclear missiles. What might happen in a crisis when someone knows you've got them and can't control them? If the Russians saw them as a threat, they didn't need to say, such a crisis would not have a happy outcome. And with an inadequate intelligence system, no satellites, and no ability to target missiles, Ukraine clearly seemed to be in much deeper water than was healthy for Ukrainians.

The Ukrainian Parliament voted to turn in their nuclear missiles in 1994, and they had done so by mid-1996. Under the trilateral agreement of 1994, the United States took the high-grade uranium from these missile warheads and reprocessed it to a lower grade fit only for nuclear reactors, then split it three ways between Ukraine, the United States, and Russsia. This was billions of dollars' worth of uranium, and it was a key political act for Ukraine to disarm unilaterally.

Nick had moved back to Ukraine full-time with Chris and Paul. And while in Ukraine, Nick was asked by friends in the Pentagon to assist on another project, as a result of which he traveled often to Germany.

In 1992, Paul Wolfowitz and General Galvin, the American commander in Europe at the time, thought that it would be a great idea to set up an institute established in the Marshall tradition, a sort of Marshall Plan that would help Eastern Europe. The idea was to create a center, like a senior university or a war college–type establishment, where people from Eastern Europe could come, both civilian and military, and learn how to develop civil-military projects, strategy, defense policy, and associated issues.

On their behalf, Nick and a few other senior American civilian and military leaders developed the concept for the Marshall Center for European Security Studies. It was approved by Secretary of Defense Cheney in late 1992, and one of Nick's jobs was to get the Army to go along with this. General Dave Maddox was now the commander of U.S. Army Europe, and he was busily closing down U.S. Army installations. But Nick and his allies convinced him to leave the lights on for a while longer while they tried to get the Marshall Center set up.

The U.S. Congress approved it, but the final resistance was from the German government. General John Shalikashvili, the Supreme Allied Commander, was unable to convince senior German generals of the importance of the Marshall Center, and just when things looked really glum, Nick got a call from the Pentagon. He was told that he knew the U.S. ambassador to Germany, and that he should try to meet with him and get him onboard to help convince the German government to let the Marshall Center be opened.

The U.S. ambassador to Germany was none other than Bob Kimmitt, class of 1969 at West Point, and Nick had been his tactical officer. So Nick went to see Bob, and they had a great meeting. And just when it had looked as if all hope was lost, Bob was able to swing it, getting the German minister of defense to agree to the Marshall Center. Secretary Aspin, the new American secretary of defense, and the German minister of defense formally opened the Marshall Center on May 5, 1993. Nick brought the Ukrainian chief of staff to the opening ceremonies, where he met the American secretary of defense. From there, Secretary Aspin went on to the Ukraine, where Nick hosted him.

The institute that Nick had set up was functioning with a small staff and two very good directors, so Nick and Chris and Paul came back to the United States. Nick continued to work as a consultant to the secretary of defense on Ukrainian matters until 1997, when Secretary Cohen gave him a special consultancy title, the "Secretary of Defense's Senior Military Assistant Representative to the Ukraine."

His work is not easy, but it is certainly fulfilling. He goes to Ukraine almost every month, sometimes spends a week there, sometimes more, depending on what's happening. He attends all the Partnership for Peace exercises, but there are two more rewarding programs in which he has played a role. One is the military education exchange, under which Ukrainian students have been sent to West Point and the Air Force and Naval academies, and also to all our other military schools at higher ranks, such as the Career School and the Army War College. But most important, Ukraine is reforming not only its military systems, but also its military education. It has added social science departments to every one of its military schools, it has linked all its military institutes with civilian universities, and it has added sociology, leadership, and languages to its military education.

There are still some choppy waters ahead for the people of Ukraine, but they are committed to a freely elected government and a market economy, and there are signs of hope. Ukraine has been militarily controlled by others since well before World War II, and now that it has its freedom as an independent state, Ukrainians are just beginning to understand all the good things that can happen. Nick does his best to help them by teaching the Ukrainian military about certain concepts that exist in the West, such as the concept of service rendered by the military to a state run by leaders elected by the population. The idea of civil-

ian control of the military is entirely new, but they're trying. They did have one civilian minister of defense who
theoretically was in charge of all the military. Unfortunately, he didn't last too long, but they are introducing a
civil service corps into the military. They have a draft, but
they want to convert into an all-volunteer force, which is
an area in which Nick is trying to help them.

Ukraine is an enormously productive agricultural country, but it is burdened by a lack of energy resources. Its
need to purchase natural gas and oil from Russia and other
former Soviet Union members has put it over a barrel
politically, but it is working hard, and Nick often finds
himself asked for help in wide areas, and he finds himself
caught up in a whole array of social sciences. The country
is, in effect, trying to start over, and Nick, a little boy when
his parents spirited him away sixty years ago, has become
a key player in bringing the things that have made America
great back to Ukraine.

Nick's long-range goal for the Ukrainians is for them to
transform their military education to the point where their
young people catch fire to serve their country. The military
has played a dominant role throughout Eastern Europe for
most of the twentieth century. But now, with national freedom from Soviet domination for Ukraine, coupled with
their economic orientation toward the West, the military is
learning and structuring internal rules that establish as the
norm the control of the military by popularly elected civilian leaders. Nick fervently hopes and believes that this will
be a successful experiment in government, and he intends
to continue to devote his best efforts to see that those
Ukrainian dreams come true.

Chapter 10:

Vietnam—Frederick M. Franks, Jr.,
Humbert Roque Versace, Larry D. Budge,
James V. Kimsey, Thomas Eugene White, Jr.,
and Eugene R. Sullivan

Fred Franks

Baseball practice started in March of 1956, and one of the hottest plebes to try out for the team was Fred Franks from Pennsylvania. He shone immediately, and within a few days, he met Red Reeder. Although the details were not clear, Fred knew that he was a retired Army colonel with a flashy military career behind him, and he had been told that Red had been a war hero of some sort during World War II. The fact that Red was writing popular novels about an imaginary cadet who played on the West Point baseball team only made him all the more attractive. It was known that he had written *Bringing Up the Brass* with his sister, which was a great book about West Point in the early twentieth century, whose centerpiece was Marty Maher.

Marty had started as a waiter in the mess hall just after the turn of the century, but eventually found himself working as a trainer in the gym. Through Marty's eyes, Red was able to tell the stories of all the great generals from World War II—Patton, Bradley, Eisenhower—as flawed young men at West Point, and how they had learned the essentials of their profession. And in time, that book was made into a great John Ford movie about West Point that came out in

1956, and the theaters were packed to watch *The Long Gray Line,* starring Tyrone Power and Maureen O'Hara. Red was also writing a series of books aimed at teenaged boys, whose hero was Cadet Clint Lane of West Point. Many American teenaged boys read those books and were hooked by them. Fred and other cadets were drawn to Red like bees to honey.

And when Red spoke, his stories could be almost magical. Probably the very first time he heard him talk, Fred was sitting on the dugout bench with two other cadets, and Red started telling a story about his time on the cadet baseball team. After a few minutes, Fred suddenly realized that his mouth was open, and he quickly closed it and swallowed. But then he was drawn right back into the story, utterly mesmerized.

That was the beginning of a long, strong, and loyal friendship. First of all, Fred found that Red knew a lot about baseball. When he was sworn in as a cadet at West Point in the summer of 1955, Fred had already shown himself in high school to be an extraordinarily gifted ballplayer who could hit, throw, catch, and run with the best of them. And while he knew that he would have to stay in the Army for three years after graduating from West Point, in the back of his mind he nourished the dream of someday playing in the major leagues. He knew before he came to West Point that there were plenty of amateur baseball teams associated with different Army units or military bases. So it was more than an idle dream that, one day, after graduating from West Point, he might complete his required service and still find a way to play for the Philadelphia Phillies.

Fred was an understated star of the plebe baseball team in 1956. In the spring of 1957, he was competing as a sophomore to play on the first-string varsity team—he was that good. One afternoon during practice, Fred and some other cadet baseball players were sitting in the dugout at Doubleday Field, watching play on the field with their feet propped up on the steps in front of them. The water cooler happened to be on the opposite end from where Red usually sat as an assistant coach. As he came down the line to get a drink, also watching the play on the field, he banged into Fred's leg with his prosthetic leg. There was a kind of hollow "thunk," and Red apologized, but Fred had felt the metal and he knew instantly Red had an artificial leg. This was a genuine surprise, for Red had never before shown any problems walking around or advising cadets on how to play the game, even demonstrating stances and so on. Later, Fred asked one of the officers assigned to the team about Red, and for the first time heard the story of Normandy and Red's Distinguished Service Cross.

It had become a tradition for some time for the New York Giants or the New York Yankees to come up to West Point before their season opened and play an exhibition game against the West Point team. In 1957, the last year before they moved to San Francisco, the Giants came up to West Point and put on quite a show. They had many stars, but Willie Mays probably shone brighter than all the rest.

Before the game, there was a certain amount of camaraderie between the Giants and the young cadets who would take them on. The Giants were first formally presented to the three general officers who were the official leaders at West Point: the superintendent, the commandant of cadets, and the dean. But West Point was very proud of Red, and given his books and the great success of the movie *The Long Gray Line,* which had been based on his book, Red was a member of the official party greeting the

Giants as well. Several senior officers made it a point to tell the Giants that Red, as a young officer newly minted out of West Point, had passed on an offer from their very team, the New York Giants, to leave the service and play for them, preferring to serve his country as a soldier.

When the game started, Fred Franks was playing right field, and the center fielder was Lenny Morella. In his first time at bat, Willie hit a monster ball deep into center field, way over Lenny's head and well over four hundred feet from home plate. As Lenny chased the ball down, Fred went over to yell at him and let him know what was happening. Fred kept turning to watch Mays run, expecting him to stop with a stand-up triple. But as Lenny got to the ball, Fred realized that he wasn't going to stop at third, but instead was going to try for a rare inside-the-park home run. Lenny got to the ball as it bounced off the wall, and Fred yelled at him to get it to the shortstop, who was the cutoff man, for Willie was going all out, and had already made the turn at third, running like blazes. Lenny picked up the ball and fired, and the shortstop turned and pegged the ball home. The catcher caught the ball and turned just in time to tag Willie Mays out as he made a headfirst slide into home plate.

Willie Mays was at the peak of his skills and his glory as a baseball player, and the Giants won by a score of 16–0. Bill Wrigley, the manager of the Giants, was furious at Mays for risking injury with that headfirst slide in what was really just an exhibition game with a bunch of college kids. But for the cadet players on the field, as well as for the stands packed full of fans, Willie Mays had just taught a great object lesson in life: Whatever you do, if you want to be a true champion, then you must go all out and do it to the best of your ability. If you want to be successful in any field of endeavor, that's just the way you have to play the game. There was no holding back or half-stepping for Willie Mays: When he came to play baseball, he played baseball.

The pitcher for the Giants was Mike McCormick, a rookie lefthander, and he was throwing smoke. The cadets, of course, had a very difficult time even getting their bats on the ball, and Red Reeder, wearing khaki pants and a black Army jacket and baseball cap, was coaching third base and encouraging what was a pretty fruitless effort. In about the third inning, one cadet finally got some solid wood and drove a hard line drive up the third-base line. Distracted by someone behind him, Red hadn't been watching, and the just-foul line drive nailed him below his left knee with a loud "Whack!" then bounced out into the infield. That was Red's artificial leg, so he felt no pain and didn't even react to the blow. Instead, he turned toward the batter, clapping his hands and encouraging him to hit the ball just as hard again, only this time into fair play. For a few seconds, the Giants in the field stood stunned in drop-jaw silence.

After they came off the field, the word was gradually spread through the Giant dugout that Red had lost a leg in Normandy as an Army colonel and had then come back to West Point, his alma mater, to write books and help out with the baseball team. The game eventually ended without Army having been able to score a single run, but they had all enjoyed the experience immensely. When the last cadet struck out, the crowd flooded onto the field, and it was mostly teenagers and younger fans thronging Willie Mays and others, calling them heroes and pleading for autographs. After a few minutes, Willie held up his arms.

"Wait a minute, kids, wait a minute! We're not heroes,

we're just baseball players! You want to talk to a hero, go talk to that colonel Reeder who was the third-base coach for West Point! He lost a leg in World War II, and he's a *real* hero!"

Red encouraged Fred in his dreams, and even talked about similar dreams he had held as a cadet. But he also talked about the Army, which had finally become Red's one true love. And he was beguiling. Fred became deeply attached to Red, a man he could always talk to. When they went on trips, Red went with the team, and to Fred and all the other cadets, he was just fun to be around. As their friendship deepened, he would become a true lodestar for Fred: He would always be there at key moments in his life if he needed help to make the right decisions.

When Fred graduated in 1959, he chose to be commissioned in the armor branch. He married his high-school sweetheart, Denise, a few days after graduation, then proceeded through certain basic Army educational assignments. Armored Basic, Airborne, and Ranger schools ate up the better part of his first year as an officer, then he was off on his first assignment with the 3rd Squadron of the 11th Armored Cavalry Regiment in Regensburg, which is in southern Germany. Fred and Denise grew up in West Wyomissing, Pennsylvania, a small town west of Reading, and both came from a long line of civilians. The farthest away from home either of them had ever been was West Point, and sailing off to Europe as passengers aboard a luxury liner, the SS *United States,* was edifying, to say the least.

The 11th ACR spent a lot of time in the field, and Fred found it a wonderful environment in which to learn the fundamentals of being an Army officer. And to tell the truth, he was just a bit surprised at how quickly he fell in love with that role. All dreams of big league baseball started to fade fast, and he kept thinking about Red and his quiet influence. Their friendship had started with the older man's baseball lore, but it had slowly evolved into his active encouragement to Fred to give the Army a fair shot as a career. And as the Army grew on him, Fred had to smile affectionately at his fresh memories of lessons learned at Doubleday Field. With the wide Atlantic Ocean between them, Fred and Red started writing letters to each other, the beginning of a life-long correspondence.

The 11th ACR drove M-48-A2 tanks and M-59 personnel carriers, and they essentially had World War II–vintage weapons and Korean War–vintage equipment. There were quite a few World War II veterans still among the ranks of his soldiers, and there was also quite a bit of rubble remaining in Germany from the last days of Hitler's defeat. But within a week of their arrival at Regensburg, Fred left on a six-week training exercise to Grafenwohr and left Denise by herself. And that was the downside of military families: long periods spent apart.

But it wasn't all bad. Fred quietly learned all about the duties and responsibilities of officers and noncommissioned officers up and down the chain of command. And gradually, he found more and more responsibility being loaded on his shoulders as a junior officer serving at a border camp. It was a load he bore easily and well.

One of the most important things he picked up was an understanding of the role of a professional noncommissioned officer. As a young platoon leader, Fred was in a training exercise at Grafenwohr. His platoon was the lead element of the squadron, and on the next morning, they were supposed to lead the unit out of the training area and into a maneuver area in the civilian countryside, where they would make contact with an "aggressor" force.

It just happened that a very dense fog had set in overnight, and while Fred's platoon was supposed to move out before dawn, he was astounded to realize that, in the dense fog and pitch black of around 4:30 in the morning, they could see nothing. And lights were reflected back, making things worse.

After a few minutes of scratching his head and wondering what to do, he realized that his sergeants were there for a reason, and that maybe he should ask them. So Fred got together with his platoon sergeant, Sergeant First Class Jules Vinson, and his scout section leader, Staff Sergeant Dewey Pons. They knew the mission, of course, and Fred got right to the point and asked them how they were going to find their way through the thick fog. Sergeant Pons said, "Don't worry, Lieutenant. My scouts have already been out, they know just how to get us out of here and to where we're going. Depend on us, and we'll get out of here with no sweat."

That was one of the most important lessons he learned as a young lieutenant: to depend on his sergeants, to make use of the trust that has to exist between officers and NCOs and to make use of those who want to help you if you will only let them. Fred and the rest of the platoon followed Sergeant Pons and his scouts, and he led them right to the point on the ground from which they were meant to launch their attack. That was a lesson he would never forget.

While he was learning to soldier, Fred did his best to be a good husband to Denise, the woman he loved who was also his very best friend. In June 1961, their angel daughter Margie was born, and all seemed right with the world. Margie was to be their only child, but they showered love on her and she immediately became the center of their little family.

This was a time when unit athletics were very big, and

there were company, regimental, divisional, and even Army corps teams in football, basketball, and baseball. And commanders felt it very important to organize the best teams possible, not only to win championships and acclaim within the peculiar world of professional military organizations, but also just to increase unit esprit de corps. In the spring of 1962, someone at Stuttgart, the VII Corps headquarters, found out that Fred had been a star on the West Point baseball team in 1959. Eventually, the word came down to the 11th ACR that they wanted him to come to Stuttgart and be the manager and the player/coach of the VII Corps baseball team. By that time, Fred had completed the three years of service that he owed the Army after graduation from West Point, and he was a first lieutenant at the border camp when he got a phone call from his squadron executive officer, Major John Barris. Barris was a World War II veteran and a serious soldier, and he passed the word that he had gotten a call from VII Corps asking for Fred to be reassigned to Stuttgart so he could manage the baseball team. He came right to the point: "Fred, you've got to decide whether you want to be a soldier or a baseball player, and I'm waiting for your answer."

But for Fred, there was no hesitation. He had had a great start in the Army. He loved what he was doing, he loved being a soldier, he loved the challenges, the service, even just being around the troops. He loved baseball too, but he loved the Army more, and the time had finally arrived when he had to choose. He decided in that instant that he wanted to be an Army officer and serve his country for the rest of his life. So he told Major Barris to tell Corps he was very honored to have been selected, but it was no contest, he was very happy where he was. Much as he loved baseball, he said, he loved the Army more, and he didn't want to get sidetracked at this early stage in his career. And that was a decision he never regretted.

In 1964, Fred Franks, by now a senior captain, was lucky enough to be assigned to teach English at West Point. In preparation for that, he was to spend two years at Columbia University in New York City earning a master's degree in English literature. While at Columbia, Fred not only completed his master's degree, but he also finished all the work for a doctorate, including passing his oral and written qualifying exams, and had to only write his dissertation to get his Ph.D. But Fred was first a soldier, so that was a task that somehow fell by the wayside.

Fred reported to West Point as an instructor of English in June 1966, and classes started in the fall. Over the summer, he got his wife and daughter settled into quarters and learned what would be expected of him when the academic year began. But he was happy to join two old friends who were also in the English department, Walt Pritchard from the class of 1957 and Lon Spurlock from the class of 1958. Fred had known them briefly when they were all cadets in the late fifties, but all three had been graduate students together at Columbia over the past two years, and they had built a special bond of friendship.

After only two years teaching at West Point, Walt Pritchard and Lon Spurlock both left in the summer of 1968 and went to Vietnam, while Fred stayed on for a third academic year. Then, in the spring of 1969, Fred learned to his great distress that Pritchard and Spurlock had both been killed, within a month of each other. Their families had stayed at West Point while they spent their year in Vietnam, and the Franks family had been very close to them. Fred and Denise helped both wives through their grief as best they could.

But then it was Fred's turn, and in June 1969, he left for Vietnam. Just as Pritchard and Spurlock had done with their families, he left Denise and Margie at West Point. If anything happened to him, they all knew, this was the right place for them to be.

Major Fred Franks landed at Long Binh in early August 1969, and he was told not to contact anyone, that orders on where he would serve and with what unit would come down for him. But he knew that the Black Horse, the 11th ACR, was nearby, and he wanted to serve with them. So he got to a phone and called them up, and told a duty officer that he had served with the Black Horse in Germany and he sure would like to join them in Vietnam. He was told not to say anything to anyone, that they would pick him up and take care of the orders after they had rescued him.

(Just so nomenclature doesn't further confuse a story already overloaded with military shorthand, some clarification of what units were called at the time is in order. Because of their direct connection to horse-mounted cavalry units of the nineteenth century, armored cavalry units in the late twentieth century designated units called "companies," "battalions," and "brigades" in any other division of the time as "troops," "squadrons," and "regiments.")

Sure enough, a jeep from the 11th ACR appeared the next day. Without so much as a "by your leave," and without even saying anything to anyone, Fred threw his duffel bag into the backseat and was whisked away. The admin people at the 11th ACR would take care of the paperwork, and no one was going to be critical of Fred later for going off to fight the war.

Next day, Fred was flown to regimental headquarters at Quang Loi, a relatively short ride by helicopter. The regimental commander at the time was Colonel Jimmy Leach, who had been a company commander in the 37th Tank Battalion in World War II. During the Battle of the Bulge in 1944–45, this was the battalion commanded by Lieutenant Colonel Creighton Abrams that led the successful deep attack of Patton's Third Army, an attack launched to rescue the 101st Airborne Division besieged by German forces at Bastogne. Abrams later rose to four-star rank, and in 1969, he was the commander of U.S. forces in Vietnam. And that feat by his 37th remained the stuff of legend. Leach still seemed to carry a little of that magic around with him, and professional soldiers who knew of the 37th, which included Fred, loved to serve under him.

The Black Horse at that time probably had twice as many majors as they needed. All of the regiment except for one squadron had moved up to Di An, but there was some administrative trouble back at Xuan Loc, the base camp of the Black Horse. It seemed that the inspector general had found some buried equipment that had mysteriously disappeared off the regiment's books, and there were a few other questionable issues that had come up. Only the 2nd Squadron had stayed there, and Leach told Fred, as his first duty, to go down to Xuan Loc and clear that mess up.

So Fred spent his first few weeks toiling in the vineyard. But while he was in Xuan Loc, he got to talk to many officers and NCOs, and he found out a lot about the enemy they were facing, their tactics, their weapons, and a lot of "lessons learned" that would be of great use to him later on. He eventually got the administrative mess cleared up, but he also felt he had learned more about combat in

Vietnam in a few weeks than he had ever learned anywhere else before arriving "in country."

The war in Vietnam was mostly an infantry war fought by individual lightly armed foot soldiers in mountainous jungles or in flooded alluvial plains. The 11th ACR, an armored brigade equipped with heavy M-48 tanks and M-113 armored personnel carriers, was unable to operate in parts of the country simply because of the terrain. But tracked vehicles were also enormously versatile, and there were many areas of the country where tanks and other armored vehicles became powerful enforcers. While their engines were loud and gave the enemy plenty of early warning of their arrival, they were tough in a fixed fight. They were frequently attacked by armor-piercing .51-caliber machine gun fire, or by rocket-propelled grenades that could easily blow through the armor of anything the Americans had, up to the heavily armored front slope of an M-48 tank, although it could even burst through the side or rear of those beasts. But the enemy seldom hung around after such attacks, for they knew they were no match for the enormous firepower of which the Black Horse, once alerted, was capable.

In the middle of August, Fred was called forward to be the all-important S-3, or operations officer, of the 2nd Squadron while the regular S-3 went on a seven-day "rest and recuperation" trip to Hawaii. That was his first taste of combat, when, riding in a helicopter above his unit, he first realized that enemy soldiers were shooting at him. And it wasn't just the awareness that he was on a battlefield where random bullets were flying past; rather, he suddenly realized that, sitting in the open door on the side of the helicopter and looking down as it lazily circled above his cav forces, the enemy soldiers were shooting at *him*, and that they wanted to kill *him!*

Needless to say, this was a mind-opening moment, and Fred's body immediately tightened up. Cold terror, unknown until now, washed over his head and shoulders and flooded through his body as he felt his heart leap into his throat. But his training quickly took over. As he felt his arms and shoulders harden, he fought off that unexpected chill of fear. He slowly flexed every muscle in his body as he sat immobile, reflected on his relative safety as a moving target, then continued his mission.

Within a week, a new squadron commander took over, Lieutenant Colonel Brookshire, and he asked Fred to stay on as squadron operations officer. Obviously, Fred had done well, for this was nothing more or less than an invitation to stay on as the key subordinate officer of the battalion commander. It was an offer to stay in the fight, and Fred was delighted to accept.

In late September, the squadron was redeployed to an area north of Saigon near the Cambodian border. Their first mission there was to open a road between the towns of An Loc and Bu Dop, and this became a long, hard fight, with enemy contact almost every day. As the S-3, Fred was usually in his helicopter several times a day, and each time generally for several hours.

The countryside was quite flat and only sparsely populated, and vegetation ranged from bare fields to elephant grass six or eight feet high all the way up to triple-canopy jungle as much as a hundred feet high or more. Fred quickly got familiar with operating in these ever-changing terrain types, and that was a good thing, for his unit would have to deal with them for the rest of the time he was in Vietnam. Getting shot at became a daily, almost routine experience, and it was no longer alarming, or even noteworthy, unless the helicopter or one of the crew members got hit.

One of Fred's subordinates in the S-3 office was Sergeant Bob Bolan, who was on his fourth one-year tour of duty in Vietnam. It was obvious that Bob had volunteered to spend this much time in Vietnam, and he was to become one of Fred's heroes. In June 1970, he would be made the command sergeant major of the squadron, and shortly thereafter, in July 1970, he would be killed in action. Bolan's assistant in 1969 was Sergeant Tommy Jones, and the three of them were a very tight and effective team.

While Fred went out on his helicopter flights to get an overview of the terrain and the operation, Sergeants Bolan and Jones kept the paperwork that was necessary for such operations going. Upon his return, he joined his sergeants in a specially configured armored operations vehicle. Basically, this was just an M-113 armored personnel carrier that was packed with radios and other equipment, and it had raised armored sides that allowed them to stand up in the middle of an operation and still remain out of the line of enemy small-arms fire.

Lieutenant Colonel Brookshire was, in Fred's estimation, a superb combat leader. His squadron command element was a very tight team, and it consisted of himself, Fred as his S-3, the four troop commanders, his artillery battery commander, the squadron sergeant major, and a few other key noncommissioned officers. And Fred quickly learned that the enlisted soldiers in the Black Horse were young men who served with great skill and courage, and at enormous self-sacrifice. They performed their duties, he would come to believe, as magnificently as men in any American war drawn from any generation ever performed their duties on any other battle front.

Fred's daily duties as squadron operations officer normally required flight in a two-man OH-6 "Loach," a light observation helicopter. In his Loach, Fred would fly just above the treetops as he helped his armored units navigate across country. When they got into contact with enemy forces, the immediate effort was directed to isolating the battlefield and then bringing in supporting artillery fire while allowing the ACR's heavy firepower to do its work.

Sometimes Fred would also act as the "forward observer" from his Loach and direct artillery fire onto suspected or actual enemy positions. The artillery they used was generally the six self-propelled 155-mm artillery battery located at their squadron command post, and usually only a few miles from the contact. The tank company usually stayed at the CP waiting to be called forward, and they moved every two or three days so that their North Vietnamese adversary could never be quite sure where they were.

Combat was a daily experience, and they knew they were opposing North Vietnamese regular army regiments. In addition, local Viet Cong would do such things as bury mines in roadways, but they were really little more than an annoyance, for they didn't have the strength to attack an armored cavalry unit. Only the North Vietnamese regulars could or would do that.

At this time, the Black Horse was operating under the operational control of the 1st Cavalry Division. Also known as the 1st Air Cavalry Division, this was primarily an infantry division with a large number of helicopters that allowed them to quickly move in force from point to point. During the road-clearing operations from An Loc to Bu Dop, Fred's squadron initially had two infantry companies of about 150 soldiers each attached to it from this 1st Cavalry Division. These soldiers would stay out on the flanks and move in an almost classic tank-infantry configuration as the armored force slowly made its way down the road.

The key component of this road-clearing effort, of course, involved clearing the vegetation on either side. This was done by a team of "Rome Plows," huge machines made in Rome, Georgia, and capable of cutting through any vegetation up to and including tree trunks. The end result was a swath that cleared both sides of the road back to a healthy distance and thus reduced the cover from which an enemy force could ambush road traffic.

While this road-clearing operation between An Loc and Bu Dop was underway, the 1st Cavalry Division called Fred one day and informed him that, since the two infantry companies were not making any enemy contact, they would be pulled back to the division and put to use somewhere else. Fred tried to convince them that the reason there was no enemy contact was the presence of the two infantry companies, but he was unsuccessful.

And sure enough, the vehicles and their crews trying to clear the roadway started getting hit by snipers and rocket-propelled grenades and small infantry unit hit-and-run attacks, which really slowed things down, first to a crawl and then to a full stop. In pretty short order, the two infantry companies came back, and the road clearing continued. Within another month, it had significantly widened the open area along the entire roadway, and this effectively eliminated the threat of ambushes between the two towns. Thereafter, Fred's 2nd Squadron stayed in the same area. They fought every day against North Vietnamese regulars trying to strangle the countryside while they, the soldiers of the Black Horse, struggled to keep the roadways open.

In February 1970, the 2nd Squadron was moved into War Zone C. This was an area with a heavy communist military presence that lay northwest of Saigon and just below the Cambodian border protrusion into South Vietnam known as "the Fishhook." The mission of Fred's squadron was to interdict the North Vietnamese who were trying to move soldiers and supplies from their sanctuary in Cambodia to an area just north of Saigon. The 2nd Squadron was able to get astride the North Vietnamese lines of communication, and they hit them hard with everything from heavy patrols and ambushes using their own armored vehicles and other weapon systems to B-52 strikes called in from the U.S. Air Force. The result was pure havoc for communist forces as the Black Horse cut them into small pieces and effectively cut them off from Cambodia.

While in War Zone C, Fred's helicopter was shot down twice, and it had also been forced down by mechanical failure on two other occasions. The first time he had been shot down was in March 1970, when a .51-caliber machine gun round had gone through the rotor blade about a foot from the rotor head. The helicopter vibrated wildly, but the pilot was able to put it on the ground safely before the blade came off. Within minutes another craft arrived and spirited them away, while a much larger cargo helicopter arrived, hooked up slings on the wounded Loach, lifted it out of harm's way and ferried it back to a U.S. repair base.

The second time was barely a month later, in April 1970, when Fred's Loach was hovering at treetop level and took some AK-47 submachine gun fire out of an area of thick jungle. Several rounds went into the engine compartment, and more smashed through the small plexiglass bubble inside which Fred and the pilot sat. The pilot got hit in the hip, and as they turned away and called for help over the radio, Fred watched the oil pressure indicator slowly drop toward zero. By the time the engine stopped, fortunately for them, they had gotten far enough away from the source of the gunfire to bounce the helicopter in just as other ships arrived to pick them up. A medevac took the pilot to a hospital, but Fred waited for another Loach. As soon as he was airborne, he went back to the site of the shoot-down and plastered the jungle with artillery fire for another twenty minutes.

In April 1970, Lieutenant Colonel Donn Starry took over as the new regimental commander. Soon after taking command, he met with Fred and told him that since he had spent his time on line he had earned the right to a "safe" staff job in the rear. But Starry had known Fred for a long time and had even watched him in action, so he also told him that, if he wanted to stay on, he was most welcome to keep his place as the squadron operations officer.

Fred knew what he loved most in life, and that was being a soldier. He also understood that the fullest life available to a soldier is to be found in war, so he never even hesitated. What he wanted most of all, he told Starry, was to stay on as the squadron operations officer. He did.

At the end of April, the Black Horse received the order to attack into Cambodia as part of a massive American effort to trap and destroy the major North Vietnamese headquarters element known to be there, which basically ran the war for the communists inside South Vietnam. Since Cambodia was a separate nation that was, in theory, not involved in the war, American forces had never before openly crossed its borders on such a large scale as the impending attack gave evidence of being. It is true that raids into Cambodia by small Special Forces units had occurred, and even large American air strikes. But never before had the United States so openly violated the theoretical neutrality of Cambodia, even though its territory was widely known to be in use by North Vietnamese forces, not only as a refuge and a marshaling area for their forces, but also as a warehouse for arms, ammunition, and other supplies. But beyond these organizational purposes, the most egregious use, according to the political thinkers in the White House and the Pentagon and the State Department who decided such things, had been the site for COSVN, the Central Office for South Vietnam which actually ran North Vietnamese forces operating inside South Vietnam.

But by 1970, President Nixon had apparently had enough of this charade, and he proposed to make a surprise invasion of Cambodia with major U.S. forces. He intended to hit COSVN and other communist forces, and hit them hard. The Black Horse was among the units that would lead the charge.

The 2nd Squadron would be the lead unit in Task Force Shoemaker, which would burst across the border on May 1. As they prepared for the move into Cambodia, Fred and others anticipated that the ground-to-air fire would be quite intense. They decided, therefore, not to use helicopters on the first day of the invasion, and Fred was part of the command group that would move right behind the lead cavalry troop that attacked into Cambodia.

On the first of May, the armored column plunged across the border. Colonel Starry, the regimental commander, had planned to be right up front during the attack, riding in his own armored personnel carrier but moving with the 2nd Squadron command element. Before they got near the border, however, his vehicle broke down, so he spent that day as a passenger in Fred's armored personnel carrier.

When they had gone no more than a few hundred meters across the border, however, they were hit by small-arms fire coming from a small village. The armored cav troop in the lead returned the fire, then tanks flanked the village and swept through it. The village, being so close to the border, had long been abandoned by civilians and was occupied only by North Vietnamese soldiers, all of whom quickly fled or died.

Over the next few days there was constant contact as the North Vietnamese hastily threw forces together in an attempt to defend their enormous expanse of supply storehouses filled with arms and equipment, as well as hospitals and motor pools and other logistical establishments. Fred's squadron suffered quite a few casualties, and many American armored vehicles were knocked out by armor-piercing weapons, particularly by rocket-propelled grenades (RPGs), of which the North Vietnamese clearly had an abundance. But the American attack, the American invasion, really, was such a surprise that the North Vietnamese could only slow it down at best. They simply did not have the force needed to stop it. So the Black Horse left the booty for following forces to collect or destroy and plunged deep into the heart of Cambodia, killing enemy soldiers and destroying their bases as they went.

There were tough times. On the second day, an American soldier in the command group was badly wounded by shrapnel from an RPG round that knocked out his armored personnel carrier. Fred was one of those who tried to help, and as they rolled him onto a poncho, blood spurted freely from his wound and soon seemed to cover everything. His shirt was removed, then a medic was on the other side of him, working furiously to try to stop the blood shooting from the jagged hole in his back. From the steady spurting, he was not having much luck finding the open artery or arteries, and Fred cringed. Then the soldier turned his head and looked Fred dead in the eye, his face inches away.

"Sir . . . how am I doing? Am I gonna be okay?"

Fred was stunned. He watched the medic shaking his head from side to side as he worked, and he felt queasy. But he also knew that encouragement and attitude can do wonders in the field of life preservation. He forced a smile.

"Yeah, you're going to be fine. You'll get some good time in the hospital with a beautiful nurse, don't worry."

Fred heard the medevac ship hammering in no more than fifty meters away. Then the medic stood up and four other soldiers hoisted the poncho on which the wounded man lay and jogged toward the waiting helicopter. Even after it took off and the noise faded to silence, Fred continued to feel terrible. It was a feeling that lasted for a very long time. Years, even. Many years.

On the third day, they decided they could start to use their helicopters again. Soon enough, Fred was aloft in his Loach, soaring out in front of their armored column to see what awaited them. They were moving along toward Highway 7, and the key town of Snuol lay ahead, which appeared to be the base area for one or two North Vietnamese regiments. The 2nd Squadron was moving very fast, trying to maintain the effect of shock and surprise on the enemy, and they had even outrun their howitzer battery. One of the battalions of the 1st Cavalry Division had air-assaulted into a nearby area, and they had brought along their 105-mm artillery battery, so on the fourth day, Fred flew over to their CP and landed. Their commanding officer was Lieutenant Colonel Jim Anderson, who had graduated from West Point in the class of 1956 and had been the platoon leader of Fred's platoon when he was a new plebe in Beast Barracks.

Fred went over to Colonel Anderson and spoke right up.

Arthur Middleton Parker III, a true officer and gentleman from South Carolina who gave his life that others might live.

Sylvanus Thayer, remembered today as the Father of West Point.

Robert Edward Lee, whose
heroic actions in Mexico
repeatedly opened the door
to American victory.

Ulysses Simpson Grant, whose aggressive actions outside
Mexico City foreshadowed his Civil War triumphs.

John Pelham, the only man below the rank of general mentioned in dispatches by General Robert E. Lee during the Civil War, a true romantic hero.

Patrick Henry O'Rorke, a man of the people who rose from quarryman to cadet to colonel of volunteers, then died at Gettysburg as he led his men in a charge.

Battle Monument.

Henry Ossian Flipper, the first African-American to graduate from West Point, had to fight a political war based on race against the fiercest hostility.

George Smith Patton, Jr.,
whose raw courage was
baptized by his own
blood in France in 1918,
truly earning him the
immortal nickname
"Old Blood and Guts."

Douglas MacArthur, whose World War I
triumphs reassured him that he was
destined for greatness.

Benjamin Oliver Davis, Jr., the man who trained and led the first all-black American fighter aircraft unit, known as the "Tuskegee Airmen," to legendary aerial exploits in Europe.

Russell Potter Reeder, Jr., the cadet baseball captain destined for greatness in the army until loss of a leg in combat forced him into retirement as an author and West Point's assistant baseball coach.

Joseph Gordon Clemons, Jr., who with his men withstood the most gruesome of combat tests on Korea's Pork Chop Hill.

Nicholas Stephen Hordij Krawciw, the Ukrainian immigrant who became an exemplary cadet, bled for his new country in war, and rose to general's rank.

Frederick Melvin Franks, Jr., yet another cadet baseball captain who lost a leg in combat, but reinforced by Red Reeder, he stayed in the army and eventually rose to four-star rank.

Trophy Point.

Humbert Rocque Versace,
the man of absolute principle
who was wounded and
captured while serving with
the Special Forces, but defied
his Viet Cong captors, who
eventually executed him.

Larry Donald Budge, Rhodes scholar and infantry company commander. He survived war, fell in love with Art Parker's widow, and built a new life with her.

James Verlin Kimsey, the streetwise city kid who retained a heart of gold and built an orphanage while fighting a war in the face of seemingly impossible odds.

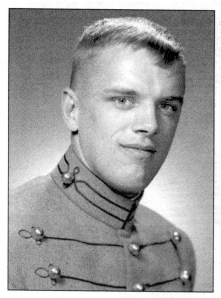

Thomas Eugene White, Jr., who became a legendary figure at West Point, then made his mark as an extraordinary armored cavalry leader in Vietnam.

Eugene Raymond Sullivan, who fought in Vietnam, then went to law school and launched a new career in the Justice Department, capped by a judgeship on a federal court of appeals.

David Leroy Ramsay,
the fighter pilot's
fighter pilot who
finally rolled those
dice in combat one
time too many.

Robert Benjamin Ramsay,
the bomber pilot who
turned from flying B-52s
on bombing missions over
Vietnam to becoming a
true pasta king in the
Midwest.

The cadet chapel at West Point rises above the academy buildings and the Hudson River.

Jason Luke Amerine, leader of the Special Forces team that led the fight against the Taliban in Afghanistan in the first days of a new century.

"Colonel Anderson, I realize you don't know me from the man in the moon, but you were my Beast Barracks platoon leader."

"Okay, what do you need?"

"Sir, I'm the S-3 of the 2nd Squadron of the 11th Cav. We outran our own artillery battery, and we could use some help from your 105s."

"Okay, we can help."

Colonel Anderson called his fire support coordinator over and said, "Give Franks whatever he needs!"

That 1st Cav artillery battery quickly went to work and that day, the 2nd Squadron got all the artillery support they needed.

By the fifth of May, Fred's squadron was just to the south of Snuol, headed north toward Highway 7, which went through a rubber plantation just south of Snuol. That day, intelligence told them that the North Vietnamese had laid an ambush along Highway 7, and that they were waiting for the Americans. In addition, intelligence confirmed that there was a North Vietnamese regiment in and around Snuol, also waiting for them. In addition, there was an airfield near Snuol that they wanted to take because they could then use it to bring in reinforcements for the 1st Cav.

The scheme of maneuver that was developed by Colonel Grail Brookshire and his staff called for the squadron to stay off the road, and rather to go up to the east, through the rubber plantation, and capture the airfield before they tried to take the town. Most of the civilians in the region had stayed in place, and Brookshire was very concerned about civilian casualties. As they developed plans and put the word out to the troops, he emphasized that concern time and again.

The 2nd Squadron of the 11th Armored Cavalry

Regiment, of which Fred was the operations officer, consisted at this time of three armored cavalry troops, Troops E, F, and G, a tank company, H Company, and their howitzer battery, which had finally caught up with them. Each cavalry troop had a combat troop strength that ranged from 120 to 130 men, mounted in 9 Sheridan light tanks, 3 armored 81-mm mortar carriers, and 20 M-113 armored personnel carriers. H Company had a total of 17 M-48 tanks, each tank with a crew of 4, and the howitzer battery had 6 self-propelled 155-mm howitzers with 6 men assigned to each gun.

Their scheme of maneuver called for Colonel Starry and Colonel Brookshire to stay with the ground maneuver element, just behind the leading cavalry troop, while Fred got in his Loach and tried to help the cavalry troop and the tank company maneuver up through the rubber plantation. It was important that Fred stay right at treetop level so that they could avoid revealing to the North Vietnamese forces where precisely they were and where they were going.

Just after Fred's pilot lifted off that day, their craft ran into a set of metal telephone wires some twenty feet above a road. They hit the Loach's plexiglass bubble right at eye level, and the effect was to stop it completely for a few seconds. The pilot, CW3 Paul Millett, instinctively gave the machine more power, and within a few anxious heartbeats, the added horses caused some of the wires to break. Then the rest slipped under the craft rather than over the top and into the transmission, where they would have caused some serious trouble. All of this only took a few seconds, but Fred swore it took an hour, and while they hesitated on the precipice, as it were, his whole life seemed to flash before his eyes. There were no such telephone wires in Vietnam that he knew of, he had never seen any or worried about them, and such a concern hadn't even entered their consciousness. But now, like a flash out of the blue, they were brought right up against it, straining against metal telephone wires that had probably been installed by the French in this strange new country of Cambodia fifty years earlier, strong wires that now threatened to turn their Loach into a ball of flame and send it hurtling toward the earth.

This was certainly a more frightening event for Fred than either of his shoot-downs had been. After they broke through, both men were still a bit shaken, but Fred figured that would be the only bad bit of luck he would hit that day.

As they raced across the treetops, they headed north toward the airfield. Then they came to the end of the jungle and were suddenly flying over open country that surrounded the airport. Looking down, Fred saw that, just past the jungle, they had flown directly above a North Vietnamese antiaircraft position. It looked like a reversed doughnut, with a circular trench four feet deep running around a mound atop which was mounted a .51-caliber machine gun. The trench enabled the crew to swing the gun around in a complete circle and shoot up at an aircraft as it approached, then follow it out as it flew away in the opposite direction from which it had arrived.

Fortunately, the North Vietnamese were as surprised as the Americans were, and there was no one manning the gun, which might have quickly knocked them from the sky. But as they wheeled over and headed back for the jungle cover, Fred pulled a can of smoke he kept in a canister by the door and threw it out to mark the area. Then he got on the radio and told Brookshire what they had found, and he quickly moved a cav troop and the tank company to their location. These forces soon took the North

Vietnamese position, and Fred had his pilot take them back there and land.

Fred was wearing the body armor that was standard at the time, consisting of a one-inch-thick steel plate strapped over his chest, abdomen, and back with a hole in the top through which you slipped your head, much like a medieval suit of armor. He got out of the Loach and strode toward the American officers he saw near the gun emplacement, concerned because the North Vietnamese were not only waiting in ambush along Highway 7, an ambush that would have stopped the 2nd Squadron cold, but they had also ringed the airport with what intelligence was telling them was a regiment-sized ambush. This anti-aircraft position was the first piece of it they had taken, and it was important to Fred to get to Brookshire and tell him they needed to try to capture prisoners here if possible so they could interrogate them.

They had taken two prisoners, but their sullen looks did not encourage Fred, and he was about to get back into his helicopter. Then someone called him and told him they had trapped two more North Vietnamese soldiers in some sort of bunker or tunnel right by the .51-caliber gun position. Fred drew his pistol and walked back there, trying to cover the troops as they removed some logs from the front of the bunker. Meanwhile, their interpreter was talking to the North Vietnamese soldiers, encouraging them to come out, but only eliciting angered responses. Back in Vietnam, someone probably would have thrown a grenade into the bunker by this time, but in Cambodia, they were trying to be very careful and capture as many prisoners as they could.

Then Fred heard people yelling behind him. He couldn't make out what they were saying, and he turned toward the voices. All he heard was confused yelling, but he saw people pointing wildly at his feet. He looked down, and on the ground saw a grenade the North Vietnamese soldiers had thrown out of their bunker that was bouncing toward his left leg. Before he could react, he was falling to his right as Colonel Donn Starry, who had grabbed his shirt at the shoulder, jerked him off his feet. Then he heard a loud bang and all the lights went out.

When he regained consciousness, he felt enormous pain in his left leg and all up his left side. Then he looked up and saw medics leaning over him, and the anxious look on the faces of other soldiers told him things were not well. He was given morphine, and he and three other wounded men were ferried out on Starry's helicopter. Over the next few days, he was treated at various American hospitals in Vietnam, then transported to Camp Zama in Japan. From his earliest moments of lucidity, he would ask the doctors for details on his wounds and finally if they thought he would lose his leg. He was told that most of the wounds he had suffered above his left knee would heal in time to the point that there would be no trace of injury left beyond some scars. As to his left foot and the lower part of the bones in his left calf, however, it was clear that they had been badly broken—most gave him some version of "very small pieces," but one slipped and described his foot and ankle as "crushed." They uniformly told him, however, that he would not lose his leg, and that eventually, he could hope to recover completely. But this, he would later learn, was just so much reassurance intended more to help him keep his spirits up than to give him any actual information about his realistic prognosis for recovery.

In June 1970, Major Fred Franks finally flew home to the United States, but on a stretcher. After they landed in

California, he was immediately sent to Valley Forge General Hospital in Phoenixville, Pennsylvania, which was the Army hospital closest to his hometown. There, he was to endure a series of nine surgical operations as the physicians attempted to improve the condition of his badly shattered foot and lower leg. He would also undergo repeated skin grafts and a radical mastoidectomy to clean out the damage done to his left eardrum and auditory canal.

Despite the physical pain, Fred was delighted to be home. His wife, Denise, drove forty-five miles each way, and she came every day to visit him. Their daughter, Margie, was in fifth grade, so she could only come to see him on weekends. But he was home with his wife and daughter, and while this hospitalization would prove to be the most trying time of his life, he knew that without Denise and Margie it would have been pure hell.

By July, he was able to ride home stretched out in the back of their station wagon for a few days at a time. He was told that he would eventually be able to spend several weeks at home healing between surgeries, but that they had to start slow. Then the surgeries on his foot and leg began in earnest, and he became much less mobile for a while.

As he was recovering from the first surgical operation at Valley Forge, Fred got a letter from Red Reeder at West Point. Fred was deeply touched, and though Red had few details on how bad his injuries were, his letter was brimming over with support. Fred wrote back right away and told him that his life was not in danger, though he was in some minor discomfort because of a light scratch on his leg. But over the next few weeks, and after several letters and more surgery, Red gradually began to understand both the seriousness of Fred's leg wound and the devastating effect it was having on Fred's morale.

Fred was going through an awful lot. He knew he was getting the best care in the best medical facility available, near his wife and daughter and parents and family friends, and those were good things. But his appetite was gone, he felt massively depressed much of the time, and the physical pain in his leg was a never-ending torture from which there was no relief. Normal amusements or even temporary distractions, such as television, or movies, or even history books, had somehow lost their appeal. All his life, he had been active, playing sports, going hunting or fishing, relishing the great outdoors, and celebrating life with physical activity. His initial service in the Army had been a dream come true. And now here he was, strapped to a bed, forgotten by the Army, and genuinely helpless.

The Army medical team running the hospital knew the poison of self-pity, and they did everything they could to keep patients busy and involved in something. But Fred still spent long hours alone when he felt the world closing in on him. Oh, he could struggle out of bed well enough, and put on normal clothes except for his left foot. So long as that was bandaged up, he could get around all right on crutches or in a wheelchair. But what a fall this had been! He had been flying high in the fullest and most robust state of health of his life, and now was broken, a pitiful, helpless victim. At first, going home was good for his morale. But even at home, all he could do was lie around and wait. Wait to heal, he knew, which was important. But time hung heavy.

And the pain endured. And the infection. Fred's left leg below the knee had been very badly damaged. Crushed, really. Great chunks of flesh and tendon as well as pieces of bone had been consumed or blown away by the explosion of the grenade. And the bones of his foot and ankle had been smashed into such tiny fragments that it was virtually impossible for surgeons to fit them back into place. The goal of the doctors was to repair his foot and lower leg enough so that it would able to bear his weight and function as a foot once again, at least to some degree. But reassembling Fred's bone pieces was like trying to fit the pieces of a tiny jigsaw puzzle back together after they had been blowtorched and then dumped in a mud puddle on a windy day. And to Fred's great added misfortune, a nasty infection had also set in, an infection that was impervious to all the antibiotics and other medications that could be mustered.

One day after an hour of rehabilitation exercises, Fred was sitting in a chair at the end of his bed reading. His next surgery wouldn't be for at least several weeks, his doctors had told him, and he was trying to read a book about the Civil War, something he normally would have enjoyed and that he now hoped would give him some escape. Then he heard something unusual and turned to see what it was. There, at the end of the ward and coming his way, was Red, and as Fred turned and looked at him, his beaming smile burst into loud laughter! Fred felt a strange and delicious sense of joy welling up from somewhere deep inside. He grabbed the left arm of the chair with his left hand and tried to push up onto his right leg, opening his right arm to Red. And then the old coach was there, hugging him and soothing him. Both their faces were wet, and neither could speak a clear word at first, so they didn't try. Good old Red!

Theirs was a relationship that defies easy description, but Red was certainly old coach, role model, father, and brother in arms to Fred, and his unexpected arrival on Fred's ward in the hospital tapped a reservoir of emotion in Fred that he had carefully protected since his wounding, so far successfully. But Red's presence was welcome and a compelling force. Red was fairly bursting with warmth, affection, and acceptance, and his words made clear his fervent and unalloyed support, a support he told Fred that he felt not only for him, but also for any other American soldiers who served in what had become, by this time, the quite unpopular war in Vietnam. On that day, it was clear that Fred was Red's hero.

The first meeting in the hospital was quite emotional, and when Red finally left, Fred felt buoyed far beyond anything he might have anticipated. And there were to be more visits. Each time, Red would listen attentively while Fred told him first of his war experiences, and then, gradually, of his concern about his future and finally, about his fear of losing his leg.

This last issue was all the more difficult because Fred knew that Red had lost his own leg below the knee in World War II, and he seemed perfectly fine. In fact, Fred hadn't even known Red was an amputee at all until Fred had bumped into him that day in the dugout. At first, Fred swore to himself that he would never even bring the issue up. But gradually, their connection grew stronger than it had ever been, even back at West Point.

At West Point in the 1950s, of course, their relationship had been their own variant on the old soldier counseling and training and educating the young cadet in preparation for a military career. But the young cadet had come of age and had been launched and commissioned. He had served in the Army as a regular Army officer leading troops in Germany, had gone to graduate school and had then come back to West Point to educate other young cadets. And finally, as a mature man, he had gone off to fight a war, and had come back not only wounded but badly damaged in a way that would necessarily change his whole life. Could their relationship accept and adapt to these dramatic swings enough to endure?

These concerns, of course, were only Red's, and they were at best but silent reflections never articulated. Instead, as Fred talked, Red listened and responded in a way in which most human beings were simply not capable. It wasn't that no others could sympathize or empathize with Fred, it was just that none of them had ever been there. The doctors may have been skilled at their craft, but they had not gone to West Point and they had not been in combat. Fred's peers may have gone to West Point and faced combat, may even have been wounded. But they hadn't faced and dreaded amputation of a leg. Only Red shared all those experiences with Fred. And only Red could truly understand.

So Fred confided in Red. He was perhaps hesitant at first, sensitive to Red's own amputation. But Red quickly laughed that concern away. And he understood completely Fred's concern. He encouraged him to do everything he could to save his leg. But if the cards were against him, he told Fred, don't give up hope. It might be that, with an artificial leg, he would be more capable of performing his duties as a soldier than he would with a mangled appendage.

While Red's visits were welcome, Fred began to be able to go home on convalescent leave for days, then weeks at a time while his body tried to heal. One day at home, his ten-year-old daughter Margie came running in the front door with the mail and said, "Daddy, Daddy, you got a letter that has five stars on it." Fred was a bit confused.

"Nah, you must be mistaken," he said as he took the envelope in his hands. But just as Margie had said, in the upper lefthand corner of the envelope were five small gold stars in a circle, and below them was the name "Omar

Bradley." General Bradley had been a four-star general during World War II, and because of his concern for the welfare of his men, he had become known as the "soldier's general." General Bradley was the last surviving five-star general, a rank that was held by only five men of the World War II generation, when the United States had fielded a ten-million-man army. During World War II, the rank had been held by George Marshall, who had commanded all American armies from the nation's capital in Washington, D.C.; Douglas MacArthur, in the Pacific Theater of Operations; Dwight Eisenhower in Europe; and Hap Arnold, who had commanded the Army Air Corps, a force that was converted into the U.S. Air Force in 1947. In 1950, Omar Bradley received his fifth star, becoming the last and youngest of that era's five-star generals. Fred was moved, for a letter to a lowly major in the hospital from General Omar Bradley was a very high honor indeed.

Inside the envelope was a personal letter from Omar Bradley, and although they had never met, he had somehow learned some things about Fred and was very complimentary to him. Fred knew that Bradley had played baseball himself as a cadet at West Point in the class of 1915, and as he read the baseball stories Bradley was telling him from more than fifty years ago, it slowly dawned on Fred that Red Reeder was the only man who could have made this happen.

At Red's next visit, Fred pulled out the letter and read it to him, and Red admitted that he had called in some chips to get that particular prize written and mailed. He never said what those chips were, but it really didn't matter. A personal letter from Omar Bradley, after all, written to an Army major recovering from wounds in 1970, was a very big deal, and the memories of Army baseball that he shared with Fred only made for that much more frosting on the cake.

As they talked, Red always encouraged Fred to fight for what he could, but he also counseled him to accept the things that were beyond his control. If it were possible to keep his leg and recover enough that it would not be a significant hindrance to his future life, then Red would urge him to fight to that end. But if things were so bad that keeping the leg would change his life and divert him from his chosen path, say a career in the Army as an armored officer, then perhaps amputation would become a reasonable outcome of the very difficult position in which Fred found himself. Then Red told him a story about amputees in the Army.

After he returned from Europe, Red faced the bitter reality that amputees were not allowed to stay on active duty. And as promising as Red's career had been, all his dreams of one day wearing general's stars had been dashed when he lost his leg. But he had thought this an administrative problem that should be rectified. After all, in Fred's case, when he was mounted in the cupola of a modern tank, Red didn't think a prosthesis would limit him as a commander in any way. This was particularly the case with modern prosthetics that allowed almost a full range of motion and use of an artificial leg.

In the years after World War II, Red began to get pretty well established back at West Point. Then one day in 1951, he was visited by none other than George Catlett Marshall, a very august figure who had been the senior five-star general of the U.S. Army during World War II. After the war, General Marshall had retired, and he was then a civilian serving as the secretary of defense. With him, General Marshall had brought Mrs. Anna Rosenberg, who was then the assistant secretary of defense for manpower.

When they arrived in Red's office, General Marshall turned to Mrs. Rosenberg and said, "This is the officer I was telling you about. If he had been in the British army, he would have been allowed to remain on active duty, and we would have had the benefit of his continuing service." Mrs. Rosenberg appeared confused and asked General Marshall why that was true. With a smile, Marshall told her that American Army regulations did not permit amputees to remain on active duty. Mrs. Rosenberg was quick with her answer of "I'll fix that!" And after that visit, Red explained, the automatic expulsion of amputees from the U.S. armed services ended. Thereafter, each amputee who sought to remain on active duty would be judged on a case-by-case basis. Fred even remembered being taught as a cadet by an amputee on active duty, George Gividan, who had lost a leg in the Korean War and yet was teaching psychology as an active duty Army captain in the infantry. Still, it was far from an appealing prospect.

In addition to surgery on his foot and leg, Fred had undergone many skin graft operations, and he spent as much time as possible trying to walk in an effort to save his foot and the lower end of his leg. That whole end of his leg just didn't work very well, and it certainly didn't look very healthy, or for that matter, look much like a foot and ankle at all. The bones in his foot and ankle had been crushed, and despite all the efforts of the doctors, simply refused to heal into anything approaching a normal, serviceable appendage. He didn't know what lay before him, but the prospects for full recovery didn't look good.

But the alternative, so far as he knew, was amputation, and like any normal human being, that was something he dreaded. He just couldn't imagine himself as an amputee, and the last thing he wanted, the nightmare that inhabited him most during his early days back in the United States, was the dread that, despite the miracles of modern medicine, he would somehow lose his leg. The doctors always seemed upbeat, and no one even mentioned that dreaded word "amputation." Fred certainly would not let it escape from his lips, afraid that just saying it might somehow set the process in motion that would end up with him living out his worst nightmares.

The other wounds Fred had suffered on May 5 were to his upper left leg, his back, his left arm, and his left hand, but none of them involved broken bones. By the late fall of 1970, these injuries had all pretty much healed. His left eardrum had been blown out, but surgery had repaired that to the point that his hearing was close to normal. All that was left was the badly mangled foot and lower leg.

In December 1970, he asked the doctors what choices lay before him. The response he got was that they could save his foot, but that they would have to continue to operate on it. It was highly unlikely, however, that they would ever be able to give him an appendage on which he could walk for any distance. And the chronic infection was the wild card. Apparently embedded in the bones of his foot and ankle, it had proven resistant to every medication then available. Fred was warned that it might stay dormant like a time bomb for a long time, and then erupt one day with no forewarning into an uncontrollable disease that could suddenly kill him.

The constant pain would almost certainly continue indefinitely, and the doctors could see no way that he would be able to function with anything approaching normalcy as an Army officer. The alternative was amputation, and they told Fred not to ignore that, as great progress had been made with artificial limbs. If he chose that path, he might find that he had an almost normal life, one very close to what he would have experienced had he never been injured.

Fred had lost forty pounds since he had been in the hospital, and he knew that he was clearly headed downhill fast. While the doctors would not formally recommend amputation, that was one of the options they presented to Fred. He drew strength from Red's visits, and he also drew strength from watching other soldiers in the hospital who had limbs amputated. There was a great deal of open camaraderie among patients of all ranks on this ward where amputation was common, and it was normal for others to give him good-natured grief. He heard a lot of, "Hey, Major, you old guys heal slow!" from young amputees already learning to use their prosthetic devices. Fred was hardly an "old guy" at thirty-four, but all of this had a positive effect on him, and he began to see that an amputation could make his life better, not worse. Fred had thought long and hard about his future, and he knew that all he wanted to do in life was to remain a soldier. And it was becoming increasingly apparent to him that, in order to save any sort of a life, particularly a career as an Army officer, he was going to have to get rid of the infected clump of flesh that had once been his left foot, ankle, and lower calf. Finally, there was only one choice for him to make.

In December 1970, Fred Franks elected to have his lower left leg amputated. The surgery took place on the Monday after the Super Bowl in January 1971, when his left leg was amputated some eight inches below the knee. Because of the virulent infection, however, the surgeons were unable to immediately repair the stump, and they had to leave it open. Even so, Fred immediately began to feel much better. He started to eat again, the constant pain was gone. While the infection was still a problem, the doctors told him that they had cut off the heart of it and they expected what was left in his system to clear up rather quickly.

That hospital time spent with young men who had been grievously wounded in service to their country also marked Fred profoundly. Most of the other patients on the ward were very young enlisted men, often teenagers, and to them, Fred really was an "old guy." But he also acted as a father figure for them, and he was able to help them through some very difficult times.

They were all badly wounded, so they needed no justification among themselves. But as a somewhat older man with a college education, Fred could also reassure them and serve as a sort of moral refuge amid the loud storm of antiwar rhetoric then booming through the land. In a rather short period, American society had turned from supporting the war in Vietnam to opposing it massively as a wicked, evil affair. And against all logic, the American people also seemed to have turned against veterans of that war, young men who had done nothing more than answer their country's call to serve. But as the men in uniform who carried out the political decisions to fight a war in Vietnam made by our nation's elected political leaders, decisions believed by antiwar activists to be wrong, even evil, Vietnam veterans were too often, and wrongly, seen as the personification of that evil.

Most young women and those young men who were lucky enough to have gone to college or somehow found another way to avoid the draft were probably the most cruel. "Baby killer!" they yelled at Vietnam veterans foolish enough to wear an old fatigue shirt in public. "Baby killer!" they screamed at young amputees on public streets. "Did you lose that arm in Vietnam?" "Yes, I did." "Serves you right, baby killer!"

Under the Constitution, of course, antiwar activists had

every political right to say, even scream, their beliefs in pretty much any public forum. Fred knew that. But he also knew that words could cut deeper into the hearts of those young veterans than any real bullet. These were young men who had offered their lives for their country and been marked and often limited for life by tragic wounds. These were the young men with whom Fred shared that hospital amputee ward. Their company was a powerful and enduring moral experience.

That was when and where what he would later call a "hot blue flame of intensity" was born in his heart, a deep commitment to serve and to do what was right for our country and for our soldiers, at whatever personal cost, come what might, for as long as he was able.

That winter, Fred was fitted with temporary prosthetic devices and began learning to walk again, although the stump was still open and draining, which was a limitation. The problem was the infection, which wouldn't go away. But the doctors finally licked it over the summer, and in September 1971, Fred underwent a revision of his stump and they finally closed it off. He was then fitted with a permanent prosthesis, and to celebrate, he and Denise and Margie ran off on a four-day escape to Disney World.

When they got back, Fred's condition was reviewed by medical boards in order to assess his physical fitness for further military service. The armor branch chief at the time was Colonel Jimmy Leach, the World War II legend who had been Fred's initial regimental commander in Vietnam. Colonel Leach was known for helping those who had been badly injured in Vietnam but wanted to remain on active duty, and he was very strongly in Fred's corner here.

The Medical Board decision was finally handed down on February 4, 1972, and it approved Fred's request to be

allowed to remain on active duty in the U.S. Army. For the
Franks family, that was truly a "Hallelujah!" day. But duty
lay ahead, and in short order, Fred was discharged from the
hospital. Then, burning with that newfound hot blue flame
of intensity, he and his family moved to Norfolk, Virginia,
where he began his next assignment as a student at the
Armed Forces Staff College.

A lieutenant general, Fred was the commander of VII
Corps in Germany when Iraq invaded Kuwait in August
1990, and he moved his forces into Saudi Arabia. He
returned to the United States many times while his forces
were still moving into position and training in Saudi
Arabia, an exercise that consumed September 1990
through February 1991. And during his trips, he several
times returned to West Point, where he visited Red Reeder
and sought the old man's counsel.

The VII Corps divisions were arrayed along the border
south of Iraq and west of Kuwait, and when the order came
down on February 25, 1991, Fred attacked with them deep
into Iraq, the famous "Hail Mary" attack or "Left Hook" that
General Schwarzkopf threw around Saddam Hussein's
forces. They went straight north for some sixty miles, then
turned due east and attacked the Iraqi Republican Guard
reserve. They blew through this and were about to cut off
from the north all Iraqi forces still inside Kuwait when they
were halted by President Bush before they reached the sea
after a "hundred-hour war," still leaving a main north-south
highway open, up which the great bulk of Iraqi forces raced.

After the war, Fred finished his tour as commander of
VII Corps and returned to the United States. One of the first
awards he received for his performance in Desert Storm
was promotion to four-star rank of full general, the highest

rank in the U.S. Army. The use of five-star rank ended in 1950, when the last man to reach that rank, Omar Bradley, was promoted. Named by the president as one of the small number of four-star generals at the top of the Army hierarchy, Fred had reached the pinnacle of success in his Army career. Red Reeder was at the promotion ceremony, beaming proudly as that fourth star was pinned on what was really his son's shoulder. And in many ways, Fred's promotion to the highest rank was a symbolic attainment of personal military success for Red too, given the long, close, and almost eerie connection that had been built up between the two men over the decades behind them.

After the ceremony, Fred assumed command of the prestigious Training and Doctrine Command, or TRADOC, headquartered in Fort Monroe, Virginia. And Red went home to West Point. In the spring of 1997, the West Point Association of Graduates announced that Red Reeder had been selected as a "Distinguished Graduate" of West Point. He was one of three such West Pointers who were honored on the Plain one Saturday morning in May 1997 at the Distinguished Graduates parade held in their honor. Benjamin O. Davis, Jr., had received this distinction in 1995, and Red stood proudly as the Corps of Cadets paraded by and saluted him. He had come a very long way.

The West Point alma mater contains the following lines:

And when our day is done,
Our course in life has run
May it be said "Well Done!"
Be thou at peace.

A few weeks after that parade, Red Reeder lay down in his bed, never to rise again. He is at peace now, but Fred carries his legacy forward, as do all other West Pointers who spend their lives promoting the dreams caught up in those three magic words, "Duty, Honor, Country."

Rocky Versace

In the early and middle 1950s, Humbert Roque Versace lived with his family in Alexandria, Virginia, and the Versace kids all went to Saint Rita's, the nearby Catholic parochial grade school. Their father was an Army officer and a West Point graduate who was often on the road, and Rocky, the oldest of five children, always filled his father's role when he was gone. A smart kid, he had a mind as quick as a whip. But he also grew increasingly opinionated and stubborn as he got older.

His best friend through grade school and high school was a neighbor named Mike Heisley. Mike was from a rather poor family, but that didn't matter to anybody. Rocky and he grew very close, and Mike was practically family. He and Rocky were always together, and Mike would often hang around the Versace house right through supper, after which they would usually study together.

After grade school, Mike and Rocky went on to Gonzaga High School in Washington, D.C., together. As close friends going through puberty at the same time, with hormones coursing madly through their bodies, they went through the normally predictable ritual combats, ranging from laughing tussles to sharp blows. But their affection endured.

By the age of sixteen, both were pushing six feet tall, but Mike was more solidly built. As they wrestled, it was clear that Mike could take Rocky, but it was the sort of thing you just didn't do with your best friend. There were times, however, when Mike would hold Rocky down and pound on his shoulder to get him to ask for mercy or agree to something outlandish. But the more he pounded on Rocky, the more Rocky refused to give in. Finally, it dawned on Mike that Rocky would *never* give in, that the pain didn't matter to him, that in order to beat him you would have to kill him because you could never break him or defeat him. Rocky would never give in.

This happened in the classroom too. Gonzaga is a Jesuit high school where Jesuit priests teach, and Rocky would occasionally get into arguments over issues in class that he simply refused to end. One example Mike remembers is of an English class in which Rocky was convinced that Shakespeare intended Brutus to be the real star of *Julius Caesar,* the play that the class was then reading. Rocky raised his hand and made that point, and the teacher, Father Daly, responded that he didn't think Rocky had understood the text completely, but that was a very good comment, well done, now let's hear from someone else.

But Rocky wouldn't let it go, and he raised his hand again.

"Mister Versace?"

"Father, I don't think you understand. When Brutus is awaiting Mark Antony and he makes his speech that starts, 'There is a tide in the affairs of men,' what he's doing is allowing the reader to look at the full Brutus, the only one of the conspirators in whom there was no guile, no sense of—"

"Mister Versace, you already said that, and I told you it was a very good comment, but that I also think you need to understand the rest of the play before you jump to a conclusion about Brutus and his moral decisions being the center of the play. Let's hear from someone else. Mister Lee?"

Rocky wasn't through.

"But, Father, you still don't understand. All you have to do is look at—"

"Mister Versace, I understand perfectly well, I have read the play many times and studied it in graduate school. Brutus is an interesting figure, but it's a play about Julius Caesar in which Brutus is a less important figure. Now let's listen to what someone else has to say. Mister Lee?"

Rocky didn't give an inch.

"Father, you just don't understand! I don't care about graduate school, and what do those people know anyway? I mean, the play is written in English by a man we can no longer question about it, and I can read the play just as well as any grad—"

Father Daly lost it.

"Mister Versace! The name of the play is *Julius Caesar*, not Brutus!"

The rest of the class recoiled before Father Daly's wave of rage, but Rocky held his ground.

"Father, that doesn't matter, the title means nothing, you have to put yourself in the—"

Now Father Daly was shaking as his face turned red.

"Mister Versace, the play means nothing! Drop it!"

"Father, that's just not right, you said yourself—"

"Silence! Not another word out of you!"

"Does that mean—"

"Mister Versace, leave my class this instant! Go!"

"Father, I don't have to do that, I'm just trying to discuss—"

Father Daly's rage was boiling over, and his extended arm pointing at the door was shaking as his balding head turned a darker shade of red.

"Get out! Get out!"

The entire class was distressed, all except Rocky, who never missed a beat.

"No, Father, I haven't done anything wrong, I'm just—"

Father Daly turned and stormed out the door himself, slamming it behind him. None of the other students were really mad at Rocky, for they had gotten out of class twenty minutes early with no homework assignment. After Father Daly was truly gone, though, there was a certain amount of laughter, and also jeering comments aimed at Rocky.

But he didn't think it was funny at all. He thought he had been wronged.

After supper two days later, Rocky's father told him they were going to Gonzaga for a meeting. Mike Heisley happened to be there studying, and when Rocky asked his father if Mike could come so they could keep working in the car, his father waved him on. Later, Rocky and his father sat in the principal's office while Father Daly let Rocky have it. But this time, Rocky just sat there quietly and took it.

Mike Heisley had been waiting in the car, and he wasn't supposed to know what was going on when they came back, so he feigned ignorance. The ride home began in silence, then Rocky's father spoke.

"This should be an important lesson to you for the rest of your life, son. The most important thing is that if you know you are right, then you should never back down. When an important principle is involved, be deaf to expediency, and never compromise on an important issue. That's why Abraham Lincoln is our greatest president, because he refused to compromise on principle. But you must also realize that you can only have so many major fights in your life, so you must choose those fights carefully. This was a case of much energy spent for little gain.

Next time, make sure you are taking on a fight that is worth your while."

After high school, Mike worked for a year to pay his first year's tuition, and then he enrolled at Georgetown. After that, he always found side jobs from which he could scrape together the money for his college education. He and Rocky stayed friends through college, and often Rocky would get tickets to football games for Mike and his girlfriend, who would later be his wife.

As they grew older, Mike noted that it was still the same old Rocky, but he was being refined. No, that wasn't right, Rocky would never allow someone else to change him, so it must be that he was refining himself. He seemed to be reading a lot more, including books on philosophy. Mike was almost floored when he brought up names like Nietzsche and Kierkegaard in their casual conversation. He knew Rocky was studying engineering at West Point, so he asked him where he was getting all this philosophical bullshit. But Rocky just laughed with Mike, ignored the question, and smoothly changed the subject.

Rocky was in the 2nd Regiment at West Point, and he lived up in old North Area. Pete Dawkins was the class president and somewhat of a bigshot because he was a star halfback on the football team and was near the top of his class academically. But to Rocky, that made not a whit of difference: To him, Pete was just Pete, this lanky guy from Michigan he had first met plebe year, a guy who could run like the wind but delighted in pranks and taking on the Tactical Department in that old cadet game of "Us" against "Them." And as young men bursting with life, it just wasn't possible to rigidly control them and make them behave the way the regulations *said* they were to behave. "You may say I cannot do such and such," cadets seemed to be saying to the Tactical Department charged with their discipline, "but catch me if you can!"

And it was in such occasional youthful celebrations of life that Rocky and Pete saw each other best. To Pete, Rocky was a very complex man whose subtleties could easily escape detection. It was easy to caricature him, but if you did that, it was also very easy to misunderstand him. To Pete, Rocky was very open and honest about virtually everything, and he just didn't care about social niceties or what people might think. If he felt something, he said it; he said what he thought and he meant what he said.

Despite such occasionally shocking candor, Pete saw Rocky as direct, honest, and utterly guileless. Because he wore his heart on his sleeve, he would sometimes be seen by others as naive, gullible, uncool. But underneath such superficialities, Pete thought Rocky was a very appealing guy and a good friend. And he had a refreshingly natural way of saying what was on his mind without caring what anyone else might feel.

This was sometimes carried to extremes. Rocky was almost always right in his assessments of things and people and appropriate actions, but sometimes he was wrong. And when that happened, he could be unbelievably pig-headed, to the point that even his friends would get furious at him. Yes, Rocky was incredibly hard-headed. And once he had his mind made up, it didn't matter how dumb it was, or how unpopular, or how courageous, he would just pound away without any willingness to compromise whatsoever.

But there was another side to Rocky as well. The summer between his sophomore and junior years at West Point, instead of going home for thirty days' leave in the summer, he chose to stay in New York City, where he worked for an orphanage and a soup kitchen. He was a very religious young man, and during the academic year he seldom missed the 6:00 A.M. mass every weekday morning in the Catholic chapel.

Then on June 3, 1959, Rocky and his classmates graduated. He took his commission in armor, went to the Armor Basic class with Nick Krawciw, then Ranger School, and finally Airborne School. His first year was spent in Korea, which was uneventful save for his first exposure to orphanages in the Third World. When he had worked in that orphanage in New York City during his summer cadet leave, the orphans there had touched his heart. But for these poor kids in Korea, things were far, far worse. He was touched by their plight and their poverty, and he started learning how to scrounge "excess" equipment for them from supply sergeants.

He came home for eighteen months with the 3rd Infantry Division at Fort Myer, Virginia, where he was a tank platoon leader. But his unit was also part of the Army's official honor guard, which did such things as march in ceremonial functions and provide the spit-and-polish individual sentries who guarded the Unknown Soldier's Tomb in Arlington Cemetery adjoining Fort Myer on a twenty-four-hour basis. A square-jawed, handsome man, Rocky was described by other officers as a "West Point cadet right out of Central Casting," and he certainly had the looks for any honor guard,

Rocky knew that a war was heating up in Vietnam, and he hungered to go to it. After about six months on the job, he even filled out the forms and volunteered to serve in Vietnam. But while that adventure was still pending, in his mind he was also testing other paths in life.

He loved to be with girls—they were fun, and at base, he knew, the attraction he felt to them was a normal red-blooded American sexual drive. But he also knew that it was an animal urge human beings share with all other animals, and that one mark of civilization is one's ability to control those biological drives.

He had always enjoyed women, but now he was beginning to think more and more of leaving the Army and becoming a Catholic priest. Before he took that step, however, he wanted to make sure he made the right choice, for it would mean taking the vow of chastity. That, for all intents and purposes, would mean giving up the company of women. And before he took that big step, he wanted to make sure he was doing the right thing.

Handsome as he was, Rocky was still a bit of an enigma to the pretty women he squired around town. One Saturday evening, for instance, he was out on his third or fourth date with a lovely young woman he had recently met at a reception. Her name was Mary Carns, she had just graduated from college in Seattle, and she was living with her parents in Virginia while she looked for a job. The two of them had really hit it off, even dazzled each other just a bit.

They ate at the Fort Myer Officers' Club, and after supper, he suggested they walk through the adjoining Arlington Cemetery to the Custis-Lee mansion, from which they would have a stunning view of Washington across the river. The evening was lovely, and Mary readily agreed. It was a long walk, but it was dreamy. She knew it was getting close to midnight and she had to be getting home soon, but the full moon created shadows on the sidewalk before them. They were holding hands as they walked, and then the moonlight danced deliciously as their walk took them under high trees. Mary moved closer and rested her head against his shoulder. She was feeling warm and happy and romantic when a loud voice shocked her.

"Halt! Who goes there?"

She was further stunned to feel Rocky's arm tighten as he suddenly stood up straight.

"Lieutenant Versace!"

"Advance one to be recognized!"

She saw a soldier some fifty feet in front of her holding a rifle out in front of him. Rocky pulled away and walked toward him. As they got closer, their voices lowered to almost a conversational tone."

"Good evening, sir."

"Good evening, Corporal. What are your orders?"

"Sir, my orders are to . . ."

She was suddenly bewildered. They had enjoyed such a lovely dinner at the Officers' Club, and their walk over was so beguiling. And when they had started on this stroll, her thoughts had been of romance, but instead he was playing soldier. Wasn't he ever off-duty?

After a few minutes, he came back to her, and they started down the path again. She was quiet for a moment, then stopped and turned and looked at him.

"Rocky . . . back there . . . why did you do that?"

Rocky laughed.

"Because he knew that I'd have court-martialed him in the morning if he wasn't ready."

She scrunched up her eyes as she looked at him. To her, Rocky's answer had been no answer at all. She had wanted to know why he had interrupted their date to test some poor, lonely soldier who had to stand guard all night in an empty cemetery, but instead he thought she wanted to know . . . what did "I'd have court-martialed him in the morning if he wasn't ready" really mean? Did it mean that Rocky was always on duty? She smiled, then turned and started walking again. Men could be pretty amazing.

*   *   *

On May 12, 1962, Rocky arrived in the Mekong River Delta town of Camau, South Vietnam. Having just spent the better part of a year in school preparing for his job as an intelligence advisor to South Vietnamese forces, he quickly fit in and worked every day at improving his command of the Vietnamese language and at learning more about the Vietnamese people. To his delight, he soon saw that his outgoing attitude toward the people was answered. He found a nearby Catholic church, and from that found a Catholic orphanage where young children whose parents had been killed by the communists did the best they could. And while the Korean orphanages had been poor, this one seemed absolutely destitute.

But Rocky was not defeated just because he was faced with a difficult problem. He immediately pitched into the problems faced by the Vietnamese people at the lowest level, setting up medical dispensaries, securing tin sheets to take the place of thatched roofs, and getting tons of bulgur wheat with which to feed family pigs. And he also started making more frequent visits to the orphanage and to the American supply depots from which he might be able to wheedle some assistance for them.

He was to spend a year and a half trying to help the South Vietnamese fend off communist invaders from the north, and that was truly what he believed. In a Christmas letter to his family, Rocky wrote: "I am convinced that your taxpayers' money is being put to a very worthy cause—that of freeing the Vietnamese people from an organized communist threat aimed at the same nasty things all communists want—at denying this country and its wonderful people a chance to better themselves. . . . Many among the poor and remote people are responding to a government that can and does help them and protect them. I have found villagers and ordinary soldiers and farmers to be wonderful people."

Rocky had made many friends among the Vietnamese, and while it was obvious that he was seeking intelligence for military reasons—to defeat the Viet Cong—it was also apparent to them that he was one of the few Americans who chose to spend most of his private time with the Vietnamese rather than with other American off-duty soldiers. And the fact that he was at the orphanage, and that he was getting used children's clothes from the United States, and used soccer balls from American schools, and other unimaginable goodies, meant that he really did win the hearts of most Vietnamese who knew about him.

When other American officers visited, Rocky would always take them to see the orphanage. He was very proud of the improvements that had been made to it through his work or through American donations. If the American guests didn't get that hint, he would always bluntly ask them for a cash donation before they left. And he almost always got it.

After his normal twelve-month tour was up, he extended for six months. But he also decided to leave the Army after his military duty in Vietnam ended and then enter the Maryknoll order and become a missionary priest. In October 1963, he had already been accepted by Maryknoll, and he had only two weeks left to go.

Then he went out on a mission with a nearby Special Forces A team and several hundred soldiers from their Civilian Irregular Defense Group (CIDG)—local men equipped, trained, and led by U.S. Army Special Forces to resist communist forces.

Rocky had gotten a tip that a small Viet Cong unit was

setting up in the village of Le Coeur and intended to use that to direct attacks against Special Forces camps. Rocky took this information to nearby Special Forces team A-23, and they devised a plan to preempt this communist move with an attack of their own.

Le Coeur was very close to the edge of the U Minh Forest, a vast forest that had remained an unconquered and safe communist base area since the days of the French. The plan was for two companies of Special Forces CIDG, with roughly one hundred soldiers in each company, to conceal themselves between Le Coeur and the U Minh Forest. Once they were in position, the third company of 120 men would hit Le Coeur from the other side and flush the Viet Cong force toward what they would think was safety in the U Minh Forest, but in reality would be the widow-making weapons of the waiting CIDG companies.

On October 29, Rocky accompanied the CIDG assault company, led by two American Special Forces soldiers, First Lieutenant Nick Rowe and Sergeant First Class Dan Pitzer. When they hit Le Coeur, they seemed to have really surprised the VC, who turned and ran. But instead of running toward the U Minh Forest and the two companies waiting in ambush, they ran off to the side and avoided the jaws of death. They were soon gone, and after the attack company swept through the small village and found nothing, they started moving back toward their camp.

But after they had moved a few kilometers, they suddenly saw an enormous force of armed men arrayed to one side of them, running to cut them off. Nick Rowe said they were still nine hundred meters or so away, and their mortar rounds were way off target. But it was clear the CIDG company wasn't going to get out the way they were going, so they pulled back to a tree line and a defensive position.

Soon they were attacked, and Rowe said he had never seen so many VC. They blocked two sides of the rectangular CIDG position and attacked from a third, almost inviting them to try to run out the fourth side. None moved, so the VC got their range with mortars, and death rained from the skies. But the CIDG men were putting out a lot of fire, and attacking VC were hit almost as soon as they showed themselves. They were hoping the other two companies would soon rescue them, but then they got word that they had been ambushed as well and were just holding on.

The firefight went on for quite a while, but finally they were running low on ammunition. So the Americans told the CIDG to start an orderly withdrawal, and that they would cover them. That was obviously the wrong thing to suggest, for Nick Rowe says the CIDG "came past us at Mach 3 and accelerating." A brief firefight ensued between the Americans and a VC squad that burst out of the trees, but a 40-mm round from an M-79 grenade launcher carried by Dan Spitzer hit the leader square in the middle of the chest and vaporized him. The VC had never seen this weapon before, and the survivors disappeared, giving the Americans a chance to pursue their CIDG troops.

They found them soon enough, hiding in a big ditch and ready to surrender after having thrown their weapons away. But the Americans got them to get up and recover their weapons, then moved them down a trail and into a cane field. But as they ran, the deep and unmistakable sound of a burst fired by a Browning Automatic Rifle (BAR) ripped the air. Rocky went down with three rounds in his leg, and as Nick Rowe reached down to help him, a grenade blast knocked him over. He and Dan Spitzer pulled Rocky off the trail and managed to get two bandages on his leg before VC soldiers came out of the canes from all around them.

Rocky, Rowe, and Spitzer were immediately stripped of their weapons, boots, and all personal possessions. Their arms were bound, and they were led off into the dark heart of the U Minh Forest.

When they finally got to a primitive camp, Rocky told their captors in Vietnamese that he was the senior officer and that he would represent himself and the other two prisoners of war, and they expected to be treated in accordance with the Geneva Convention on prisoners of war. He was told that they were not prisoners of war, they were war criminals, and there would be no special rules to protect them. And his captors marked him already as a "troublemaker."

So began a period of almost unimaginable suffering for the prisoners. But through it all, Rocky remained true to his principles and would not even bend. The VC told Rocky that they knew he was a captain and an intelligence officer, that Nick was a lieutenant and Dan a sergeant. But they were only fighters, while he knew about intelligence, about VC plans and American plans. He could make life much easier for himself if he would just tell them things they already knew.

But Rocky would only give the limited information permitted by the Geneva Convention and nothing more. He told his captors that as long as he was true to God and true to himself, what was waiting for him after this life was far better than anything that could happen now. So he told them that they might as well kill him then and there if the price of his life was getting more from him than his name, rank, and serial number.

During this period, the three Americans were together, and they subsisted on a diet of rice with vegetables and an occasional morsel of fish. Rocky's untreated leg became swollen and was clearly infected, so he was taken into a sort of dispensary hut, where the VC tried primitive treatment on it. But one night, when all the VC were asleep, he crawled out of the hut and into the swamp and jungle all around. The next day, his guards followed his bloody path and caught him, dragging him ruthlessly back to camp, where he was put in leg shackles and then into isolation inside a bamboo cage six feet long, two feet wide, and three feet high. He was repeatedly beaten, and put on a starvation diet of rice and salt. In the swampy area where their camp was situated, all the VC had mosquito nets in which they slept every night. Only the good Americans were given mosquito nets, and Rocky almost never. Every morning, his face and every exposed patch of skin was swollen by painful, maddening mosquito bites.

In 1968, Phung Van Tuong, a man who had been a VC guard in Rocky's camp from 1963 through 1965, turned himself in to the government of South Vietnam. He told them that Rocky had tried to escape four times, and that each time he had been beaten and then put in irons in an isolation box and had his diet cut back to only small amounts of rice. He was considered a very bad prisoner by the VC.

But endurance was not enough for Rocky. He continually complained that their wounds were not being treated properly, or that they weren't being fed adequately, that they received no mail from home or even Red Cross packages—the list went on and on. Every time he did this, of curse, he was soundly beaten and placed in leg irons inside the isolation box. And when complaints continued in the form of yells in fluent Vietnamese from inside the box, they gagged him, but all that did was muffle the sound. The bottom line was, he just wouldn't stop! And if the VC thought mere physical pain would shut him up, well, these people simply didn't know Rocky Versace!

Eventually, the communists started sending political officers into the camp for "reeducation" of the prisoners. This meant that the Americans would be subjected to constant and repetitive dry narrations of Vietnamese history and Marxism from the VC perspective. The idea was that if the Americans heard this story line repeated often enough over a long enough period, they would eventually come to believe it whether it was true or not. And since they weren't doing anything anyway, they might as well get some "reeducation."

Rocky refused to attend such classes, insisting it was a violation of the Geneva Convention. The VC first said "fine," and he spent the first few classes in the isolation cage in irons. For Nick Rowe and Dan Spitzer, those classes were just something to endure. But after they had given Rocky the alternative of attending the classes or doing leg-irons-in-the-cage time and Rocky chose the latter, they began to get angry. Finally, the VC decided that Rocky must take the classes. Sometimes it took two VC to drag him to the classes. And once the three men were in their places, the teacher began reciting Marxist cant in English, probably without even realizing what he was saying. He was stunned to hear Rocky challenge him on a particular tenet of Marxist history.

This was to go on without end. Rocky didn't really know much about Marxist history or theory, but he had read some critical reviews, and these strange facts just kept jumping into his mind and out of his mouth.

At first, these outbursts were tolerated and ignored. But as the teacher began to ask the other VC if they knew anything about this crazy American and whether he was right in what he said about Marx or Lenin, to his amazement, Rocky interrupted him in fluent Vietnamese. And then, when two older men came to camp together to educate this difficult American, they had been warned that he spoke Vietnamese, so they tried to confer in front of him in French. And when he shouted them down in a better French than they spoke, they had him thrown back into the detention box.

Finally, Rocky was taken away from the other two Americans, although he was kept nearby. Nick and Dan often saw him from a distance, and they heard him singing, usually changing the words to popular songs to send them messages about his morale and state of health and ask about theirs. The last they were to hear from him was his loud rendition of "God Bless America" from inside a detention box they could just make out fifty or sixty feet away.

After that, the VC decided to separate Rocky completely from all other Americans, so they tied his hands behind his back, looped a noose over his head, and led him down the trail like an animal in a visiting circus.

But this was just what the American intelligence had hoped for. While the prisoners were kept in the sparsely populated heart of the U Minh Forest, there was little chance for the tip needed to launch a rescue mission that might free one or all of the captive Americans. But once they were out in the farmed area, there were always people playing both sides of the street, even in the areas most strongly dominated by the communists.

And so, in late 1964, intelligence reports kept coming in about a particular American. Captain Jack Nicholson from West Point's class of 1956 was an advisor in the region where Rocky was being held, and his record of the reports he was receiving then bear repeating.

By spring of 1964 the farmers were talking about one US prisoner in particular. They said he was treated very poorly, led through the area with a rope around his neck, hands tied, bare footed, head swollen and yellow in color (jaundice) and hair white. They stated that this prisoner not only resisted the Viet Cong attempts to get him to admit war crimes and aggression, he would verbally counter their assertions convincingly and in a loud voice so the local villagers could hear. The local rice farmers were surprised at his strength of character and his unwavering commitment to "his" God and the United States. The villagers' descriptions of Versace and his resistance became a topic of conversation we could count on hearing as we periodically operated in these remote farming areas. Villagers described Versace's deteriorating physical condition and added that the worse he appeared physically, the more he smiled and talked about God and America. Our interpreters told us that Captain Versace was impressing the villagers with his faith and inner strength, to the chagrin of his VC captors, who were reported to be making his existence even more miserable in their attempts to break his will and exploit him.

On three specific occasions between December 1963 and September 1964, we conducted operations throughout Phing Dinh Province in attempts to rescue Captain Versace. On one occasion, we found cooking fires and heated food that had been hastily abandoned by the VC. A US door gunner named Christmas was shot dead as we departed that particular area. On another occasion in late summer 1964, at a place called Seven Canals, we suffered 120 casualties one night in an attempt to reach an area where US captives reportedly were being paraded through the villages. Needless to say, we were not successful.

On September 29, 1965, Radio Hanoi announced that Captain Versace had been executed in retaliation for the killing of suspected communist sympathizers by South Vietnam.

After his death, Rocky's loss was deeply mourned by many. Because he stood up for what was right in the face of the most threatening opposition imaginable, he eventually paid for his rock-hard principles of proper behavior under pressure, the true code of a West Pointer, with his life. The way in which he refused to bend, willingly facing the consequences of his actions in the most brutal treatment imaginable by his captors, up to and including death, showed others what full commitment to duty, honor, country really meant.

In 1968, Nick Rowe was able to overcome his guard, run into a clearing and wave his arms wildly when an American helicopter flew over low. They saw him, landed, and picked him up. Within a short time, he was in President Nixon's office, and when he told the president of Rocky's trials and performance under pressure, he told the president he thought Rocky should receive the Medal of Honor. Nixon told his assistants to make sure that happened, but political resistance by antiwar activists could not be overcome, and the effort died. But Nick told of Rocky's heroism in great detail in his wonderful memoir, *Five Years to Freedom*. In 1988, Colonel Nick Rowe was serving in the Philippines when a communist rebel sniper shot and killed him in his car while he was on his way to work.

Those who knew Rocky hold that his actions showed the highest moral and physical courage imaginable. His classmate, Pete Dawkins, has said he believes that Rocky is a saint for his unwavering moral resolution in the face of great adversity leading to death.

Over time, a number of Rocky's old friends and admirers, most but not all of them military veterans, looked for a way to commemorate his gift of his life for his country. They were able get his story widely told, and they tried to get a new public elementary school in Alexandria named after Rocky. Although the Alexandria School Board rebuffed that effort, the Alexandria City Council was so impressed by the outpouring of support shown for Rocky more than thirty years after his death that they agreed to construct a memorial to Rocky and the sixty-three other Alexandrians who lost their lives in the Vietnam War.

The result will be the Rocky Versace Plaza and Vietnam Veterans Memorial, the space for which was dedicated on Veterans' Day, November 11, 2000.

Ultimately, Rocky's supporters were able to get the Army to nominate him for a Medal of Honor. In the spring of 2002, President Bush plans to present that award to Rocky posthumously at a White House ceremony.

Many individuals worked to advance Rocky's cause, most of them over many years: his twin brothers Steve and Dick, his youngest brother Mike, his sister Trilby, and John Gurr, Nick Rowe, Joe Flynn, Phil and Mike Faber, Bill Schwartz, Pete Dawkins, Mike and Tony Heisley, Mike Kentes, Duane Frederic, Bill Boykin, Ken Bowra—the list goes on and on. But the sense of loss among his friends endures. Mike Heisley is today a very wealthy man who owns many businesses and, wanting an NBA team, bought the Vancouver Grizzlies, then moved them to Memphis. He readily acknowledges that Rocky was one of the small number of men he ever looked up to and on whom he modeled himself.

"It just doesn't seem fair," he says. "When I got out of college, I got married, had five kids, and earned a billion dollars, while Rocky went off to war, got shot and wounded, was captured and tortured beyond belief, and when they finally realized that he wouldn't let them break him, they had to kill him."

Larry Budge

Larry was born an only child in Logan, Utah, in 1939. His parents actually lived on a ranch in Paris, Idaho, but the hospital was in Logan, Utah, so that's where Larry came into the world. His father was an ROTC officer during World War II, but he got out after the war and went back to the family ranch. Agriculturally, this was a marginal area with a short growing season, and times were tough. After two years, the Army asked Larry's father if he wanted to become an officer again, and he did. The Budge family began to make the frequent moves that are a traditional part of the military profession, and his father stayed in the Army until after Larry graduated from West Point in 1961.

As a plebe and a yearling, Larry played lacrosse, and he had the occasional girlfriend here and there. But he was very smart, and with a little application, he found that his grades went up. With a *lot* of application, they soared! So mostly, Larry studied. And he did very well. He graduated number three in his class, but he had also applied for and won a Rhodes Scholarship at Oxford.

Rhodes Scholarships were first established for the education of American college graduates at Oxford by Cecil Rhodes in 1902. Rhodes wanted only the finest young Americans, so he specified that the recipients were to be chosen on the basis of their demonstrated prowess in the fields of academics, leadership, and athletics. Individuals must apply for the scholarships, but an endorsement of their application is required from their college. Since "college degrees" were required of all applicants and West Point only granted diplomas rather than degrees until 1925, graduates of the Academy were simply not eligible for Rhodes Scholarships for the first twenty-two years of their existence. But West Point has made up some ground in that time, and in the year 2000, is ranked fourth nationally (behind only Harvard, Yale, and Princeton) among American colleges in the total number of Rhodes Scholarships that have been granted to its graduates.

After graduation leave, he went to Parachute School, then in September sailed to England with the rest of the Rhodes Scholars on the SS *United States*, a luxury cruise liner. Once at Oxford, Larry was in his milieu, and he relished the academic life he found there. He studied philosophy, politics, and economics, and after three years, he received a second-class degree, which is a grade that is probably equivalent to an American graduate school "Gentleman's B."

Over the three years, Larry took courses in what are known as eight "fields." These consisted of two in philosophy, two in politics, two in economics, and two that he could choose from a wide array of offerings. For those two fields, he chose to study international relations.

Larry met ten or twelve British officers who had come back to Oxford to get their degrees, and one of them invited Larry to join him at his regiment during his second summer at Oxford. Larry saw this as a splendid opportunity, and he went to the U.S. embassy in London, where he sought permission from the American military attaché, who was technically responsible for him, and got it. So he went to Cyprus and for three months served as an infantry platoon commander with the Green Jackets, a British light infantry battalion on Cyprus.

Most of their time was spent training for things like riot control and crowd dispersal. But one of the things in which Larry got involved that he enjoyed and from which he learned a great deal involved teaching the soldiers to swim. These men, most of whom had enlisted in London and had never been in water over their heads, couldn't swim at all, so this was quite an important skill for them to acquire. The sergeants did virtually all of the instruction, however, and the officers were only there to fill a sort of general supervisory role.

The Royal Army had a saying that the role of the officer was to teach the men how to die. But some important things underlie this saying. First of all, the British army at the time had a very professional noncommissioned officer corps, and the NCOs were primarily responsible for all training of the individual soldiers. The officers were responsible for leadership in a tactical situation or in any other kind of difficulty. It wasn't until the last year of World War I, for instance, that British officers carried personal weapons. Until then, they carried riding crops, canes, umbrellas, or some other sort of implement in their hand with which to give direction.

At the end of the swimming lessons, the men would be required, as a test of their prowess, to swim out to a float a hundred meters or so out in the bay, swim around it, and swim back to the beach. After all this time of simply observing, it was time for the officer to lead the way in the dangerous part. So Lieutenant Larry Budge swam out to the float at the head of his platoon, swam around it, then led them back to shore. This, of course, was what leadership was all about.

After his three-year stint at Oxford was up, Larry came back to the United States as a newly promoted captain in the infantry. He first attended Infantry Officer Basic Training at Fort Benning, Georgia, then in March 1965 moved on to his first assignment with the 5th Mechanized Infantry in Fort Carson, Colorado. When he arrived, he was given the choice of being either the Motor Pool Office or the Assistant S-3 (Training and Operations) Air. Larry knew that no one wanted to work in the motor pool, so he took the slot at S-3 Air.

Within a few months, by June 1965, he was company commander of A Company. But his company shrank in one day from 130 men to thirty men, because the one hundred he lost were going to fill up the 1st Infantry Division that was about to go to Vietnam. In the fall, the 5th Mech went through what the Army then called a "train and retain" cycle. This meant that they had to put together a basic training course for new soldiers, then connect that to another course they structured for advanced individual training.

The new recruits who arrived at Fort Carson had been in the Army for less than a week. As they got off the bus, they were put through the basic training course. Those who would serve in the infantry stayed at Fort Carson and went on to the next stage, which was the advanced individual training course. After that, volunteers were sought to make up a new infantry battalion at Fort Carson. Once that battalion had been formed, it would be going to Vietnam, where it would become part of the 1st Cavalry Division (Airmobile), commonly referred to as the "1st Air Cav." This division had gone to Vietnam in the summer of 1965, but had gone with only eight infantry battalions instead of the nine it should have had to fill out its three brigades. This new battalion was designated the 5th Battalion of the 7th Cavalry, and it would join the 3rd Brigade of the 1st Cavalry Division.

Larry, of course, had volunteered to join this new battalion, and in January 1966, he was given command of an infantry company. The battalion went through basic unit training, followed by advanced unit training, then in June 1966 they sailed for Vietnam aboard the USS *Gaffey*, a naval transport ship.

In July 1966, the 5th Battalion of the 7th Cavalry arrived in the Vietnamese port city of Qui Nhon. They were picked up by U.S. Air Force C-130 cargo aircraft and transported to An Khe, where they joined the 3rd Brigade of the 1st Air Cav. Unlike American units that would later serve in Vietnam, or even those that were first deployed there from the States, this unit had been formed and had trained together. This was important, for in the small rifle units, almost everyone knew almost everyone else. A healthy thing, this, for fighting alongside strangers is not always the safest way to go to war.

In Vietnam, the 1st Cav had a range of missions. Since the 5th of the 7th was a new battalion, they started out by securing the road from An Khe to Pleiku. The VC were periodically trying to cut that road, and the missions they performed consisted of patrolling and clearing once contact had been made, but there were no major unit engagements with enemy forces as yet. Within a few months, the entire division was moved east toward the coast, to a place north of Qui Nhon that they named Landing Zone (LZ) English. The division "forward" was set up there, and a basic "search and destroy" operation was launched from there that lasted for about four months. This operation took place first in the coastal plain that surrounded LZ English, and then they moved up into the Central Highlands to their west. This was an area that Bernard Fall wrote about in his famous book about the French Indochina war entitled *Street Without Joy*: the Highway 1 corridor running north and south near the coast and a historically safe base area for communist revolutionaries. The opponents that the 1st Cav faced consisted of local Viet Cong, but also of North Vietnamese Army forces guided and supported by the local indigenous population. It was not a pleasant time for the American soldiers.

In October 1966, Larry learned that his company was to be sent to the north and operate on this coastal plain in an exploratory manner. Helicopters would fly them north of a certain river, beyond which no American forces had as yet operated, and they were told to move across country and simply see if they could develop any armed opposition. Larry's commanders simply wanted to see how strong communist forces were in the area. If the enemy wanted to protect the area north of the river, Larry and his company should be able to stir up some action.

On the given morning, the helicopters landed them on an open field within sight of the ocean. As the airships left, Larry and his company began to move inland across the alluvial plain. Most of the landscape consisted of rice paddies separated by dikes and brief stretches of woods, and the countryside was dotted with villages and hamlets whose population was known to strongly support the communist side.

Within minutes, the long-departed helicopters were no more than a hammering memory. They had been moving for a few hours and had gone quite a few miles when they suddenly found their lead element under fire from a communist infantry force of unknown size. Although this would later be determined to be a specific Viet Cong heavy weapons company, they simply didn't know what they were facing at the time.

As he started to deploy part of his infantry company to come around and attack from his left, Larry initially expected that they had hit a small force that would quickly withdraw as they attacked. But his men met opposition on the left, and when another platoon moved to the right, it, too, ran into enemy fire. The initial burst of fire in the center was maintained, and the communists appeared willing to engage with Larry and fight. Clearly, they had run into a major enemy force, and Larry suddenly realized that he might need all the help that he could get.

In 1966, the 1st Air Cav was a new type of army organization that had been organized specifically for the war in Vietnam, and it depended on its mobility for success in the heavy jungle and mountainous terrain where it operated. But because it represented a profound change from traditional infantry tactics, in that its units moved into battle by helicopter rather than on foot or in trucks, it naturally had some conceptual adversaries. There was the lingering fear advanced by some traditionalists that was a function of the fact that helicopters could each carry no more than a half-dozen armed and equipped soldiers. And with such a rapid and long-range movement from point to point capability, a small infantry unit could easily outrun its support and end up suffering heavy defeat.

In a situation like that in which Larry now found himself, the conservative planners back in the States had predicted doom brought on by the high speed and long-range ability to deploy that new-fangled helicopters gave. The Air Cav's conceptual enemies weren't arguing for a return to mules and horses, but to many in the Old Guard who had marched through Europe in World War II, boots seemed a far safer way of moving troops around than anything that actually flew and landed in jungle clearings.

The Air Cav's battlefield success, therefore, was most important to the Army leadership that had launched it. Its sponsors went all the way up the Army chain of command, and because this high-mobility idea was new and so precarious, they had been careful to see that it always had ready access to all sorts of fire support for its operations in Vietnam. On this particular day, Larry had more than 140 men under him, which seemed to satisfy concerns about the perilous fate of a half-dozen men dropped off by a helicopter, all alone in the heart of enemy country. But his company was obviously opposed by a major communist unit that meant to stay and fight. That day, Larry was to make use of most of the fire support that was available to him.

The artillery support he or his artillery forward observer called in and adjusted ranged from the Air Cav's own 105-mm and 155-mm guns through nearby seven-inch guns of another American unit all the way up to naval gunfire from U.S. warships just offshore. From the air, they used Army attack helicopter gunships firing machine guns and rockets and U.S. Air Force F-100 fighter-bombers delivering bombs and napalm.

It was a long, hard fight, with both sides well hunkered down. But only the Americans were able to deliver heavy artillery fire and air support on their adversaries, and these had a telling effect. As nightfall approached, the infantry gunfire faded and then stopped. Probing attacks and forays forward by squads from Larry's company found that enemy forces seemed to have withdrawn. The full result of the day's fighting wasn't actually known until the next morning, when what they found made them feel that Larry's company and their supporting fire had completely disrupted the ability of that VC heavy weapons company to act as an effective fighting force.

The Americans recovered the bodies of almost fifty enemy soldiers, and countless blood trails showed where other dead or wounded had been dragged. Official papers found on some of these bodies told Larry that they had been going against a specific VC heavy weapons company, but the rest of the company escaped, no doubt with many wounded. In the final analysis, they probably got away because Larry's battalion commander, looking on the scene from his helicopter above, had anticipated the enemy withdrawal and had used transport helicopters to put his scout platoon into a position from which he thought they could cut them off. But the VC knew right away where the Americans were setting up a blocking position, and they were therefore able to simply slip around it. That, of course, was part of the price you paid when you went against a foe with complete support of the local populace, including soldiers in their ranks who had grown up locally and knew the terrain intimately.

That was the biggest fight Larry's company was involved in while he was company commander. He had suffered three men killed and another half-dozen wounded, but at the end of the day, it was the enemy that had withdrawn from the field of battle, not him. In fact, the results were so impressive that, years later, this battle would be presented as a model in the infantry advanced course taught to field-grade officers at Fort Benning. The official report Larry later wrote, along with maps and the reports of others, ranging from Larry's battalion and brigade commanders to the artillery, helicopter, and Air Force pilots engaged, enabled the use of the battle as an example of how an infantry company that was heavily engaged with an adversary of similar size could effectively use different types of fire support to its advantage and win.

After this operation, Larry took his company on patrols up into the mountains that were near the coast, and contact with enemy soldiers was always fleeting: a few bursts of fire from the bad guys, and then they were gone. In December, Larry's company went back to An Khe and operated on what was known as the Green Line. This meant they would conduct patrols out from An Khe and provide basic security for the main division base.

The basic defense posture called for an infantry battalion to be located at An Khe, which would patrol out from the base at night, usually moving to a prearranged site along a trail or at a stream crossing, where they would set up an ambush. But these patrols never went farther away from the perimeter than the seven-kilometer range of their supporting artillery. The actual fighting positions located around the perimeter, meanwhile, would be filled by the support troops from the base camp, who would pull twelve hours of guard duty. That meant that, if there were four soldiers in a given position, three of them would sleep while one would stay awake on guard, looking out over the perimeter with his weapon ready for the three hours of his shift, after which he would awaken his replacement.

After Larry had been a company commander in combat for six months, he was rotated to the division staff, where he was made the briefing officer for the G-3, or Division Operations. But this only lasted for about two weeks, when he was asked if he wanted to be General Westmoreland's aide de camp.

General Westmoreland was the commanding general for all American military forces in Vietnam, and Larry knew that his aide de camp was a captain who had to be something very special. The man selected would replace a captain named Bill Carpenter, who had graduated from West Point in 1960, one year before Larry. Carpenter had become famous nationally in those days as the "Lonesome End," the star receiver of the Army football team who never went near the huddle. When Army had the ball, he would just stay out on the flank between plays and run. Normally, a defensive back would stay with him, and he was only a ruse on most plays.

It was a mystery to the crowd, as well as to the other team, how Army was able to coordinate a long pass play when the receiver (there were usually only one or two who went downfield in those days) never came near the huddle. But they had a simple signaling system that involved the stance of the halfbacks to tell Carpenter when they were going to throw him the ball and what pattern to run.

So it was clear why Carpenter had become Westmoreland's aide, but Larry was completely mystified about how his name had come up. Sure, he had graduated from West Point, and had done very well academically. But he was a rather quiet man, and certainly had not been one of those big loud rah-rah guys who made their presence known both at West Point and as junior Army officers.

But this was an opportunity Larry wasn't going to miss. He accepted the offer, and next morning, his meager possessions packed in his duffel bag, he was on a plane to Saigon.

For the next six months, Larry was always at General

Westmoreland's side. Larry's job was multifaceted, but he was kept very busy, mostly taking care of detailed preparations for General Westmoreland's trips. They traveled around Vietnam and the Pacific region a lot, and even made two trips back to Washington, D.C., that lasted several days each. And while he may have worn fatigues every day, that was about the only real-world connection he felt to his days in the field.

Six months slipped by very quickly. Larry came home and went right to the Advanced Course of the Infantry School at Fort Benning, Georgia. After that, he went to West Point and began teaching in the social sciences department.

While Art Parker was in Vietnam, his wife Connie and their son Chip were living in an apartment in her hometown of Saint Mary's, West Virginia. On May 26, 1968, an urgent telegram from the Army was brought to her apartment. While Connie was not there, Saint Mary's was such a small town that the delivery boy knew where Connie's parents lived, so he took it there. They redirected it to Charleston, where Connie and Chip were visiting Art's parents, and within hours it reached Connie just as a similar telegram reached Art's parents. The message was that Art had suffered a compound skull fracture and was in "grave condition." As a nurse, Connie knew this wasn't good. She immediately called Bill Rennagel, one of Art's classmates from West Point, who had already lost an arm in Vietnam. He was then working in the Pentagon office that coordinated contacts between casualties of the war who were still in Vietnam and their families in the States. As soon as Connie called him, Bill was able to learn that Art had not regained consciousness, but he was still alive, and he was receiving treatment on the USS *Sanctuary*, a

U.S. Navy hospital ship in Vietnamese waters. Connie's reaction was that she wanted to be with Art immediately: She was a nurse, she could help deliver the medical care that was keeping him alive. Bill tried to console her and told her that it just wasn't possible for her to fly to Vietnam, but that he would call her every morning with an update. As soon as they could transport Art back to the United States, Bill assured her, Connie would be able to be with him. But until then, she could only wait.

The next morning, Bill called with the news that Art had first been evacuated to an Army field hospital, where they had performed a tracheotomy and removed the upper back of his skullcap so that his brain had room to swell. He had then been flown to the *Sanctuary*, which had superior medical facilities. On his second day on the hospital ship, Connie learned, they had operated on Art twice, but his outlook was not good.

During this time, Connie prayed as she had never prayed before, begging God to let Art come home alive no matter how bad his condition was. But she was still a nurse, and she knew that a head injury of the sort he had suffered would either kill Art or turn him into a bedridden ghost who might never regain consciousness. Even if he lived, she was afraid that he would be limited to little more than suffering and, eventually, a painful death. For the first time, she began to feel that it was wrong of her to plead with God to keep Art alive. Agony in a hospital bed with most of his bodily functions gone wasn't the sort of life that he would have wanted. She couldn't stop thinking about all the medical possibilities, given Art's condition, and all of them were grim. Her anxiety grew as her mind raced, but she just couldn't think about anything else. This isn't right, she felt, this isn't what Art would want.

On the night of that second day after Connie had learned of Art's perilous condition, she finally turned the corner and stopped praying for Art to stay alive. She knew deep inside that she had to accept reality, and through a mist of unstoppable tears, she finally prayed only for strength as she let Art go.

The third morning was Memorial Day, but there was no nine o'clock phone call from Washington. At first, Connie began to rationalize that it was because of the national holiday. But she became increasingly anxious, and finally, as noon approached, she was sitting in the kitchen of Art's parents' house when a man in an Army uniform walked by the window. Before the doorbell even rang, she knew. It was some poor guy from the Citadel who recited the required lines of bereavement on behalf of the president of the United States. After he had informed her of Art's death, Connie was assured that the Army would help her with all the details of the funeral, but that she would make all the decisions.

It was a crushing blow, though it was not unexpected. And and even as a knife went through Connie's heart, she also dimly perceived that her prayers had truly been answered, that the three days Art had stayed alive had been given to her so that she could build up enough strength to accept his passing. And Connie was suddenly a very strong person, something she didn't know about herself.

It was Art's wish to be buried in South Carolina, and Connie saw to that. When the assistance officer arrived days later, he was a poor little second lieutenant, and the first words out of his mouth were, "I've never done this before." Connie was ready for him.

"Well, neither have I, so we're going to do it my way. Now let's start with the pallbearers. I have here a list I made up of the people I want to be the pallbearers."

The lieutenant smiled uneasily.

"Ma'am, you can't do it that way, the Army sends its own—"

"Lieutenant, you don't understand. This is the way it's going to be, and I don't care how you do it, but I want you to get it done, do you understand?"

Connie felt like she was beating up the poor lieutenant, but Bill Rennagel called and told her they could make it all work. Art was buried in Lake City, South Carolina, a place he truly loved and where he had told Connie he wanted to be buried. He did not want to be buried at West Point, even though that was where Connie would have chosen. The final resting place he got was the one he chose in South Carolina. He loved it so . . .

Connie took Chip back to Saint Mary's and her apartment. She started working again as a nurse in the local hospital, but it just wasn't the same as it had been before. Chip was the center of her life, but things just didn't feel right. A few months after Art's funeral, Connie and Chip went to West Point, where they received Art's medals for his service at an official ceremony. And while she was there, she looked around. She found out that a few other young widows and their children had moved back to West Point, just to be near their friends. And she began to think about that.

By the spring of 1969, Connie Parker had realized that she didn't want to stay in West Virginia, she really wanted to see the friends she had made in the Army, she wanted to be with Art's classmates and their wives, the only people in the world who could really understand how she felt and who could really console her. Oh, her parents had been very compassionate, as had Art's parents. But she longed for the company of the young men and women her age she had met in the Army before Art went off to war.

Once she had decided, she made a few phone calls, and

sure enough, support was there. She readily secured a part-time position working as a nurse at the West Point hospital, and soon enough, she and Chip were living in a townhouse just outside the gates of West Point in Cornwall, New York. They were right between the townhouses of two waiting wives whose West Point graduate husbands were then serving in Vietnam.

Within a few months, Connie got an invitation out of the blue to attend the Thayer Award dinner. This was a formal award given by West Point each year to a public figure who was not a West Point graduate, and it was presented at a formal dinner that always generated a certain amount of media attention. Connie had no idea how she had gotten the invitation, and she certainly had no intention of going. But her next-door neighbor told her she would watch Chip, that Connie needed to get out and meet some people socially at West Point. So Connie went.

She was seated next to Bill and Louisa Heiberg. Bill was a major who had graduated from West Point in 1961 and was teaching in the social sciences department, they had a baby Chip's age, and Connie really hit it off right away with both of them. After a while, Bill told Connie that he had a classmate who was a bachelor teaching social sciences named Larry Budge. Larry was supposed to have come to this dinner, but instead he had been dating a woman down in New York City fifty miles to the south, and it was apparent that he had skipped the dinner to go spend the weekend in the city. But now Bill and Louisa had a plan, although Connie proved to be very reluctant. She didn't want a romantic relationship just yet, she told them: The only social life she really wanted was with good friends. It took them several months, but eventually they got Connie to agree to go out to dinner with them and Larry Budge.

On the day of the big dinner date, the Heibergs' son developed a fever, so plans changed to "dinner at the Heiberg house." That evening, Larry showed up, they smiled and got in Larry's car, and silence descended on them. Connie was a bit rattled, but what could she say? She just didn't know how to date anymore. She was a widow not yet twenty-five who had buried her husband less than two years ago, she was going out with a thirty-year-old bachelor, and as she tried to think of something cute to say, all she could think about was Chip. Larry, for his part, said almost nothing. It was the longest car ride of Connie's life.

But once they got to the Heibergs', everything changed. Larry and Connie both laughed a lot over dinner, and to their great surprise, they found that they liked a lot of the same things. They especially enjoyed each other's company, and they began to take occasional walks around West Point together in the afternoon. Larry was teaching international relations and comparative politics, and he spent a lot of time preparing for class in his room at the Bachelor Officers' Quarters. But Connie's open-hearted goodness, and yes, her occasional spontaneous peals of laughter, were refreshing, even beguiling.

Larry was really impressed by Connie's personal courage. Here she was, a widow at twenty-four, but she didn't seem to hold the slightest bitterness toward the Army or West Point. One would have expected a young woman like that to stay home with her parents and let herself be consoled by them and family friends for a long time. But instead, Connie had come back to West Point.

After a few weeks, Larry broke up with his girlfriend in the city and began to see more and more of Connie. But then academics and final exams ended in June 1969, followed by June Week, the annual week given over at the Academy to graduation and reunion. Once that had ended, Larry went down to Washington for a three-month temporary assignment in the International Security Affairs Directorate, one of the policymaking organizations within the Department of Defense.

Soon after he arrived, the Navy captain who ran the East Asia–Pacific "desk" went off to the National War College, and Larry took that job on a temporary basis. He was to spend most of his time that summer working on a National Security Study Memorandum (NSSM) on post-Vietnam Asia policy. Nixon was president at the time, and Henry Kissinger, his national security advisor, had set up the NSSM system to examine a broad range of national security issues. NSSMs were detailed papers developed and coordinated by temporary interagency groups whose members represented all the major policy players on a given issue. It soon became clear, at least in regard to post-Vietnam Asian policy, that Kissinger was paying little attention to the NSSM system. As the NSSM working group wound up its work, Nixon announced the policy of "Vietnamization"—a major policy shift designed to get the United States out of Vietnam, a change that had never even been considered by the working group. Larry had to smile as he reflected on what was going on all around him: The NSSMs were not unlike the Harvard term papers that Kissinger-the-professor had assigned his students, except that their primary purpose was to keep the policy people busy while Kissinger-the-national-security-advisor ran the war.

And he missed Connie. They only spoke on the phone occasionally, as these were still the days of very expensive long-distance phone calls. They wrote regularly, and yes, he missed her warmth, her comfort, her person.

But Larry was still a bachelor, and he and Connie had not made any sort of formal commitment to each other. Although he was very fond of her, Washington, D.C., was an interesting town with a number of attractions, not the least of which was a large array of beautiful women. Although Larry was kept quite busy at the Pentagon that summer, he did find time to go out on a number of dates.

One of these dates was with a woman we'll call Carol, and Carol turned out to be both interesting and fun. They were to go out together on several evenings that summer, and Larry was surprised to find how much he enjoyed himself. The last evening they were together, just before Labor Day weekend, Larry sort of surprised himself by inviting her to come up to West Point and go to the West Point Homecoming football game and celebrations with him in October. But as he drove north the next day, he began to realize that he had put himself into a potentially difficult position.

As soon as he got back to West Point, Larry called Connie and then went over to see her. He was engulfed by her warmth, and he had soon completely forgotten that he had invited Carol up for Homecoming. But after a few days of classes, he got a letter from her confirming that she hadn't forgotten him, and that she would be arriving for that big football weekend in just about another month.

Unfortunately, Larry treated this looming crisis the way most people initially treat problems of any sort: He ignored it and hoped it would go away. But another letter told him it wouldn't go away. He thought about it, then realized that he still had three more weeks, hell, three and a half. He knew he would find a way to get out of this predicament, he just couldn't think what that might be— so he ignored it and hoped it would go away.

It didn't go away. Connie had been invited by a young captain to go to the Homecoming game and parties with him, but she had already been to two games with Larry, they went out together several times each week, and she was sure Larry would invite her to Homecoming. So she had said "No" to the captain and just waited for Larry to invite her.

Larry handled this one badly. He didn't have the gumption to uninvite Carol and just tell her that he was involved with another woman—and technically he wasn't, as they had made no agreements on exclusivity or anything of the sort. So he kept rolling over as Carol's letters arrived unfolding her plans for the two of them that weekend. He didn't say anything to Connie until the Friday afternoon before the game, an hour before Carol was scheduled to arrive and go out to dinner with him. He called Connie on the phone, and after some uncomfortable chat, he told her.

"Connie, there's something I need to tell you about this weekend. I . . . I . . . there is this woman I met in Washington last summer and I . . . I invited her up for the game this weekend, and she will get here pretty soon, so . . ."

Larry heard only silence.

"Connie?"

"Yes?"

"Oh, I thought . . . I didn't know if you heard what I said . . ."

"I heard."

"Oh. Well, I guess that's all I wanted to tell you. I didn't want you to be hurt or anything . . ."

"Hurt? Why should I be hurt?"

"Well, not hurt, I guess. I don't know, we've seen a lot of each other, and I just thought . . ."

"You thought what?"

"I . . . I don't know, I just want you to enjoy yourself, that's all . . ."

"I will, Larry, don't worry about me. Have a nice weekend."

Click.

It was without any doubt the longest weekend of Larry's life. He tried not to look around at the game or at the parties to see if Connie was there, but he cringed every time he turned. His male friends were happy to meet Carol, but all their wives seemed just a bit icy—was this that secret entente that all women everywhere seemed to have going for them?

Larry was very unhappy and confused during the whole weekend. He had handled it poorly, he knew, very poorly indeed, and he regretted having invited Carol up more than he could say. Of course, there was no one for him to express that regret to, so he just bottled it up. He smiled as needed, made small talk as necessary, but the weekend was a dreadful failure. When he waved goodbye to Carol on Sunday, it was the last time he would ever see her.

After Homecoming, Larry pursued Connie relentlessly. Nearly every weekend, he took her down to New York City, an hour south, for an evening of dinner and theater. They would also often spend all of a Saturday or a Sunday together, usually on long walks and picnics at Round Pond with Chip and their basset hound Demetrius, or taking a lunch aboard a sailboat on Lake Popolopen. Larry taught Connie how to play tennis on the West Point tennis courts and how to ski at the Victor Constant ski slope, a private West Point retreat with short lift lines. Larry was the officer in charge for the cadet parachute club, and Connie and Chip often went out and watched them jump. Chip was allowed to help Larry pack his gear after he had jumped, and he relished being involved in such manly affairs. But one day as he was trying to help, he pulled the wrong handle, and Larry's reserve parachute ballooned out. The cadets all froze, fearing a reaction from Larry that might have been as fierce as the one they would have expected themselves for such a blunder. But instead, Larry smiled at Chip.

"What a big strong boy you are to be able to open that parachute!"

All tension disappeared instantly, and the cadets joined the laughter.

They spent Christmas and New Year's of '69–'70 together, and in the spring declared to each other their love. In late September 1970, Larry finally got around to "popping the question." But he was still a soldier first, and social niceties were not his strong area. His proposal was less than "storybook."

One evening Larry announced to Connie that Allen Francis, a colleague of his on the West Point faculty, was taking his wife Mary on a ski trip to Switzerland over the Christmas break. He said that he had been invited to accompany them, and that was something he really wanted to do. Then he asked Connie if she would come with him. Allen and Mary Francis were good friends they often saw socially, and Connie was thrilled. But when she answered him, it was with an eye to the real world in which they lived.

"Larry, I'd love to come, but my parents would never understand if I asked them to take care of my three-year-old son over Christmas while I went on a trip to Europe."

"What if we were married?"

"Are you kidding?"

"No."

"Is that a proposal?"

"Yes."

"Okay. I accept."

They were married December 12, 1970, in the middle of a raging snowstorm. Larry taught cadets for the next week, and they had an early Christmas with Chip. Then Chip stayed with Connie's parents while they went on a two-week ski trip to Davos, Switzerland, with Allen and Mary Francis. The trip, in Connie's words, was simply wonderful.

The following summer, Larry went to the nine-month Command and General Staff College at Fort Leavenworth, Kansas, and he and Connie knew a time of unalloyed marital bliss together. When his orders for Vietnam arrived, it was clear that he would not be going to an American fighting unit, as such units had all been withdrawn. But in order to avoid the vagaries of the Army personnel system, he wrote his friend Bill Stofft, who had been another major on the West Point social sciences faculty with him and was then already in Vietnam working for the pacification program.

Larry asked Bill for advice on assignments—that was the way you did it, no one would be so gauche as to come right out and ask for help getting a good job—and Bill replied that the Pacification Studies Group where he worked had an opening. Larry liked the prospect, so Bill set the wheels in motion for Larry's assignment to the group.

In July 1972, the time arrived. Larry got on that plane and, once again, Connie was left behind by the man she loved as he flew off to the war in Vietnam.

Larry Budge went right to work with the Pacification Studies Group in Saigon. This organization was part of CORDS (Civil Operations and Revolutionary Development Support), which was the Military Advisory Command, Vietnam (MACV) element in charge of "nation-building" within South Vietnam. The goal of CORDS was really quite simple, but its implementation was both complex and difficult: They wanted to find a way or ways of supporting and promoting with the populace the form of government then existing in South Vietnam, which was slowly but surely moving toward widely based enfranchisement of the civilian population and ultimate popular sovereignty. This effort was being conducted in the face of ferocious opposition, both political and military, from communist forces based in North Vietnam who wanted to establish their own form of Marxist-based government in its place.

This was a highly political job, and in many ways, it was right up Larry's alley: It was a real-world application of much of the political theory that Larry had been teaching to the cadets at West Point. The Pacification Studies Group was a small think tank, which supported the pacification and "nation-building" effort by doing studies and analysis and by conducting surveys among the South Vietnamese on the progress of the pacification effort. While the topics for the surveys came from within CORDS, the surveys were administered by a dozen or so very talented Vietnamese known as "the Hoods."

These men included a doctor, some lawyers, and a number of men who had been in prison for what were clearly political reasons. Not only were these Vietnamese men not political stooges of the existing government in South Vietnam, they had even been chosen by the Americans because of their independence from governmental pressures. In fact, Larry was to learn, there were several Vietnamese working for the group who were not in jail only because they worked for the Americans.

The Hoods were sent out into the countryside each

month, wearing civilian clothes, and armed only with a notebook and a series of survey questions. Their job was to take a bus or sampan or other low-level transportation into the area from which information was sought. Once arrived, they would simply go into a teahouse, say, and just sit there and sip tea. As local people came in, they would engage them in conversation. Over the course of twenty or thirty minutes, they would find ways of asking some or all of the questions that they had been given in Saigon.

These men did not carry clipboards or anything of the sort that would give away their mission. Rather, they posed as simple civilians, low-level bureaucrats for some private Vietnamese company who were just passing through to check on the rice harvest or the fertilizer supply or something similarly innocuous.

After their conversations ended, they would leave and go to a private setting, where they would fill out the survey form and perhaps make notes on other issues that might have come up. They would then go on to the next public setting where they might interview another local citizen.

Every American of political importance who came to Saigon was briefed on the progress of the pacification program, which was considered an overwhelming success by the entire American community in Saigon. The briefing focused on Long An Province, a heavily farmed and bountiful province in the heart of the rice-growing Mekong Delta south of Saigon, which was touted as one of the great success stories of the pacification program. The briefing would start with the history.

In 1963, the visitors were told, an American couldn't spend a night in Long An without the real fear of being killed, and even the Vietnamese army or governmental figures were at a similar high risk. In fact, a graphic tale about the early days of the American war in Vietnam was told in a book entitled *War Comes to Long An*, which most senior Americans coming to Vietnam had read before they arrived. It told how American helicopters were shot down and South Vietnamese Army forces with American advisors accompanying them were badly mauled by a much smaller Viet Cong unit. It was truly a terrifying prospect, and the whole province was considered a safe operating base for communist forces.

In 1965, the political sympathies of Vietnamese peasants living on or near the land they farmed in the Mekong Delta were measured and recorded under the "Hamlet Evaluation System." In Long An Province, the hamlets and villages were all colored red, meaning that they were under strong communist military control. But when the American 9th Infantry Division arrived in the delta that year, they began to engage and defeat communist forces, and the American assessment of political control, measured *inter alia* by frequency of armed conflict, began to shift, first from red to yellow, indicating an improving security environment. Over the next few years, the coloration of the maps continued to shift, from yellow to green, indicating that the security environment and hence political support in Long An Province had shifted strongly toward the South Vietnamese government. By 1972, the maps used in the briefing for the important visitors showed that all of Long An Province was green.

Not everyone in the group was comfortable with this latest assessment, and it generated quite a bit of discussion among the Americans. Finally, Larry's boss, a civilian named H. Lee Braddock whom Larry both liked and respected professionally, said, "Okay, send in the Hoods, let them find out what's going on." And they did.

They came back after three or four weeks, and they told
the Americans that the reason the map was green was that
the Viet Cong owned the whole province, and they didn't
have to fight, they didn't have to engage in violence, they
simply owned the whole place.

Late in the fall, Larry and a man named Jack Pellicci
were selected by the head of CORDS to design the small
U.S. organization that would remain after the American
forces left under the provisions of the peace agreement
then being negotiated in Paris. The director of CORDS,
George Jacobson, told Larry and Jack to travel around
Vietnam and talk to people, and then come up with a
design for the structure of Americans in CORDS that
should be left behind.

Early in 1973, as part of the Paris Accords, the Four
Party Joint Military Commission was organized in Saigon.
Major General Gilbert H. Woodward, who was the chief of
staff for the Military Advisory Command, Vietnam
(MACV), became the American delegate, and he selected
Major Paul Miles to be his secretary for the commission
meetings. Miles than accompanied Woodward back to
Paris to get briefed on what would be needed for the com-
mission. When they returned to Saigon, it was clear that
General Woodward needed another very smart major to act
as his second secretary. And Paul knew just where to go to
find one.

Paul had graduated from West Point in 1960, one year
ahead of Larry. But he had also won a Rhodes Scholarship
right after graduation, and the years he spent at Oxford had
overlapped with those of Larry, which had allowed them to
get to know each other well. He showed up one day in
Larry's office and asked him if he wanted the job. He did.

The duties of the secretaries meant that, during formal

meetings, one of them would sit in the meeting room at the table with General Woodward and take notes. The other would sit in a back room listening to the meeting over a headset. Afterward, they would together come up with their account of the meeting, and they would then write the message that went back to Henry Kissinger every evening. The purpose was to try to decide who controlled what pieces of the ground in South Vietnam. Larry left in May 1973, after ten months in Vietnam, but the Joint Military Commission went on for several years.

Larry's first assignment back in the United States was to Infantry Branch, where he managed files of men going to Army schools. He was a bit surprised that the Army had found a job for him that made little use of his acquired skills, but he had no options.

At first, the job was simply boring. Then it became tedious, and after only weeks, Larry knew that it was soul-destroying. He tried to find another job, and even got people in the Pentagon to say they would hire him if he could get released. But the general who ran Infantry Branch found out about his unrest and told him he was there for three years: Get used to it and stop fighting the problem.

For the first time Larry was actually thinking about leaving the Army and going to Harvard Business School. Then along came Lieutenant Colonel Peter Dawkins, West Point class of '59 and a Rhodes Scholar. His time at Oxford had overlapped with Larry's and they were good friends.

Pete told Larry that Congress had established a committee to review the military academies, and he had been named to the committee. He asked Larry if he would like to be the secretary for the commission, and Larry jumped at the chance. So directions came down to Infantry Branch to transfer Larry to serve on the commission, which threw them into a tizzy. They finally came to Larry with the proposal that, if he would turn down the commission post and stay for three more months so that they could get his replacement, they would let him go back to serve with troops.

That was all Larry wanted anyway, so he quickly agreed. Meanwhile, unbeknownst to Infantry Branch, the other services had insisted that the secretary of the commission should come from a service other than the Army. One of the other services eventually filled the secretary post, but by that time, it no longer mattered to Larry, for he was out of Washington and on his way to Fort Carson, Colorado, and duty with soldiers.

In January 1976, a son was born to Larry and Connie. They named him Stephen, and he and Chip grew up the closest of brothers.

Jim Kimsey

Growing up in Washington, D.C., in a family without much money, James Verlin Kimsey won a scholarship to Gonzaga College high school, a Jesuit institution for boys renowned for both the education and the discipline that it established in its graduates. For three years, Jim's academic grades were fine, but during the fall of his senior year, he was becoming somewhat of a discipline problem. He was a handful, a truly disruptive influence in many of his classes, and some of the school administrators were looking for a way they could pressure him into adhering a bit more to the straight and narrow line.

Finally, at the end of October, he was called in to talk to the dean, who started by reminding Jim that he was on a full scholarship. A requirement of the scholarship, he continued, was that Jim's grades had to be maintained above a certain level, and if they dropped below that level, he might lose his scholarship. Jim nodded. That was nothing new, and he wondered why he had been called in.

The drone continued. Jim had been somewhat of a problem in some of his classes lately, so the administration had decided to apply a new academic scholarship rule. The new rule, he was informed, was that the required minimum grade level would be raised to an average just above his present average. He would have to study hard for the rest of the semester, the dean warned, because if he didn't bring his grades up just a few notches, he might lose the scholarship and not be allowed to continue through his senior year and graduate.

Suddenly Jim saw what was going on. He asked the dean if this new minimum-grade standard applied to all students on scholarships or just to him. The dean smiled as he told him that it only applied to him. Then Jim erupted.

Down the hall, the windows rattled, and the air was blue with four-letter words that came streaming out of Jim's mouth. The dean tried to quiet him, then raised his own voice. Soon they were yelling at each other, then Jim stormed out the door, slamming it behind him.

Well, that was the end of him at Gonzaga. He knew that before he even hit the street, but he didn't care. He was steaming as he walked, but he soon suppressed his anger. He stopped in a bar he sometimes hung around on Fourteenth Street, in a rough part of town. This was long before anyone cared about clients having to be of a certain age, and his first beer cooled him down. The second was even better, and then he decided to tell the owner how he could save some money on storage. Within hours, he was on the payroll.

He worked late that night, and when he got home just before midnight, his mother was waiting for him. He told her what had happened at Gonzaga, though he omitted the part about taking the job in the bar. When he finally went to bed, she was in tears.

After a month or so in the bar, Jim was starting to wonder if he had done the right thing by dropping out of high school when he had been so close to getting his degree. Then one evening his mother asked him to come with her the next morning to visit another school. What could he say, this was his mother, and even though he thought of himself as a tough city kid, he was only seventeen.

The next morning, he dressed in a coat and tie, the clothes he had worn to Gonzaga for more than three years. He got on the bus with his mother, and as they rode, he tried to guess where they might be going. When they got off and started walking down Vermont Avenue, he knew where they were going: Saint John's military school, a Catholic boys' high school run by the Christian Brothers and Gonzaga's big crosstown rival.

Sure enough, his mother had arranged everything. When she and Jim walked in, they met with an administrative officer who told Jim he understood the whole story. If he could pass a test they would give him, he would be admitted to Saint John's on a full scholarship for the last semester of his senior year. He would be a special student and would not be required to wear the uniform or go through any of the military training the other students took. What did he think?

Jim looked at his mother's pleading face, and there really wasn't any question.

"Sure," he said, "I'll take the test."

He did very well on the test, and the next thing he knew, he was enrolled for the second semester. He was immediately glad he didn't have to do any of the military stuff, though, which he really thought was just so much Mickey Mouse. So he took the courses, and as winter turned to spring in 1957, he did quite well. He also made new friends, and soon had in many ways turned the page on his three years at Gonzaga.

After graduation, Jim won a scholarship to Georgetown University in Washington, D.C. He walked through the doors that opened before him, and soon found himself enrolled at Georgetown in an A.B. Honors course. This meant that he could graduate in five years with a master's degree in some field of liberal arts. And he was doing very well in that program until he started getting distracted. It wasn't just the booze and the girls, they were always there. No, this was something else, something completely new and different.

The first thing was a new John Ford movie he saw called *The Long Gray Line*, starring Tyrone Power and Maureen O'Hara. This was the first time he had really paid any attention to West Point, and all of a sudden it seemed kind of neat. Then there was a TV series about West Point that was on every Wednesday night, telling about the personal lives and adventures of cadets. That was neat too. In fact, it was so neat that he found himself watching every episode almost religiously. He was young. There was glamour.

This started him thinking about what he was going to do when he got out of college. The master's degree would allow him to become some kind of academic administrator or to teach. But now he realized that he didn't want to do either of those things. In fact, if he kept going to Georgetown, he realized he was drinking so much booze that he could well graduate with cirrhosis of the liver. What he really wanted to do was to go to West Pont and become a soldier. But how would he do that? Getting an appointment to West Point was a very difficult task in those days.

Jim had an aunt who lived in Montana, and he put out the word on the family net that he wanted to go to West Point. And in 1958, Senator Murray of Montana announced that anyone who wanted his appointment to West Point would have to take a test. No favoritism would be shown, his office said, and any American eligible for West Point could apply. The one who got the best score would win the appointment. So Jim applied, took the test, and won the appointment. And there not only was no political favoritism shown, Jim did all this without ever even meeting Senator Murray.

Only in America.

Jim was quite enthused before he got to West Point. But the first days of Beast Barracks were very depressing. This wasn't at all what he had expected. No matter how depressed and unhappy he got, however, he never forgot some important events that had preceded his donning cadet gray.

When he first decided he wanted to go to West Point, many people told him he would never get in. Then when he did get in, many more told him he would never stay, that he just didn't have whatever it took. "You'll never make it," they said. What they meant was, "You don't have any of that magic that it takes. That place is just too hard for normal people. I couldn't do it, and you're no better than I am. You'll be back on the block in no time, a washout just like I've always said you are."

Unhappy as he was during all four years, Jim was always inhabited by visions of "I told you so" from the

Greek chorus that would await him when he returned to Washington without a West Point degree. So he stuck it out. And over those four years, he spent much of his time trying to find the outer limits of the envelope and then testing them, seeing how hard he could push without getting thrown out.

They never caught him for any big stuff, and he graduated in 1962.

But once he was commissioned in the infantry and actually started being a soldier with the 82nd Airborne Division at Fort Bragg, North Carolina, he found that he enjoyed it, that it was downright fun.

As he looked around, however, he also realized that there were a lot of other young lieutenants like him who seemed to be very careful in everything they did, and he never really understood why. Were they afraid of being themselves?

He later realized that, had he stayed in the Army, he would have had a hard time making general officer, simply because he was too big an iconoclast, and he had a very hard time not saying what he thought. Over time, he would realize that such candor could limit your progress in a bureaucratic organization like the Army. But as a young officer, he stayed pure, and he called 'em like he saw 'em.

The 82nd reorganized, and as a first lieutenant, Jim was made an infantry company commander, which was quite unusual at the time. Jim was good, and he knew it. But a little cockiness was almost required of a company commander of the toughest fighting men in the world. He was married, and his first son, Michael, was born at Fort Bragg. But any true infantryman was always listening for the sound of the guns, and they were booming ever so softly in far-off Vietnam. Without telling his wife, he volunteered for service there, and he had some friends in Washington who promised to make it happen, although it would take a few months to get the paperwork routed through the right offices in the Pentagon.

Sure enough, the orders came down, and Jim was packing his bags in April 1965 when, to everyone's surprise, a group of communist rebels in the nation of the Dominican Republic started shooting up the government. President Lyndon Johnson was not ready for another communist dictator like Castro in his backyard, so he threw his Immediate Ready Force, a battalion of the 82nd, in there right away. Their orders were to crush the communists. And what do you know, Jim's company was the first infantry company on the ground and operational. They had their hands full right away.

But American firepower was effective, and his riflemen drove the rebels before them. And as soon as Jim's men were deployed and fighting, other companies from the 82nd began appearing right beside them and expanding the fight.

These rebels operated in the countryside, but their main political base was in the capital city, Santo Domingo, and that was their refuge as well. So the American forces started by dividing Santo Domingo in half and clearing the rebels out of the inland section. Once they had done that, they swept through the other half and drove the rebels up against the sea, where they crushed them.

The hot combat where American lives were at risk mostly occurred during the first few weeks, and Jim lost a handful of men from his company. After that, it was almost a mop-up, and as the number of American combat soldiers in the small country went up, the risk to him and his men went down. He had had his first taste of combat, and he had relished it. There had been a few sweaty-pits moments, of course, like that moment about 3:00 A.M. when he saw four men crawling down an alley toward him and he wasn't sure whether they were good guys or bad guys. They turned out to be good guys who didn't know he was in front of them, and he was glad he had held his fire. But of such tense moments—thrilling, really, with life itself at risk—an infantry leader's life is made.

As the fighting lessened and the rebel areas were cordoned off, American political leaders began to fly in. And because Jim's company had been the first to arrive, they had set up their command post right next to the airport. That wasn't a problem, except that colonels and generals and strange people in civilian clothes began appearing in his command tent and using his radios. Then they had a telephone switchboard set up, and he had to detail soldiers from his company to man it. He wished he had set up a few hundred yards away, but when they arrived, that had not been a choice.

During the day, Jim was usually off with his men killing rebels or scaring the hell out of them. He and a few other officers and senior NCOs in his company slept on cots right there in the headquarters tent, but they usually weren't around while civilians were there during the day. And while some civilians might have sat on their cots, no one had ever really disturbed them.

The cots were all covered with poncho liners, a lightweight camouflage-colored miracle cloth covering that was six feet square and weighed less than a pound. And most important, it would keep you warm even if you and/or it were wet. But one afternoon, he was standing inside the tent explaining something to two sergeants when a civilian in a blue suit came in. He was a well-known political appointee, but he had obviously just stepped in some dogshit outside, and it was all over the side of his shoe. He didn't even acknowledge that Jim and the other soldiers were even inside the same tent, and without so much as a "by your leave," he walked over to Jim's cot, pulled his poncho liner down and wiped the dogshit off his shoe with it. Then he walked out the back and toward an adjoining tent where some meeting was going on.

Jim was stunned, and as the politician walked past, he called to him.

"Hey!"

No response. Jim took several steps behind the politico and raised his voice.

"Hey!"

Suddenly a three-star general was in front of him, blocking his way with the palm of his right hand open toward him. It was the commander of the XVIII Airborne Corps.

"At ease, Lieutenant."

"Sir, that guy just—"

"I said *at ease, Lieutenant!*"

That was the first time that Jim saw the American political feeding chain in operation. Senior officers tell junior officers what to do, political appointees tell senior officers what to do, and who told political appointees what to do? As far as he could see, it was rich civilians. So how did you get membership in that class?

In the summer of 1965, Jim returned to Fort Bragg from the Dominican Republic, but he was only on the ground long enough to kiss his wife goodbye, then he was back on a plane and headed for Vietnam.

His orders said that he was to be an advisor in Hau

Nghia Province. But an entire American advisory team, a captain, a lieutenant, and a slew of sergeants, had just been wiped out in Duc Pho District in northernmost I Corps area, so that overcame mere written orders. Jim was a brand-new captain, and as soon as he got off the plane, they grabbed him. An advisory team of eight men was quickly thrown together, he was made the commander, and he led them back into Duc Pho.

The small town of Duc Pho was surrounded by concertina barbed wire and bunkered defensive positions manned by South Vietnamese Regional Force Popular Force troops. These were really little more than a poorly armed local militia, but they controlled the town and went on operations to fight communist soldiers every day. And they paid a blood price for that every day also.

The rural population of Duc Pho was heavily supportive of the communists, and for an American, Duc Pho was one of the most dangerous places in all of South Vietnam. The previous American team commander who had been killed was a Captain Rod, and he was from New Orleans. Before his death, he had written home about all the orphans in the province, most of whose parents had been killed by American firepower. After his letters had been passed around local churches, modest contributions of used clothing were sent to Duc Pho for the orphans. But after his death, he became a martyr, and suddenly the flow of packages ballooned.

This quickly became a problem for Jim. It wasn't just that the Vietnamese had no use for mittens and scarves. More important, he was going out on daily operations with his Ruff Puff troops, and so were his men, and they had no time to sort mail. Duc Pho was a dangerous place. In addition to local sympathy for communist insurgents, there were major

American units operating both to their north and to their south. To the communists, Duc Pho was a sort of haven area, where neither American Marines operating to their north nor Air Cav troops operating with their helicopters to their south would bother them. Consequently, the region was flooded with communist soldiers, both Viet Cong and North Vietnamese regulars. All these hardened regulars had to worry about in Duc Pho was the local, poorly armed RFPF units.

Yawn.

Jim's fighting force would suffer six or eight casualties every week. These were usually Vietnamese Ruff Puff soldiers, but Americans went down as well. Sometimes his weekly casualties were much higher, even ranging up into the hundreds. Duc Pho was a very important communist base area, and for Jim as an American commander, that meant a lot of very bad days. People above him realized this, of course, and a few years later, one brigade of the U.S. Americal Division would be assigned to operate there. They would have their hands full.

But while the VC and the NVA were trying to kill Jim and his men, Captain Rod's martyrdom had gotten Catholic Church authorities involved in the orphanage project he had proposed. Jim was kept in the loop on this, and they eventually told him they were going to build the orphanage, but that it would probably be built in Saigon or in Da Nang, big cities that were then safe from communist military threats.

Jim was a bit surprised to hear this, so he wrote back and said that if they really were going to build an orphanage, it should be built in Duc Pho, because that's where all the orphans were who had gotten Captain Rod started down this path, and where he had been killed. His ulterior motive, of course, was to get the orphanage started, and then use its presence to bring the political pressure needed for a large American infantry unit to operate regularly there and protect it. And if they did that, they would also necessarily protect Duc Pho, thus accomplishing his larger mission.

Meanwhile, Jim had bunkerized the small house in which the American team lived with sandbags. His only ace in the hole guaranteeing his survival and that of his American team for a while was a Navy destroyer that came offshore near them about two or three days each month. They had a computerized firing system known as the Naval Tactical Data System, or NTDS, and it was extremely accurate. Every time it came by, Jim made a point of calling in its fire, and he regularly wowed the locals with its accuracy. But he also put out the word that this American ship was out there all the time, and that if they didn't hear from Jim every hour, that would mean he had been overrun by communists, and they would fire all their guns on the small town, destroying everyone and everything in it.

The district chief was stunned when he heard that, and he asked Jim what would happen if his radio didn't work. Jim told him that would be too bad and the town would be destroyed. This was the craziest thing the district chief had ever heard. But everyone else heard it too, which meant the communists got the word. They had all seen the accuracy and destructive power of the naval guns, and maybe this crazy American was telling the truth. Jim remains convinced that is the only reason he survived a year as an advisor in Duc Pho, that he and his team were not overrun some night and killed like Captain Rod and his team right before him had been. And maybe it is.

Meanwhile, the Catholic Relief Services were not saying anything more to Jim about where they would build the orphanage. So he decided he had to act, and he started telling them, through the mail, through the American Military Command, through the embassy, through every means he could think of, that if they did not build the orphanage in Duc Pho, they would be breaking faith with the martyred Captain Rod, with the people of New Orleans who were making all these contributions, with the orphans of Duc Pho who had first awakened Captain Rod's sympathy, on and on. Finally, an American working for Catholic Relief Services called him down to Saigon. When he got there, he was told that they were going to turn all their money over to him, and he was to build the orphanage himself.

Jim was a bit surprised. But it was a challenge: In the middle of a war, in the middle of a population that leaned heavily toward their communist enemies, he was supposed to find the people and the materials required to build an orphanage. Okay, he said. I can do that.

There were lots of American support troops in Saigon, and before he went back to Duc Pho, Jim visited an American Engineer battalion and was able to get a modest drawing set and some paper. When he got back to Duc Pho, he started making some sketches, just as he had done in civil engineering classes back at West Point. The drawings were rough, true, but he got the idea across.

The final design was for a U-shaped building that would house and educate about a hundred kids. It included a big kitchen, a dining area, classrooms, and dormitories. Then he spoke with his local Vietnamese contacts, and they were able to get an architect and several local construction companies involved. Catholic Relief Services had given him many thousands of dollars to build the orphanage, and American money was the all-important ingredient.

There was no doubt at all that the construction companies in Duc Pho, the laborers, and maybe even the architect brought in to do the drawings were at least communist sympathizers, if not active agents or even Viet Cong soldiers on the side. But hey, everybody's got to eat! This was a legitimate construction job, bricks and mortar and stucco, and these people, communist or not, could do the work. And on their side, if the job brought money into the community to pay for legitimate work, no local communists would challenge the source of that money.

Within a few months, the orphanage was finished, and it was a beauty! He called the Catholic Relief Services guy in Saigon and told him it was ready, all they had to do was send some people up to Duc Pho to run it.

"Not a chance!" he said. "I can't send anybody to Duc Pho, it's too dangerous. You built it, now you run it!"

Jim was stunned.

"What the hell are you talking about?" he said. "I can't run this place, I've got a war to fight, remember? You paid for it, now get somebody up here to run it!"

"We paid for it, Captain, but you were the one who insisted it be built in Duc Pho, and you built it! This was all your idea, now you run it!"

"Wait a minute, now. You refuse to send somebody up here to run this place, right?"

"Captain, you don't know what people in Saigon think of your town. I don't have enough money to pay anyone to even *visit* Duc Pho, and anyone taking a job there would be getting a sure death sentence."

"All right, let me tell you what I'm going to do. If you don't have somebody up here in three days to run this orphanage, I know where there's a Buddhist monastery about thirty kilometers south of here, and I'm going to offer it to them. I'll give them the building, the operating money, everything. I think they might be very pleased to get this beautiful brand-new building for free and do with it whatever they saw fit."

There was silence on the other end of the phone.

"You wouldn't dare! You . . . you'll get excommunicated!"

"Really? Does that mean I'll get to go to Rome and all that? Tell me something that scares me."

"You . . . you can't do this!"

"Try me."

Click.

Two days later, a helicopter landed just before dark, and four little Vietnamese nuns got out. They all wore black habits with funny starched white headdresses under their black veils. The oldest one was Sister Colette, the mother superior, and the three younger ones were a nurse, a cook, and a teacher. Jim took them into the orphanage and showed them around, and they seemed delighted.

That night, Duc Pho was mortared by the communists, which usually happened a few times each month. Jim and his team felt secure in their bunkered house as explosions and tracer fire lit up the night, and he sort of expected the nuns to show up from the orphanage and ask for shelter. He even predicted to one of his team members that the next morning they would come begging for a helicopter to get them out of there. But they heard nothing from them all night.

Next morning, bright and early, there was a knock on the door. Sure enough, it was the mother superior. But she never mentioned leaving. Instead, she had a punch list. She and her three assistants had spent the night inspecting the orphanage in exquisite detail, and this was the list of changes Captain Kimsey would have to make before the children could be brought in.

"But, Mother Superior," he protested, "I gave all the money that was left back to Catholic Services, and that guy in Saigon said that he gave it to you. You own the place now, so bring your own people in to fix those things!"

"Ah no, Captain," she soothed, "that money is for the children. You built the orphanage, now you must make these final repairs."

Jim had to smile. Man, she was one tough cookie! In the end, he brought back the Vietnamese construction companies who had built the place, and they made the final repairs on the punch list to the satisfaction of the mother superior.

The dedication took place in June 1966, and it was a major deal. A dozen Army officers flew in by helicopter for the ceremony, and so did Big Lew Walt, the Marine lieutenant general who was the senior Marine in Vietnam.

It is important to remember here that the town of Duc Pho was an island in the middle of a red lake. The only safe way for Americans to drive on the few roads that ran across country outside of town might have been in an armored convoy. Walt arrived in a two-seat glass bubble Loach helicopter, and as he was landing, his pilot was shot in the belly. He was quickly hustled off to a hospital in another helicopter, and this evidence of enemy snipers on the loose was a bit of a damper on the celebrations for most Americans. But for Jim and his team, hey, this was just another day at the office.

The orphanage was filled up with kids right away, but the Ruff Puff operations were a steady drain. On one of his last operations, an American sergeant right behind him got his position overrun, and Jim really didn't think he would live through that day. He had been through some similar dicey moments before, and you learned how to control your body even when you were gorging on adrenaline. But the cold certainty you were going to die was never pleasant. Later on, you didn't even want to remember it.

Somehow he survived, and then it was time for him to go home. He went by the orphanage he had built one last time, and in her very gentle way, the mother superior thanked him. Then she asked him for one hundred dollars as a parting gift. Jim was a captain in the Army with a wife and two sons waiting for him, and he was only clearing about five hundred or so a month. But how could he refuse? He wrote the check, and it actually felt good to give this money to Sister Colette.

Back in the United States, Jim was stationed at Fort Lewis, Washington, where he stayed for two years. Then, in 1968, he went back to Vietnam, where he was promoted to major.

Jim's orders were to an American division, probably in an operations shop. But when he was processing in, there was a flag on his file, and he was sent to an office in another building.

When he was in Duc Pho on his first tour, in addition to the Ruff Puffs and the orphanage, he had also done a great deal of work with and for the Central Intelligence Agency. He had gotten to know a number of people in that way, and on a few occasions he had shown that in his spine there was some steel.

Arriving in that office in Saigon, he was surprised to find his old friend Ace Ellis from the CIA. Ace told him that there was a special CIA program being set up called Operation Phoenix. Bill Colby was running it, and he wanted ed someone he could trust to travel around the country as his personal agent. Ace had told Colby that Jim Kimsey was the right guy for this job. Colby said that he wanted Jim, but only if Jim wanted the job. Was he interested?

Jim could only smile.

"Do I want to be Colby's CIA agent traveling around the country, or do I want to be a staff officer somewhere inside the Great Green Killing Machine? What do you think, Ace?"

And so it was that Jim became Colby's agent. His job was going to meetings in Saigon and traveling to every one of the forty-four provinces in South Vietnam and overseeing the establishment or checking on the mechanics of Operation Phoenix in every one of them. It was a fun year, and it went by fast.

He sat in some meetings that were boring, and some others that were startling for the detachment from reality conveyed by the principals. In one such meeting in Saigon, he couldn't believe his ears when three generals and their staffs congratulated each other for their ideas for the Accelerated Pacification Program. After they had slapped each other on the back for a while, he finally raised his hand.

"Yes, Major?"

"Sir, in order to understand the Vietnamese kids, you've got to try to put yourself in their place. Its simply unrealistic to think they will choose a government backed up by the guns of big white foreigners who are taking over their countryside and killing their young men. Now if I was a fifteen-year-old Vietnamese boy, I would sure as hell be a Viet Cong. To those kids, the VC are like Robin Hood, and they are fighting against the Americans just like their fathers and grandfathers fought against the French. To them we're just the same, a bunch of big white guys who come in and push them around, while the VC spin that old dream of nationalism and freedom from foreign oppression. Those kids don't know what communism is, and they don't care. They just want to get rid of us, that's all."

There was an uncomfortable silence, then one of the two-star generals growled at him.

"What's the matter with you, Major, are you some kinda communist?"

That was the last time he volunteered anything at an Army meeting. He did get back to Duc Pho, and was delighted to see how great the kids looked after just a few years, and at how much the orphanage was flourishing. Those four nuns had taken a hundred undernourished, scruffy, lice-ridden kids with no hope and transformed them into healthy children with a real chance for happiness and fulfillment. That was a wonderful object lesson in life.

The orphanage had also become the economic epicenter of the countryside, with many small enterprises running, including an ice-making business that was selling ice to American units nearby. The mother superior asked him for one hundred dollars on each of his three visits, and even though it was still a lot of money to him, he was happy to give it to her.

He stood in front of the orphanage alone a few times and just drank it in. No, it wasn't the Taj Mahal, it wasn't the Eiffel Tower, it wasn't even, by American standards, a very modern building. But he had built it. It was funny, but no matter what else he might do in life, he knew that he had built this building, he had come up with the design in his head, made the first drawings, and then was the general contractor who put it up. And now it was there, alive, breathing, and providing safety and sustenance for kids— its purpose, after all, and a much-needed one. He was very happy to have been able to play even this one small role, an act to help a few unfortunate Vietnamese orphans. It had been a challenge, and meeting it had been rewarding and fun. But he didn't need anyone to know about it, for this was the sort of charitable act the performance of which is its only meaningful reward. He just loved to see this building overflowing with happy children, where before there had been nothing.

Before he got back to the States, Jim had decided to leave the Army. So he did, moving his wife and kids back to Washington, D.C., with no plan other than to somehow go into business. He had two thousand dollars saved from Vietnam, and he used to walk down the streets in Washington looking for a business or a building he could buy. This was 1970, when the real estate market was reeling, and finally he found a place. His plan was to put a bar and restaurant downstairs and lease the top floor to stockbrokers. He had borrowed to the hilt, and while the building was being renovated, someone suggested he put a ticker tape above the bar to attract the stockbrokers from upstairs. It may have been a joke, but Jim thought it was a great idea, so he did it, the first one in the country. *Time* and *Newsweek* picked up the story, and overnight, The Exchange, which they named the new place, was jammed.

That led to other bar and restaurant deals, and pretty soon, he owned six in Washington, D.C. This was a guy with no business school or even business experience before he came out of the Army. But he knew all about people under pressure and how they acted—remember the threat of the orphanage being given to the Buddhists—and he thrived.

A West Point classmate of his in San Francisco suggested he get involved in a small company that downloaded video games over the telephone, and he did. It was up and down for a while, and eventually turned into a real fiasco. Then in 1985, he took what he had learned, started something called Quantum Computer Services, and dressed it up to attract venture capital. He was fascinated with technology, and he jumped right in with both feet.

Their resources were originally limited to $10 million in venture capital, so they weren't able to hire a lot of people or set up a big operation. They had to ask computer manufacturers to promote their services, and they preferred to be seen as a little fish for a while. But the important thing was to watch how the river was flowing. IBM was King Kong for a long time, but then the river changed course on them. The same thing happened to Sears, which invested $1.5 billion in Prodigy and watched its investment limp along. But Quantum Computer Services kept skating along just under the radar.

A number of years later, Jim changed the corporate name to America Online, and he hired Steve Case as a twenty-four-year-old marketing intern. He believes one of his best moves ever was to work with Steve and then turn him loose.

As the founding chief executive officer of AOL and now its chairman emeritus, Jim has obviously made a lot of money. But he also remembers how low on the totem pole he started, and he has a few goals left in life. One of them was no doubt deeply affected by his involvement with the orphanage in Duc Pho, whose beautiful building, I am sorry to report, was confiscated by the state and turned into the local Communist party headquarters. The orphanage itself was moved, and the nuns stayed with the children. Under communist rule, however, their freedom of action has been greatly reduced.

An enduring belief of Jim Kimsey is that if the difficulties faced by poor children can be resolved early, it will help them avoid many age-old problems. For instance, he feels that all children should be able to get a good education so as to increase their future opportunities. The literacy level in the United States, believe it or not, is lower than that in Vietnam or in Ireland, two countries with far fewer resources at their disposal. Jim believes this is a function of cultural attitudes and the commitment in those countries to education, a commitment he wants to help instill here. But the present evidence in that area is quite glum. The money spent per student in Kimsey's home town of Washington, D.C., is the highest in the country, yet it has the lowest performance results.

And that's what keeps Jim busy these days. His latest challenge is to find ways in which technology can help resolve the enormous education problems we face in this country. That sounds like a daunting task. But then, anybody can do the easy things. And given his track record so far, he probably represents more promise of success in as yet unanticipated ways than anyone else who has tackled that immense nest of complex problems.

Thomas Eugene White

Thomas Eugene White had grown up in Detroit, the son of a bus driver, and West Point had been his youthful dream. It took him three tries to get in, though, and the only reason he finally made it was that the young men appointed by his congressman ahead of him had failed the stringent entrance exams.

As a new senior in the summer of 1966, Tom was greatly concerned about trying to rebuild spirit in his senior year. Cadet social opportunities at West Point have always been rather limited, and we did lead a rather Spartan life—class all day including Saturday morning, then mandatory sports and/or parades, supper, then everyone in his room studying and subject to surprise inspections by cadets on duty to catch infractions. On Sunday morning, all cadets were required to attend chapel, to which we marched in formation. Saturday afternoon after parade and inspection, Saturday evening until the midnight room checks, and Sunday afternoon after chapel until supper were periods allocated to cadet "free" time. But even then, few cadets were allowed to go off-post, and cadet possession of alcohol and "public displays of affection" with girls were both fiercely prohibited. When detected, both resulted in truly draconian punishment.

One of the few acceptable distractions for cadets was football. Through the first six decades of the twentieth century, Army had always had a nationally ranked football team, one that was often ranked in the national top ten at the end of the season. Three Army players won the Heisman Trophy, and occasionally Army went through the season without losing a single game. Football, in other words, was our Great Palliative, a psychic salve commonly used by cadets to ease the harshness of our daily lives, the pain and as-yet-undetectable gain that ran with us through the long endurance race known as a West Point education.

There was no question but that the previous football season had caught West Point in the spirit doldrums, with Army losing games it should have easily won and even the final game against Navy ending in a dismal 7–7 tie. After that game, both the Army and the Navy coaches were fired. Tom wasn't sure what he could do, but he wanted to find something to make the football season fun again.

The Tactical Department had not been impressed by Tom White's deportment, and like Ulysses S. Grant, and Dwight D. Eisenhower, he held the lowly rank of cadet sergeant when he graduated. But that mattered to him not at all. As part of his spirit-building effort, he had decided to become a cadet cheerleader, officially known as the Rabble Rousers, during his senior year. What that meant most of all for him was that it would get him permission to conduct pep rallies in the mess hall on Friday nights before football games.

All meals were mandatory then, and we ate in Washington Hall, a cavernous place with ceilings fully thirty feet high and enormous murals or stained-glass windows on the ends of three long wings that met almost in the form of a "T." The main entrance is an immense enclosed sallyport at the meeting point of these wings, and above that sallyport is a balcony, twenty or more feet above ground-floor level, where the officer in charge, or OC, sat, surveying all cadets below him, and ate his meal. The OC was an officer from the Tactical Department who was detailed for a twenty-four-hour tour of duty in charge of the discipline of the Corps of Cadets, and he would pull surprise inspections, walking into cadet rooms day or night to make sure everyone was where they were supposed to be and everything was under control. He was a man to be generally avoided by all cadets if possible. The wall corners are immense stone pillars supporting the roof, and hanging down some ten feet from that roof are huge, ornate wrought-iron chandeliers studded with lights. It is almost a gothic hall, one that seemed more appropriate for a king's castle in the twelfth century, maybe for the Knights of the Round Table, than for . . .

Tom's first idea for the skits involved him and another

cadet doing a takeoff on the Batman-and-Robin television show then popular. The heroes would be "A Man" and "B Squad." Tom would play A Man, the Batman role representing in vague conceptual manner the Army "First Team," the best West Point had to offer. He coerced and dragooned his roommate, Bill Gonser, into playing a supporting Robin role as B Squad, who represented the B squad on all West Point sports teams. The B squad was a sort of junior varsity, and their primary role was to give the A squad, the first team, an opponent against whom they could test themselves. They were basically the carp in every sport on whom the game fish warmed up, a bunch of guys who let themselves get beat up so that the first team would compete better on weekends against other colleges, and they were very average cadets, the much-beloved heart of the Corps.

For the first such skit, Tom was able to get approval to have an artillery piece rolled inside the wide, sallyportlike main entrance for the skit. But what he didn't tell anyone, including the other Rabble Rousers, who had gotten approval for the skit from the commandant's office, was that he had also gotten one of the blank shells filled just with powder. These were fired by the reveille cannon every morning on Trophy Point at 5:50, a predawn *"Boom!"* that reverberated all across the enormous military post at West Point.

When the meal was well underway and the moment for the skit was approaching, Tom had the wide doors opened and the cannon was wheeled in. No big deal, everyone thought, an artillery piece, we see those things all the time. Wonder what they will do with it?

When all were seated, Tom went over to the open breech of the gun, pulled the blank shell out of a laundry bag and slipped it into the breech, then slammed it shut and pulled the lanyard.

BOOM!

The deafening noise stunned everyone as flame shot out the muzzle and white smoke and hot cordite billowed through the mess hall. Waiters dropped trays laden with food, windows were shattered and blown from their wrought-iron casings, and cadets standing nearby were literally bowled over by the concussion. There was an instant of stark silence as Tom stood there reeling, physically stunned and deafened, a loud ringing noise inside his head paralyzing him.

But then at the far ends of the three wings of the mess hall, cadets stood up waving their napkins in the air and started cheering. Within seconds, all the cadets in the mess hall were standing on their chairs and yelling like banshees. Tom was still in shock, but warmth gradually washed over him, and an inextinguishable grin split his face.

Tom was called into the commandant's office the next day, chewed out for his thoughtless behavior, and strictly forbidden to try anything like that again. He would be allowed to continue to put on skits, but each would have to receive the formal approval from the commandant's office every Friday afternoon before supper formation. And he was warned not to try going beyond what was approved.

Tom was meek and apologetic to the officers, because he wanted to be allowed to continue to put on skits. But when he left he remained unrepentant, for he knew he had struck a chord with the cadets.

Thereafter, a formal description of the upcoming skit was delivered to the commandant's office sometime Friday afternoon, and it always came back to him before supper formation with the stamp of approval. The actual skit they performed that night, of course, always varied in some way from what had been approved. But because the skits quickly became an enormous boost to spirit and morale, no one ever challenged him on that.

The skits were put on right under the OC's balcony, in a large open area in front of the entrance and at the meeting point of each of the wings, so that all cadets, no matter where seated, could see them. A Man and B Squad both wore black Zorro masks and capes and black wrestling tights, and each had a large yellow "A" or "B" painted in the center of his black wrestling team jersey.

The villain in these skits would represent the football opponent on the next day, such as a ten-foot ball of wastepaper painted orange and rolled around to represent the Syracuse Orangemen, or a guy whose shoulders carried a two-foot red cylinder topped with a cardboard bird's head and waving ten-foot-long cardboard-and-paper wings from each arm as the Boston College Eagle, intentionally made to look more like a buzzard. For the University of Pittsburgh, the villain was "H.A." for "Hairy Armpit," and A Man and B Squad rolled in a giant papier-mâché can of Right Guard and chased him around the mess hall with it. The villain would usually exchange challenges of some sort with A Man and B Squad, then the characters would run around the mess hall, and at the end, A Man and B Squad would always emerge victorious.

To add a little mystery to the skits, they started changing the way in which A Man would enter the mess hall. The first time, he simply came racing in the main entrance, and in later skits, he would come in the large doors on either wing. Eventually, he would even come racing in from the kitchen, where cadets normally never set foot. But before the Navy game, the last and biggest game on Army's schedule every year, Tom wanted to do something different.

Finally, he decided he would come in on an aerial "slide-for-life" contraption, using a rope suspended from the OC's balcony and connected to one of the huge pillars several hundred feet away. They rigged up a heavy cargo hawser from the balcony and secured it to one of the pillars about ten feet above the floor, so that it took a hard downslope from the OC balcony. Then they suspended the small, wheeled trapeze from it. All A Man had to do was slip over the edge of the balcony, grab the bar of the trapeze below the rope, and slide for life high above the cadets eating at their mess-hall tables.

When it was time for the skit at the end of supper that night, A Man suddenly appeared on the OC balcony. He posed briefly amid applause, then reached over the edge of the balcony, grabbed the triangle with both hands, and swung over the side. It was the ride of his life.

The cadets who fixed the rope thought they had stretched it pretty tight, but they had never tested it. Tom was over twenty feet above the ground floor when he left the balcony. But as his legs followed his shoulders and torso over the side, they swung down in a whiplike arc below the rope, the wheels on the trapeze handle racing madly. He cringed in terror as he felt his weight pull the rope down, and he sank sharply, a human missile flashing through space. He thought at first he might hit the tables below as he felt his body swing down and forward hard. Although his descent stopped well above the tables, he was going much faster than he had dreamed possible, a giant human pendulum ten feet long hurtling across the mess hall as he swung. His cape spread out wide behind him on each downswing, and then enveloped him as his body swung back below the rope and back up, then cyclically down again. As the distance from his launch pad grew, his speed increased, and tables below cleared as cadets cringed or hustled out from below him.

He realized in a flash that the one cadet who had agreed to stop him at the bottom of the rope before he hit the pillar would not be able to arrest the enormous momentum he was building up, and he cringed wide-eyed as the massive marble column raced toward him. And when he got to the end of the line, no cadet was there to cushion the blow, only cold, hard stone.

He slammed into the pillar like Wiley Coyote, the impact knocking his breath out in an audible *whoof!* He fell from the rope to the floor, stunned and deafened, with unexpected stars ringing through his head.

But the Corps of Cadets loved it! A Man was helped to his feet, and as he brushed dust from his chest, the cadets around him started clapping and cheering. He quickly recovered his senses, now buoyed as whoops and wild applause suddenly filled the mess hall. As he gingerly started to trot back between tables toward the OC balcony, the cheers became deafening, and then cadets all around him were standing up and roaring. Now *this*, he thought, was *exactly* what he had wanted to call back from the dead. The pains he had felt in his legs and side after he hit the pillar magically disappeared.

The Navy game was the next afternoon, and for half-time, Tom White had come up with a wild skit for the Rabble Rousers. They got one of their number all dressed up in a Navy cheerleader costume, and he came down onto the field from under the stands on the Navy side just before the first half ended. When the final whistle was blown and the teams had gone to their locker rooms, several Rabble

Rousers went running out to midfield and went through a ritualistic sort of taunting of the Navy side. At this point, the still-unrecognized Rabble Rouser in disguise on the Navy side went running out to challenge the Army taunters, yelling wildly at them and waving his arms. Some of the Navy cheerleaders saw through this right away as an Army prank, but others, and virtually all of the crowd, were surprised, thinking that he was a Navy cheerleader who had apparently gone berserk! The Rabble Rousers threw him on the ground at midfield, where most of his body was hidden from the crowd by those of the Rabble Rousers. They went through the motions of beating him, then a great spray of red liquid came gushing up into the air from his chest. The crowd on both sides of the field was stunned, not sure they could believe what they were seeing: Were the Rabble Rousers really *killing* a Navy cheerleader, right here in the middle of the field?

Then an Army Military Police sedan raced out to midfield and the trunk popped open. The Rabble Rousers lifted the body of the "Navy cheerleader" from the ground, with what looked like red blood still spraying out from his chest. They threw him into the trunk of the MP sedan, slammed it shut, and it sped from the field. Several real Navy cheerleaders had even started out on the field, afraid that something had gone terribly wrong and one of their own was being killed before their very eyes in some tragic mixup. But as the sedan sped from the field, they realized that they had been had, and they turned sheepishly back to their own side.

Army beat Navy that day, capping a triumphant Army season with a record of eight victories and only two defeats. But those two Army losses came to perennial powers Notre

Dame and Tennessee, and Tom White's efforts to revive spirit at West Point had known undreamed-of success.

In the summer of 1968, Lieutenant Colonel John McEnery commanded the 3rd Squadron of the 11th Armored Cavalry Regiment in Vietnam. They were then operating in the III Corps area, about fifty miles north of Saigon, in relatively open country. His largest armored vehicles were M-48 tanks, each armed with a 90-mm main gun and two machine guns. The treads of these forty-ton steel monsters made almost all terrain passable, and they easily smashed through the thickest jungle, knocking over thick trees like a car driving through a cane field. The only real danger they faced was getting mired in a deep stretch of mud.

In June, McEnery had a sudden requirement to attach one five-tank platoon to a cavalry troop of more lightly armed and armored tracked fighting vehicles and send them from position A to an operation at location B some miles away. While there were no paved roads for this movement, there were dirt roads, which should help them with navigation. The area between A and B was mixed jungle, so it didn't look as if there would be any problem with navigation, and the cav troop commander, Captain Smith, was very good with a map and a compass. But they were in the middle of rainy season, which meant daily rain and cloudy skies. McEnery didn't care so much about the rain except that it made the ground quite soft, and he was concerned about some of his tanks getting stuck as they moved, out in the middle of nowhere.

The tank platoon leader was Lieutenant Tom White and the Ranger tab on his shoulder indicated that he had been through a grueling nine weeks in which map reading and compass use were necessarily mastered by the students. When Lieutenant White moved out with Captain Smith, everything went well until the tanks began to get stuck in a swampy area. They could get through the area, but it took time, and they often had to have one tank pull another through a bad part. The cav troop, with much lighter vehicles, had blown right through this, and Captain Smith was concerned that they would arrive too late for the operation. After a while, he saw that it would take the tanks another hour or more, so he told White to follow when he got all his tanks out of the muck: "Just keep heading east on this trail for a coupla clicks, then turn right and head south on the main dirt road, you'll see, just follow our tracks."

And that's what White and his tanks did. But it seemed like every few hundred yards there would be a trail of some sort going off to the right, and most of these had tracks from armored vehicles. How was he supposed to know where to turn?

Unfortunately for Lieutenant White, one of those "trails" was the road where he was supposed to turn. Instead, he kept going straight until he came to a main dirt road with lots of tread tracks, and he turned his platoon of tanks south on it. But he had come several kilometers too far, and the farther he moved south, the farther he moved from possible arrival at B. He finally stopped when he got to a river that looked as if it was a quarter-mile wide, and he knew that wasn't right. Tom did a detailed map check with his platoon sergeant and decided he had missed the correct turnoff south, so he began to backtrack. But after only a few kilometers, one of his tanks ran out of gas. He was down on the ground conferring with his platoon sergeant when Colonel McEnery's helicopter arrived.

Lieutenant White was embarrassed, but he and his tanks

were safe, and McEnery was greatly relieved. After going through a brief map drill with White, McEnery had fuel brought to their location. It was too late for White's platoon to play a role in the operation at B, so McEnery told him to go back to A. But before he left, he told White that he was only going to give his tanks enough fuel to get back to A, just so he wouldn't have to take the chance of having White end up somewhere in Cambodia.

This was a typical stunt for a young lieutenant, but in combat, the squadron commander had every right to relieve Lieutenant White of command right on the spot. Had McEnery been a lesser man, he might have done just that. But he knew this was a very important lesson for White, and he also knew that sometimes it is hard to learn unless and until you fail. This was a lesson Tom White would never forget.

Tom White quickly became a very good tank platoon leader. The U.S. troops received intelligence information on possible enemy locations every day from higher headquarters, much of it gleaned from intercepted radio conversations between communist forces. But the intelligence leads also could be provided by other sensory devices, such as "people sniffers," sophisticated equipment that hung from helicopters passing slowly over heavy jungle canopies and able to detect the presence of multiple points of uric acid on the ground below.

This was usually reported to American units on the ground as a possible enemy force location, for the multiple uric acid points were often an indication that a number of men were pissing on the ground, a common need for members of a military force moving through the jungle. Sometimes these people sniffers were right and American troops were able to surprise large Viet Cong or North

Vietnamese Army formations. Sometimes it was just a troop of monkeys. And still other times, they never knew, because by the time they got there, the uric acid producers had moved on.

But some of their best intelligence came from recently captured prisoners of war, or from turncoats, or from local residents who turned informer because of their own hidden agendas. This sort of human intelligence usually resulted in a higher number of contacts with enemy forces. And contacts were the key opening to the dance of death with their enemy.

The motto of the 11th ACR in Vietnam was "Find the Bastards, then Pile On!" The 11th ACR was made up of three squadrons of tanks and armored fighting vehicles, and their success in finding the enemy and piling on was often a function of the performance of the regiment's most mobile strike force and primary reconnaissance agent, its Air Cavalry troop.

Larger than a normal troop, the Air Cav troop consisted of twenty-six helicopters and some three hundred personnel. An unusually large unit for a troop or company designation, Air Cav troops were normally commanded by a major rather than a captain. In the spring of 1969, the Air Cav troop of the 11th ACR was commanded by Major John Bahnsen, known to his friends by his high-school nickname of "Doc."

The Air Cav troop consisted of three main components. First was a platoon of nine scout helicopters, the small two-seat OH-6 Loaches, each with a distinctive transparent plastic bubble over the crew compartment. These were known as "White Birds," and their primary mission was to find the enemy on the ground. They often did this just by "trolling"—flying low and slow over an area where enemy presence was suspected, hoping to draw fire from the ground. When trolling, of course, the White Bird was usually flying only one hundred feet or so above the ground, and the pilot always had to hope that the guy on the ground didn't get off a lucky shot. As an added precaution enabling flight crews to better hear gunfire, one of Doc's first acts when he took over was to instruct that all doors be removed from all helicopters.

Once they drew fire, they normally would drop smoke. They made this easier by removing the cotter pin from a smoke grenade and placing it inside a can of slightly larger size. This can, in turn, stood upright by the pilot's foot, specially wired to the floor, and he had only to hit it with a twist of his foot to knock it over and dump its contents out the door. As it flipped over and down, the smoke grenade then fell free and blossomed. It was a quick, convenient way to mark a spot on the ground from a slow-flying White Bird.

The second element of the Air Cav troop was made up of nine AH-1G Cobra gunships known as "Red Birds." One Red Bird was almost always aloft with each White Bird, forming a "Pink Team" (Red plus White). The Red Birds were each armed with a 7.62-mm minigun mounted inside the nose. This was a machine gun with a rotating barrel based on the Gatling gun principle that could fire six thousand rounds per minute. Every fifth round was a red tracer, but the rate of fire was so fast that a simple burst looked like a red probe coming out of the Cobra nose and pulverizing whatever it touched.

The Cobra also fired 2.75-inch rockets slung in rocket pods of sixteen each, normally one pod on each side. These were usually fired in pairs, and their impact point would be "walked" up into the desired target, although it was possible to fire more at once, up to the entire sixteen in each pod. These pods were about half the circumference of a commonplace fifty-five-gallon barrel, although they were just as long. The warheads on these rockets could be high explosive, which burst into jagged chunks of shrapnel, or flechettes, tiny steel arrows that were devastating against troops in the open.

The third element of the Air Cav troop was the "aero rifle platoon," which was basically an infantry platoon made up of about thirty-five infantrymen. The unit was called the "ARP," the men in it were called "ARPs," and the six lift ships, UH-1D Hueys, used to carry them into battle, were the "Blue Birds." There were two more Hueys in the Air Cav troop used as C&C (command and control) ships by the commander, making the total twenty-six helicopters. And most of the three hundred men in the Air Cav troop played crucially important roles in maintaining and repairing these workhorses.

When a White Bird drew fire and had kicked smoke, its Red Bird partner flying in wide circles up at one thousand or fifteen hundred feet was normally called down to chew up the adjoining real estate with minigun or rockets or both. If enemy presence such as a bunker complex was then seen or suspected, the next step was usually to call in artillery and see if it could develop things further.

Ordinarily, artillery and air support could not be used together, and the Air Force had very strict rules in Vietnam about stopping all friendly artillery fire before their fighter-bombers went to work in a given area. But with the helicopters of an Air Cav troop, it was an entirely different situation. The White Birds usually called in and adjusted the artillery fire, and they couldn't do that without keeping the target area in sight. But they knew the gun-to-target line, so they just stayed five hundred meters or so off to one side of that and watched developments on the ground. If they saw enemy soldiers, or indications of a bunker complex, they would report that to their troop commander, Major Bahnsen.

Usually already aloft in one of his ships, he would respond to these calls by coming over to take his own look. If he agreed that the target on the ground looked like potential enemy contact, he would first call the ARPs and alert them to be ready for an insertion. Next, he called the regimental operations officer, or S-3, and told him the same thing. The regimental commander at the time was Colonel George S. Patton, son of "Old Blood and Guts," and a man eager to make enemy contact as much and as often as possible. Whenever his S-3 got such a message, Colonel Patton soon knew of it. An acetate-covered map of their area of operations was kept updated in the S-3 shop at all times, and as soon as the potential contact was sent in, the S-3 determined which armored troop from the three squadrons on the ground was closest. That troop was immediately alerted to be ready to "pile on."

When Major Bahnsen had determined there was a contact to be made on the ground, he called for his ARPs. While they saddled up and loaded into their Blue Birds, six to seven men per ship, Bahnsen found a relatively clear area near the proposed contact point and put artillery fire on it to clear a helicopter landing zone. By the time this LZ had been prepared, the Blue Birds were on their way. After landing, the ARP spread out, then followed directions from the air and approached the suspected contact point, a platoon of riflemen on an aggressive recon run.

At this point, the ARP leader, a lieutenant, became all-important to American actions. As he was the only cav commander on the ground and the one with the closest and best view of the situation, Bahnsen depended absolutely on his judgment for their next move.

If it had been a moving infantry unit that fired on the White Bird, for instance, he would search the area for a while, with his focus on uncovering a classic VC or NVA bunker complex. These were bunkers that protruded only a foot or so above ground level. They were usually made of sandbags with timber reinforcement, and they always had thick overhead cover, with firing apertures just above the ground. They were heavily camouflaged and easy to miss if you didn't know what to look for. But when such a complex was discovered, it was invariably found to be simply laid out, but masterful in its interlocking fields of fire, lethal in its killing zones.

The armored units in the 11th ACR were normally moving around during the day, often following up intelligence leads and trying to develop contact themselves. But they had neither the vision nor the mobility that were added by the helicopters in the Air Cav troop. And for a group of soldiers on the ground trying to avoid contact in the jungle with a unit of enemy tracked and armored vehicles, the noise made by their engines, let alone by the trees they knock down as they move, give plenty of warning of their proximity long before they come within fighting distance. That makes Colonel Patton's statement that 80 percent of the 11th ACR's contacts with the enemy were initiated by his Air Cav troop somewhat more understandable. And that's why he loved the ARPs.

But when the ARP was in contact and called for reinforcements, the call went through Bahnsen, who relayed it to the regimental S-3. The nearest armored troop, alerted earlier, was then directed by Regiment to move in and "pile on." Normally, they tried not to get the ARP into contact unless reinforcement could reach them quickly, usually within an hour. And the reinforcement consisted, most of the time, of what was called a "cross-attached troop" of tanks and armored cavalry assault vehicles armed only with machine guns and known by their acronym of ACAVs moving through the jungle in a box formation.

This box would be led by a platoon of five M-48 tanks moving side by side. These monsters were almost unstoppable, and as they busted through the jungle, even huge trees that blocked their paths went down quickly. But they couldn't move through thick jungle fast, and even moving as little as five kilometers could take as much as an hour or more.

The sides and back of this armored box would consist of a line of six or eight ACAVs, with the troop commander moving in the center of this box in his ACAV. The five tanks on one side of the box led the way, firing their main guns as they moved forward, while the lighter weapons of the ACAVs covered the flanks and rear. The ACAV was really just an old M-113 armored personnel carrier that had been jazzed up a bit and fitted with new radios and machine guns.

As the cross-attached troop got moving, Bahnsen would tell the ARP leader on the ground how long it would be until they arrived, with updates starting maybe at "they are two clicks (kilometers) away," "one click," "a half click," "two hundred meters," "one hundred meters," all the way down to "they are on your left rear and you should see them now." And next was the tricky part, when the ARPs had to break contact and slip back between the five tanks leading the formation.

This was a dangerous time for the ARPs, because they had to leave whatever cover they had found and get back behind the protection of the tanks. Since they couldn't risk turning their backs on the enemy and they couldn't walk backward as fast as they might have run forward, this could be a sweaty-pits moment. But if the contact was heavy, the ARPs would almost certainly have artillery fire going in, and even when the artillery fire was lifted, gunships could still be making runs across the front of the tanks and at least keeping enemy heads down.

Once the ARPs were behind the tanks, the box formation moved forward over enemy ground. If any enemy soldiers tried to slip out the sides, White Birds on station there would call down their Red Birds to rip into them. As they moved forward, the ACAVs and Sheridan light tanks would hose down the areas on either side of the enemy position with heavy automatic weapons fire. The M-48 tanks used their main guns and machine guns to destroy any enemy resistance to their front, and if it was a bunker complex, their weight easily crushed the structures and anything still inside.

This was not the "Slaughter of the Unarmed Innocents," however. Communist forces in Vietnam used AK-47 assault rifles and RPD machine guns against American infantry, and many say that, at the infantry level, American infantry forces armed with M-16 rifles and much-slower-firing M-60 machine guns were significantly outgunned here. As far as the tanks and other armored vehicles were concerned, the communists had an enormous supply of rocket-propelled grenades, or RPGs. These light, shoulder-fired weapons could pierce any American armored vehicle in Vietnam. The great danger with M-48s if this happened turned on the fact that their engines burned gasoline rather than diesel fuel. If an RPG went through the armor of an M-48 and somehow ignited the gasoline, all crew members had to get out and away quickly. In fact, in one operation where Bahnsen tried to "pile on" with a cross-attached troop led by five tanks, one of them fell into a crater and turned on its side, while three of the four others were pierced by RPGs and burst into flames. So despite the fact that the U.S. Army brought heavy armor into play, this was still that most unpredictable of events, a war, and there were always plenty of nightmares available for both sides.

Tom White served five months on line, first as a tank platoon leader, then as an ACAV platoon leader. Ordinarily, he would have been transferred to some sort of desk job in the rear after six months on line. But then the ARP leader was wounded, and Major Bahnsen, who had watched White in action, approached him and asked if he would take the job. White never even hesitated.

After he took over, White made a major effort to restore esprit and elitism to the ARP, and already a master salesman, he was wildly successful. He put the word out in the regiment that the ARPs would soon gain renown throughout America as the best crack troops in the U.S. Army, or something like that, that he wanted only the toughest, best soldiers to volunteer for the ARP, that not all applicants would be accepted, and that he would be conducting interviews at such and such a time in such and such a place.

When the moment arrived, he was stunned to see a long line waiting for him. And for a while, the whole "elite volunteers" thing seemed to be working. But as the fighting went on, the ARPs began to take a lot of casualties, and "elitism" became a harder sell. After he took over the ARP, White led it for ninety days, and Bahnsen estimates that he was in contact with the enemy, meaning the ARP was exchanging gunfire with communist soldiers, for sixty of those days. White was awarded a Silver Star and other medals for his heroism, but medals say less than a company commander. And "Doc" Bahnsen said that White was the best combat platoon leader he ever saw during two years of combat duty in Vietnam: "Cool, fearless, absolutely reliable under fire, I could always count on him to give me an accurate picture of the situation on the ground. He led from the front, and he was a fearless combat platoon leader. I saw a lot of really superb combat platoon leaders, and Tom White was clearly the best of all of them—a cut above."

After ninety days commanding the ARP, Tom White was finally pulled back to work on the Air Cav troop staff for his last two months. And then he went home. He would stay on active duty in the Army until he was promoted to brigadier general, more than twenty years later. But then, after ten years in the private sector, he came back home to his first love, the Army: in 2001, Thomas Eugene White was sworn in to office as President Bush's secretary of the Army.

Gene Sullivan

Gene Sullivan was the second of three sons of a policeman in St. Louis, Missouri. He grew up in an Irish Catholic neighborhood that voted heavily Democratic, and after high school, he studied engineering at a nearby small college. But during his first year there, he competed for an appointment to West Point from his congresswoman. When he won it, he was delighted.

Sworn in as a cadet in 1960, Gene was average: In the top third of the class academically, he did well in some courses, not so well in others. But athletics were all-important in that era, and Gene had decided that he would win a varsity letter in some sport while he was a cadet. Never a great athlete in high school, he targeted lacrosse, a highly regional eastern sport that few other cadets had ever played before coming to West Point.

For the plebe athletic teams, formal testing took place in the first week of Beast Barracks. Gene was ready, and when lacrosse tryouts were announced, he showed up and just about knocked himself out. But he didn't make the cut.

Tryouts were repeated at the end of August. Same resolve, same result.

Disheartened, he stayed busy as the rest of the Corps of Cadets returned to West Point and classes began after Labor Day. A week later, the final tryout for the plebe lacrosse team took place, and once again, Gene was there, racing madly around the field and trying to impress the coaches. But once again, he didn't make the cut.

In late September, his hopes were waning, so he decided on a bold stroke: He called the head varsity lacrosse coach, Ace Adams, at his home one night and asked for permission to try out one more time. He told him that he had gained five more pounds since his last cut, and because he was now somewhat heavier, perhaps this time the coach would see potential that he might have missed in earlier tryouts.

Needless to say, the coach was astounded.

"Sullivan, report to practice tomorrow, I have to see what you look like."

Gene showed up, and although he was brand-new to the sport and probably wasn't very good, he seems to have impressed Coach Adams with his enthusiasm and determination. Adams put Gene on the off-season plebe team for the fall.

Throughout the winter, Gene worked on his stick work in the squash courts, and by spring practice, he had gotten so good that he won a position as a starting midfielder on the plebe team. In his second year, he made the varsity team. He won a gold Navy Star on his varsity letter in his junior year when the Army team upset Navy, the national champion that year. His persistence in making the West Point plebe and varsity lacrosse teams exemplify the personal motto he had adopted from Hannibal: "I will find a way, or make one."

After graduation, Gene went through Airborne and Ranger schools, and then, in 1964, at the height of the Cold War but before U.S. troops had been committed to Vietnam, he was assigned to be a tank platoon leader with the 3rd Armored Division in Kirchgoens, Germany. Gene spent a lot of time training in the field, but he also had a certain amount of free time, and he had left no romantic connections back in the States. So one weekend, he drove up to Denmark, pursuing Lis Johansen, a Danish model he had met in Heidelberg.

He went to her home and found that her family was at a summer beach resort nearby. With no real directions or address beyond the name of the town, Gene drove around the resort for several hours until, out of the blue, he saw her on the street. After dating her for a year, they were married, and then he was assigned as a Ranger instructor at Fort Benning, Georgia. In 1968, he received his orders to Vietnam.

He served first with the 2nd Squadron, 1st Armored Cavalry Regiment. That cav squadron was attached to the 4th Infantry Division up in the Central Highlands, and it operated primarily out of Firebase Blackhawk, near the Mang Yang Pass and about halfway between An Khe and Pleiku. That was the area where the French "Groupe Mobiliere 100" was slaughtered in the early 1950s, and the rusted-out carcasses of their armored vehicles were still there.

Gene was an assistant S-3, or operations officer, and his unit's mission consisted primarily of running road-clearing operations. Every morning, they would open up sections of the highway between An Khe and Pleiku. It was important that they take certain specific steps in doing this that involved coordination of artillery fire, helicopter missions, and armored vehicle movement. But after a while, it was not terribly exciting. It was, in an anonymous assessment of Vietnam that can be slipped in almost anywhere, "sheer boredom interspersed with moments of stark terror."

One particular incident occurred during a road-clearing operation that was a rare experience for any soldier in any war—a face-to-face meeting with an enemy soldier on the battlefield without combat. The incident happened just after daybreak in the Highlands near Pleiku. Gene was the ranking officer in a Huey helicopter conducting a road-clearing reconnaissance of Highway 19 in the Central Highlands. The chopper was flying at top speed at treetop level—a favored tactic to evade enemy ground fire. As the Huey crested a ridge overlooking a small village sitting astride the highway, the right door gunner spotted a figure in a rice paddy next to the village wearing a khaki shirt and trousers—the typical uniform of a North Vietnamese soldier. The door gunner requested permission to open fire with his M-60 machine gun. The first target of the day. Gene shouted over the intercom of the chopper,

"Negative to fire. I see no weapon. Pilot, circle back for another look."

On the second pass of the village, Gene could not see any visible weapon on the khaki-uniformed man. The suspected NVA soldier was stopped dead in his tracks, with his arms raised, about halfway across the paddy and about one hundred meters from the safety of the thick vegetation of the jungle bordering the rice paddy.

The situation was fast-moving. Gene ordered the chopper to land in order to check out what they had discovered.

As the Huey put down, Gene jumped out, cursing his decision to go "light" that morning—he had left his M-16 and web gear with hand grenades back at the firebase. All he had was his .45-caliber pistol and two extra clips—twenty-one rounds total.

When Gene exited the chopper, it immediately took off. (A chopper on the ground this close to the village or the jungle was a sitting duck for any enemy machine gun or rocket-propelled grenade.) Gene approached the suspect cautiously. The Huey began a wide circling of the paddy two hundred meters off the ground, using its left M-60 door gun to give protective covering fire if necessary.

The constant roar of the circling chopper made Gene shout at the frightened Vietnamese as he came near, *"Do you speak English?"*

The Vietnamese man let loose a torrent of Vietnamese words. Gene knew immediately that communication would be difficult. He tried the few French words he knew, but there was no luck there either. Gene patted him down and searched his pockets. Nothing. No weapon, no papers, no maps, nothing to indicate whether he was a soldier or not. He was in his late twenties, Gene's age. Both men realized, of course, that there were normally no young able-bodied men in a village like this, for they had all been drafted into the Viet Cong or into the South Vietnamese Army. Then there were the rubber tire tread sandals and the khaki clothes—definite identifiers of a regular NVA trooper.

Gene thought out his options. The man was probably a low-level soldier who was visiting his wife or family in the village, had overslept, and was making his way back to his unit in the jungle. Gene reasoned that if he brought the young man back to the firebase, it would almost certainly be a death warrant for this man. There would be an immediate turnover to the local South Vietnamese Army unit, where he would be tortured and killed, or less likely sold back to his family for a hefty bribe.

Gene knew he had to make a decision quickly. Even though the Huey was moving, it remained very vulnerable in its predictable circular pattern close to the ground. Moreover, Gene was alone and underarmed on the ground. There was little time.

Gene looked the Vietnamese man in the eyes. He saw the fear, and he suddenly realized that the man's life depended on his next move. His voice was stern: "You Viet Cong?"

The Vietnamese man screamed his response:

"Me no Viet Cong !"

Then Gene knew what he would do. He shouted as if making a legal proclamation, "You no VC!"

Gene held up his arm and signaled the chopper to land. At the same time, he pointed to the Vietnamese man to go. The VC suspect walked quickly, with his arms still up, to the tree line, and then he was gone.

The Huey broke out of the holding pattern, made a wide loop over the village, and flared in for a landing. Gene got on board, put his crew helmet on, and hooked up to the intercom, announcing his verdict to the crew as the Huey quickly lifted off: "Let's go. He was OK. No problem."

After six months with a combat unit, Gene was transferred to a rear-area staff position. The job was as the aide to General Abrams's science advisor, Doctor Niels Wikner, a civilian scientist who was known as the "Doctor Strangelove" of Vietnam. He was a brilliant man, a civilian who filled a three-star general equivalent slot, and he oversaw the introduction of all the new scientific equipment and weapons systems, such as the surveillance devices used on the Ho Chi Minh Trail.

For Gene, the biggest change associated with this new job was not its relative security. Far more important was the sudden luxurious feel of working in a mud-free, air-conditioned office on the first floor of MACV headquarters. He just couldn't believe the joy of air-conditioning and flush toilets. He liked it so much that he decided to live there, right in his office.

When he first arrived from the Central Highlands, he had brought all his field gear with him, including his sleeping bag and rubber air mattress, known commonly in the field in Vietnam as one's "rubber lady." He kept everything—helmet, weapon, rucksack, canteens, grenades, all that crap—under his desk. And when everyone left the office each night, he just pushed two desks together, blew up his rubber lady, and slept in his sleeping bag on top of the desks. Early next morning, he went down the hall, shaved and showered, went to the snack bar for breakfast, rearranged his sleeping area, and was always the first one in the office. It was a great life, living down the hall from the snack bar in air-conditioned splendor. Besides, the added benefit was that he had the second floor of MACV headquarters as overhead mortar protection. He was in hog heaven!

After about a month, unfortunately, his cover got blown when a combat-wise colonel on the staff asked him, since he was the last one at the office each night and the first one there in the morning, where he lived. When Gene told him, he didn't think it was funny, let alone appropriate, for an officer to be living in the office. He ordered him to get a BOQ (Bachelor Officers' Quarters) room in Saigon, where he then slept each night, in an un-air-conditioned room at the Missouri BOQ.

But living in Saigon and sleeping in a bed between sheets with a shower and a flush toilet right down the hall, he felt a little bit useless in the war, so he volunteered to serve as a door gunner at night with an attack helicopter unit. He went on a number of missions patrolling the Saigon River during curfew hours, looking for enemy resupply sampans. It was scary work, but it was also a rush. Sitting behind that M-60 machine gun mounted in the open side of the helicopter, hammering enemy sampans on the dark river below while hoping desperately that he wouldn't get hit by their return fire—it was a strange feeling, it let him feel as if he were once again actually involved in fighting the war. And truth be told, it was a good feeling. But after he came home, there weren't very many people he could tell about that who would understand.

Before returning from Vietnam, Gene had decided to go to law school. As a member of the Cadet Honor Committee back at West Point, he had developed a passion for seeing that justice was done when someone was accused of an honor violation. After graduation, his life experiences had expanded dramatically, of course, and he began to realize how important it was for a person to know his or her individual rights so that no one could take advantage of him. This realization led him to apply to the judge advocate general "excess leave for law school" program, and to apply to Georgetown law school at the same time. The JAG turned him down, but Georgetown accepted him, so once he had gotten home safely, he resigned his active duty commission, although he stayed in the reserves. But within days of returning from Vietnam, he began his first year of law school.

He did very well at Georgetown, and because his grades

during his first year were in the top 5 percent of his class, he was an editor of the law review. During his senior year, he competed for a one-year clerkship with a federal judge in St. Louis, which he won. After that, he returned to Washington, D.C., where he joined the law firm of Patton, Boggs LLP in 1972. But he hadn't been practicing long when he got a call from Jerry Murphy, a prosecutor he had met the previous year in St. Louis.

Jerry asked him if he was interested in joining the Nixon defense team. Gene could hardly believe his ears. Although he had been raised in a working-class Democratic family, this was the lawyer's dream come true—he would be one of a small team of lawyers working against the impeachment of the president, and there would be legions of lawyers opposing him.

There were plenty of smart young lawyers in this country at that time. But Jerry Murphy got him an interview with Jim St. Clair, who had just been hired by Nixon as his primary criminal defense lawyer. Jim, one of the top criminal attorneys in the country, had come down from Boston, and he was looking for ten young lawyers to help him. Two days after St. Clair met Gene, he hired him.

The political litmus test Gene knew was coming did worry him a bit. Patton, Boggs was well known as a heavily Democratic law firm, although they were smart enough to employ a smattering of well-connected Republicans. But Jim St. Clair was looking for professionals, and he never even asked Gene about his personal politics. The interesting byproduct of that is that anyone who worked in the Nixon White House was seen thereafter by the public as a strong Republican for life, which happened to be accurate in Gene's case.

But as soon as he signed in, Gene felt as if he had

entered a whirlwind, and working on the president's legal defense team really did put him right at the center of the Watergate storm. And being a White House attorney while Congress is attempting to impeach the president is a unique experience. First of all, the defense team was very small—Nixon only had ten defense lawyers most of the time. And the team was opposed by three separate governmental prosecution groups of lawyers. The Watergate prosecutor, Leon Jaworski, had over one hundred prosecutors working for him. John Dorr, the Democratic counsel to the House Judiciary Committee, had almost a hundred staff attorneys under his control, including Hillary Rodham (later Hillary Clinton). And the Senate Watergate Committee had another thirty-odd attorneys. This was quite an attack force, and the Nixon team worked twelve-hour-plus days seven days a week, with numerous overnighters. Gene hardly got to see his family while he was in the White House, but it was an invaluable legal experience. Most assignments for the next day were given out in the evening, after the end-of-the-working-day strategy meeting among Nixon, Haig, Buzhardt, and St. Clair. And Buzhardt and Haig, of course, were, like Gene, West Point graduates.

At these Watergate strategy meetings, Nixon and his three key players would plan the actions of the defense team for the following day. For instance, if, during the day, the House Judiciary Committee had requested documents from the White House, the president and his advisors would discuss their response and then decide on a plan of action. The members of the defense team were then called in and briefed by Jim St. Clair. If a legal memo was needed, it would be assigned to one or a group of lawyers, and they would immediately start work on it. The ad hoc team then worked on it until it was finished, even if it took all night. Literally. If they needed typing done, White House secretaries would be called in from their homes, sometimes at two in the morning, to do the work.

Understandably, the White House staff was most responsive to the president's needs during this crisis. On one of those all-too-common overnighters, they would finish the assigned legal work by seven in the morning or so, then turn it in to Jim St. Clair, who was usually there by seven-thirty. Once he was briefed and accepted the product, the exhausted lawyers were allowed to go home for a shower and a few hours of sleep, then back to the White House. For Gene and the rest of the Nixon defense team, it was a very consuming job, but it was the only job any of them ever knew where they saw the results of their day's work, or at least the press's interpretation of that work, reported on the seven o'clock news every night.

Early on, Gene learned that the media were key elements in the Watergate story, and he became very wary of the press. In fact, Jim St. Clair told the defense team right away and in no uncertain terms that they weren't allowed to speak to reporters or any news media representatives at all. They were told to refer all media requests to Ron Ziegler, who was Nixon's press secretary.

It was only a few weeks after Gene started working in the White House that he had his first clash with the anti-Nixon press. He was at a Georgetown cocktail party, and as he stood with a small group of strangers, he was challenged for his role in defending Nixon.

"How could you work for that SOB Nixon, who is obviously guilty?"

Gene was offended by that comment, and he explained to these people that, in America, a defendant is innocent until proven guilty, and every accused has the right to a lawyer. He unfortunately made the mistake of going a little bit too far when he said, "Even the Boston Strangler had a right to a lawyer and a strong defense."

One member of the group said, "Wow, that's a great quote, and I think I'm going to use it as the lead in a story I'm writing about Nixon that will be in tomorrow's paper. I think the lead will be 'Nixon lawyer compares his client to Boston Strangler.'" Dreading the answer, Gene felt his heart pound as he asked him where he worked.

"The Washington Post."

Gene stopped breathing. He immediately left the group and searched for the host, a senior partner at Patton, Boggs, the powerful law firm he had left to join the Nixon defense team. The host eventually saved Gene's bacon by finding the reporter and dissuading him from using either Gene's name or his wonderful sound bite about Nixon and the Boston Strangler. But even after that, he remained uneasy for weeks. He really feared that the quotation would find its way into a banner headline on the front page of *The Washington Post* and would cost him his job in the White House. After that, he kept his distance from all members of the media during the rest of his time in the White House.

As the Watergate controversy neared the endgame, Gene worked as part of a team preparing the reply brief of the president to be filed in the Supreme Court. For him, it was a wonderful but terrible time. It was wonderful because he got to work with Professor Charles Allen Wright of the University of Texas, the foremost authority in the nation on the operation of federal courts. Wright was hired as a White House consultant to be in charge of preparing the White House reply brief, and he selected Gene as one of his small team to write it.

They were under tremendous pressure to get the brief done in three days, and the team literally worked night and day to get a draft to Wright. He would then meet with Gene and other lawyers individually to discuss the portions of the brief he had assigned to each of them. For Gene, it was Rule 17, the scope of the subpoena that had been served on President Nixon to produce the Watergate tapes.

Wright's directions to the lawyers were quite impressive. He had a photographic mind, and he would say things like, "This is a good point, Gene, and if you look at the case of *U.S. v. Penrose*, in volume 145 of the *Federal Reporter* 2nd, you will find some support for this idea of yours." That was amazing because he would remember not only the name of the case in which support might be found on a particular issue, but also the volume number of the *Federal Reporter* 2nd in which the case appears. Professor Wright had a remarkable intellect, and Gene found it delightful to be exposed to him on such a close professional basis. The terrible part of working with him was that their time constraints and the magnitude of the constitutional crisis in which they were engaged created enormous pressure.

They got the brief in with only a few minutes to spare. Of course, the irony of that high-pressure exercise is in the rumor heard years later that, before the brief was even filed, the law clerks of the Supreme Court justices had started circulating drafts of an opinion holding against Nixon.

In July 1974, the Supreme Court delivered an opinion that ruled unanimously against Nixon. On August 9, 1974, Nixon resigned the presidency and left Washington.

After their client, the president, was gone, the ten White House lawyers entered a sort of political wasteland. Gene was fortunate enough to be hired as a nonpolitical trial attorney in the Justice Department, where he worked for eight years. When President Reagan was elected, he learned that the Pentagon was looking for conservative Republican lawyers who had military experience. That Gene had served in Vietnam strengthened his hand, so he reentered the political lists and was eventually selected to be the deputy general counsel and later the general counsel of the Air Force. And one day, he would become a federal appeals court judge in Washington, D.C.

Chapter 11:

David Leroy Ramsay and Robert Benjamin Ramsay

UNTIL 1947, THE AIR FORCE WAS PART of the Army. The U.S. Air Force Academy was established only in 1955, with its first class graduating in 1959. Throughout the 1960s and 1970s, the Air Force was dominated by West Point graduates, and it was very easy for a certain number of West Pointers to take their commissions at graduation in the U.S. Air Force. This was the case with Dave Ramsay, class of 1964, who had served as an enlisted man in the U.S. Air Force before winning an appointment to West Point. During his senior year, Dave was a cadet company commander and also captain of the USMA track team.

In the early morning hours of August 12, 1970, the rain was beginning to pound down on the airstrip at Da Nang as Captain David L. Ramsay slipped under the open canopy and dropped into his front pilot's seat, a rodeo bull rider slipping down to fork the monster. For Dave, still a young fire-eating fighter pilot with the 4th Tactical Fighter Squadron, 366th Tactical Fighter Wing, this was his equivalent of just another day in the office. The difference, of course, was that he never knew for sure if he would come back. But like most young fighter pilots, he thought himself immortal, and he never really considered going down in flames. Oh, he knew somewhere in the back of his mind that he might not make it, but that was just one of the risks he ran every time he took off on a mission like this and rolled those dice.

Smooth and sleek and slick in the rain, dull earth-brown and jungle-green camouflage colors coating its sensual curves and jagged edges, the F-4 Phantom fighter with its strangely squared shark tail loomed menacingly. This was the true lead stallion of its time, unrivaled in the air. Manned by a crew of two, it was highly versatile, able to drop loads of bombs with precision on targets below, or when friendly assets were threatened, to smash into enemy fighter planes and knock them flaming from the sky. And it could take a beating, often able to soak up ground fire like raindrops and never even flinch. But the full capabilities of this airship were only available to the very best pilots.

Some flew the Phantom by the numbers, like a refrigerator, relying on its durability to get them home. These, more often than not, would be survivors. But a select few were true artists able to draw the full tonal range out of this latter-day Stradivarius. Dave was a gymnast on the high wire, no net below, fully confident of his mastery of the art of F-4 flying—a bit cocky, perhaps, laughing in the face of the life-and-death risks he ran every day.

This mission, Dave would be carrying two canisters of napalm on each of his outboard stations, left and right, under his wings. At each of the inboard stations, also left and right, he would be carrying three five-hundred-pound "Snake Eye" bombs that would sprout "high drag" fins when, flying at low altitude for accuracy, he released them, thus giving him enough time to get away before they blew ㄴ up along with his target. These munitions were destined for a target in Cambodia, and centerline under his fuselage, he carried a fuel tank that would get him there.

So today he'd be a bomber. He had flown a number of different missions in the past, carrying just air-to-air missiles and guns rather than bombs, as fighter escort for B-52 heavy bombers or F-105 fighter-bombers. His job then had been to defend these, his wards, from North Vietnamese MIG fighter aircraft that might be scrambled to intercept them. While that had not happened yet, it remained his dream as the ultimate test of his skills as a fighter pilot—a test, he hoped, that still awaited him.

In fact, during the Vietnam War, the F-4 was the first choice of the Air Force for defense against enemy fighters. But on this day, as on most, Dave would fly in the ground attack mode.

Since his fellow crew member, Captain Jim Schindler, was already in his backseat with his canopy closed, Dave moved the lever that brought his massive canopy down and hermetically sealed them in. The aircraft was parked in a heavily sandbagged and covered shelter, and he normally would have kept his canopy open until just before takeoff. But given the wind, he knew the drumming rain they would taxi through would blow in on him, so he sealed off that annoyance. The sound and feel of rain and wind outside were replaced, canopy closed, by the familiar hard contours of the seat and the soft whir of electronics. The loud racket of jeeps and trucks and machinery on the tarmac to their front was now dramatically muffled, and as Dave pulled on his helmet and oxygen mask, was finally silenced. His fingers flew almost without thought as he began the routine of connecting himself to his aircraft.

Each F-4 Phantom was flown by a pilot in the front seat of the cockpit. In the seat directly behind him rode a weapons systems operator, or "WSO"—but he was more commonly referred to as a "GIB," for "guy in back." Both men had flight and weapon system controls in case of emergencies, but the pilot in front usually flew the plane, the GIB ran the radar, the radio, and the navigation systems. And most important in combat, the GIB was another pair of eyes.

Dave and his GIB were strapped in by belts and harnesses, plugged in by wires, vented by hoses. Their helmets hooked them again into the aircraft, but also were their connection to the outside world, and so were essential—as were the G-suit, the survival vest, the parachute harness, the pistol holster, and the good-luck charms many men carried in one of their zippered pockets or around their neck. Dave carried Saint Christopher on his beaded dog tag chain.

"Gunfighter Two Six" would be his radio call sign on the mission for which he was now preparing. Dave was almost halfway through his one-year tour of duty as an F-4 fighter-bomber pilot flying combat strike missions in North and South Vietnam, Laos, and Cambodia. It was rainy and windy and rotten in Da Nang, but his mission was in Cambodia, several hundred miles away. He was the commander of a flight of two F-4s, and all four crewmen in these aircraft silently hoped and expected that the weather would be clearer there.

The mission for which they had just been briefed would be against a North Vietnamese gun site, that of a ZPU 4-23. This was a Soviet 23-mm gun with four barrels. While only every fifth round was a red tracer, the rate of fire was such that, when you were its target, it felt like a firehose of cherry balls was spewing out at you. This gun's particular presence had been unsuspected until it had nailed an F-4 from the same 366th Tactical Fighter Wing, known as "Gunfighters," as it attacked a nearby truck park and ammunition dump the day before. As it made its diving attack, the F-4 was hit, and its pilot tried to nurse it back to altitude and get away. Within a few miles, however, it had disintegrated in an explosion of flames over the jungle, immolating its crew. The wingman of this F-4 had attacked the gun position immediately, but he was also badly hit himself and had to limp to the much closer airbase in Bien Hoa, South Vietnam. Today, Dave's Gunfighter flight would be seeking to wreak unit vengeance on this now-pinpointed gun site.

For this particular mission, Dave was especially grim. Not only were the crew members of the plane that had been blown up part of his 4th Tactical Fighter Squadron, but the pilot had also lived right across the hall from Dave in the Squadron Quarters at Da Nang, and he was "one of the guys." He was a major who had been in the Air Force for more than ten years, and he was, in Dave's estimation, as fine an F-4 pilot as any in the Air Force. That opinion was based on the experience of flying with him in combat. But now he was gone, and Dave felt helpless. They would try to knock out the gun that had killed him, of course, but Dave felt that even that was a rather futile gesture: he would still be dead, and there was nothing they could do about that. Sometimes this job could be very depressing.

But Dave coolly walled off his emotions as he prepared for the mission they had just been assigned. Theirs was part of a major, wide-ranging, continuing attack against targets in Cambodia by many American aircraft over a several-week period. A surprise incursion into Cambodia had been launched by the U.S. Army on May 1, 1970, causing the enemy forces stationed there to really scramble. Waves of American troops had poured into that country in an effort to destroy the North Vietnamese communist facilities that, with virtual impunity until that point, had been supporting the war they were waging in adjoining South Vietnam. But the domestic political uproar in the United States that followed this bold stroke by President Nixon, little more than a year after he had been sworn into office, forced him to reconsider. In the face of heated opposition that too often lurched into violence on American streets and college campuses, Nixon reduced the goals and duration of this military spoiling attack. By June 30—two months after the operation began—all American troops had withdrawn their heavy footprint from Cambodian soil.

Communist forces, of course, in the face of this precipitous American withdrawal, were now virtually assured that no ground attack would recur, and their facilities began to spring up in Cambodia again like dandelions in the spring. But the political dangers associated with sending American soldiers back there on the ground did not apply to strike missions by fast-moving American aircraft. And that's where the Gunfighters came in.

This was nothing new, of course: airplanes had long dropped bombs in Cambodia as part of the fight against communist forces in South Vietnam, and their fleeting presence had never been a cause for any sort of political unrest back home. But in the wake of the withdrawal by U.S. ground forces and with the array of new and promising targets, Cambodian air space became somewhat crowded with heavily armed American combat aircraft.

Dave started the engines and he and his GIB went through the long list of systems checks. Once that had been completed, Dave talked to the tower, and then their aircraft, heavily weighed down with bombs and napalm and 20-mm Gatling gun ammunition that had been loaded within the past few hours, was directed down the ramp to the arming area. There, the arming crew swarmed under and around their aircraft, pulling safety pins and making the final safety checks.

Dave's GIB this particular day, Jim Schindler, was about to finish his tour and rotate back to "the World," where he would become an instructor pilot for the T-37 trainer at Maxwell Air Force Base in Montgomery, Alabama. After a year of such combat missions, he had become very good at his job. But this was their first time together in the same aircraft on a mission, so Dave went over some basics with him.

Even though they were only a few feet away from each other, their equipment and the configuration of the F-4 cockpit was such that communication between them was virtually impossible except over their radio intercom. Their intercom microphones and speakers were the same as for their radios, mounted inside their oxygen masks and helmets respectively. The pilot and GIB were usually on "hot mike" when they were in their aircraft: Unlike plane-to-plane or plane-to-ground communication, they didn't have to push a button to transmit, they just talked.

"Okay, Jim, first time out together, we need to go over some basics. Now if we take fire, remember that as long as I'm still talking and moving around, I'll fly the aircraft, you run the weapons. But if we get hit bad and you don't get any response from me over the intercom, then you just take over. If we're hit so bad that you can't control the aircraft at all, why, then you just turn that T-handle in front of you and punch me out right away. But if you've got any control at all, just do whatever you can to get some altitude, and once we're up some, you just go ahead and punch me out then, and I'll do the same for you, okay?"

The "T-handle" was the latest in emergency equipment. It was a selector in the ejection system that allowed the GIB to eject the front-seater along with himself. The front-seater always took the GIB with him if he initiated the ejection. This coordination between pilot and GIB was quite routine but essential.

"Roger."

Then a thumbs-up to the arming crew, and the tower cleared them onto the runway. Fully loaded with fuel and bristling with bombs and guns, they paused at the end of the runway.

When the tower cleared him, Dave moved the throttles all the way forward and went into afterburner, and the aircraft leaped forward with a deafening roar. Within seconds, they saw only a blur of the tower and ramp area, with the runway lights whipping by as the overpowering roar of the two J-79 engines reverberated through their bodies. Then they were airborne, and the grinding and rumbling of their fire-breathing beast smoothed almost as soon as they left the friction of the ground.

Dave's heart rose and soared with their craft—God, he loved to fly! Just as smoothly as he breathed he raised the landing gear, cleaned up the flaps, came out of afterburner, and established a nice rate of climb through the overcast. Then, suddenly and without warning, like night to day, they popped out of the rain clouds and into the clean clear.

Below them now was an endless field of fluffy black, white, and gray snow, far beyond anything the Alps or even Disney had ever dreamed of. It was an overwhelming sight, and no matter how many times he went up, this vista of forever always moved Dave, especially in the moonlight on a night mission—ah, there was true heaven. But they were embarking on serious business now, and Dave was able to calmly restrain the thrills that coursed through his life lines as they soared free, high above this obscure corner of Asia.

When Dave had been commissioned into the Air Force back in 1964, more than six years ago now, his fantasies had only vaguely resembled the realities he now knew intimately. In his senior year, he had been captain of the West Point track team, and he had loved running and racing other men with a passion that defied description. But when he graduated and went to flight school, he was overwhelmed: The rush he found there shrank something as silly as flexing your body's natural muscles to laughable insignificance. Yes, his body had always worked well, and when properly conditioned, he could run very fast. But now, as a fighter pilot, he rode the latest, hottest steel product of the brightest minds in America, hurtling through the sky at barely believable speed, armed with potent weaponry that could destroy virtually any adversary that might oppose him. Yes, running was great, but flying these gorgeous, lethal beasts was . . . was . . . what was the word? Stupefying? Overwhelming? Monstrous? Spectacular?

No, none of them fit. For him, flying a hot fighter was just the greatest thing attainable by man. And he still marveled that he had somehow been selected as one of the small number of young American warriors entrusted with this phenomenally expensive, phenomenally potent fire-breathing, swept-wing dragon, a beast he would control and direct to the destruction of enemy capabilities in whatever way he was directed.

The few times anyone might mention it, like maybe his wife Liz's family or other civilians who knew little of the military, he had to admit that, yes, maybe there was something a little bit unusual in a man for whom running was almost second nature falling so deeply in love with flying. He did still run when he had time, but that was just for the exercise and maybe also because his body loved it so. But the clean competitive edge, the raw lust he had once felt when racing against another man and testing his muscles and his lungs and his heart, had been replaced completely by a love for mastering the three-dimensional sky in his fleeting craft. There were no limits out there, just you, and the sky, and your airplane. And as an American fighter pilot aloft, all restraints of the earth loosed, it was easy to let yourself go a little bit and feel like God.

Yes, there were many other good pilots out there. But Dave worked hard every day at becoming the very best.

While a senior at West Point, Dave had risen to the rank of cadet captain and company commander, and thus was responsible for the hundred or so cadets of all classes who lived under his command in New South Barracks. He was thus chosen by West Point as being among the 5 or 10 percent of his class who showed the highest promise for a future Army career of note. He was a marked man, and many expected him to one day become a high-ranking general, including himself.

Having served as an enlisted man in the Air Force before receiving an appointment to West Point, he was allowed to choose Air Force blue over Army green at graduation. He had taken his commission in that branch, married his beloved Penn State coed Liz, then soared off to flight school, from which he graduated at the top of his class.

And Dave had soon become a fighter pilot's fighter pilot. That meant, first of all, that he was a "good stick"— that he could fly his monstrous aircraft with the grace and control that the finest gymnast, ballerina, or toreador use to control their bodies at their moments of truth. But, perhaps more important, it also meant that he had the true attitude of a fighter pilot: the sort of "can do" self-confidence that allowed him to fly the highest-risk missions without elevating his pulse or respiration a whit, to stare death in the face repeatedly and without any concern whatever. If he died in the act, well, then, he died, but he would not allow that probability, however high, to deter him in the slightest from the fullness—the joy—of his total performance of the most daring mission.

You didn't have to be a fighter pilot to live with that attitude, of course, or even fly at all. Dave had known people from truck drivers to barmaids who had it, and he had also met men who had flown fighters for twenty years and did *not* have it.

But over the years since World War II, as airplanes had become more complex, this most-desired fighter pilot's attitude now had to be carefully joined with long and very difficult technical schooling in the specific mechanics of high-tech aircraft and the skills needed to fly them. The modern fighter pilot had to brave the risks of this most perilous and cerebral craft, where the slightest inattention to detail, the tiniest miscalculation made among myriad moving-target decisions, could turn one into toast.

Being a fighter pilot really was a joy to Dave, who had spent years as an instructor pilot teaching others to fly. His last assignment in the States had been at George Air Force Base, out northeast of Los Angeles in the high California desert. He and his wife, Liz, had driven all the way from Texas, and when they arrived, before they did anything else—eat, find a motel, look into housing, even formally sign in as having arrived—Dave drove straight to the end of the runway. For an hour, he and Liz sat there while, over their heads, the mighty F-4 Phantoms took off with deafening roars, afterburners blazing and bellowing.

And now, as a fighter pilot flying high-risk combat missions, Dave had truly arrived. His actual skill as a "good stick" had long been noted in the records, and after his tour in Vietnam he was scheduled to join the Air Force's finest: the Thunderbirds, the selected half-dozen fighter pilots who put on aerobatic displays for foreign dignitaries and for the Great American Public at air shows held across the country.

He had been told by senior personnel officers that service in Vietnam was unimportant to his career in the Air Force, that the numbers were such that he could easily shoot to the top without it. But deep inside, he knew his nation was at war and that was the circumstance for which he had been preparing all his professional life.

In fact, it would have been quite easy for him to have avoided the war in Vietnam, and he had to fight just to get assigned there, in the process playing every card he held. This included using the influence of a three-star general who had been impressed by him, and when his orders finally came through, he had been delighted. Liz was not, and their newborn daughter Nicole no doubt weighed heavy on her mind. But she kept quiet in the face of her husband's exuberance.

Liz wrote to Dave every day, and sometimes he even got audiotapes and photos. These really made his heart sing, especially pictures of their angel baby, Nicole. He wasn't nearly as regular as Liz with the mail, but he tried hard. When he tried to tell her about his work, Dave's routine on tapes or letters was to give Liz as much detail on an actual mission as he thought she could understand. This basically meant any unusual or interesting things they had seen from the air, the kinds of targets they had gone after, and their success rate. So far, from the feedback he got from her, she loved hearing about his missions, as did their friends and family. With that kind of reassurance, he never tired of sharing his experiences with her. He had a little cassette recorder in his room, and he often found himself talking to her on it.

"The roads that we hit are down in valleys, and in the hills that surround the valleys are caves, and in those caves they've got guns. And those guns shoot *down* at you, so you've got to use every trick in the book to protect yourself. But we can do it."

He would now be able to give her an even better feel for the missions, as he had made some tapes of his cockpit conversations.

"A lot of guys take their cassette recorders up with them, and I wanted to do that, so I had a special connection made over at the communications shop, and it just plugs into my microphone and earphone jack, so I made some tapes of some missions and I'll send them to you so you can hear what was actually going on. And then I can try to explain some of the stuff to you, because I'm sure it will all sound like Greek to you. It did to me for a while, too."

And he decided to tell her about his Night Owl missions.

"We've been flying at night, sometimes a couple, three times a week, it depends. Kind of wild, really. We flew night before last. It was a two-ship flight, and the lead airplane had flares and bombs and I had wall-to-wall napalms. That means that every station I could hang a bomb on, I was carrying napalm. That's quite a bit of napalm. We went into some valley. Pitch black. Dropping flares and dropping napalm. You talk about something hairy—but it was okay."

Millions of years ago, as plates of the earth shifted and edged over each other, mountains were born. The rocky spine of the Indochinese dragon that then erupted from the earth kept its sharp edges longer than other mountain ranges because they had formed more recently and were made of a particular type of limestone known as karst, one of the hardest forms, and thus most impervious to wind and water. In the Laotian and Vietnamese hinterlands, angular karst formations rise five thousand feet, sometimes higher, into the air. These mountains form long, irregular ridgelines, with occasional lonely pillars of stone vaulting up into the sky from flat valley floor. And the cliff faces are most impressive, one might even say intimidating. To a U.S. Air Force pilot flying a low-level Night Owl mission with limited visibility, they were also quite deadly.

The normal Night Owl mission consisted of two F-4 aircraft loaded with ordnance and flares. When they approached a target area, one plane would fly over the suspected target area at about five or six thousand feet and drop one or more flares in parachutes. The descent of this burning magnesium packet usually took a minute or more, during which time it cast an eerie light over areas many hundreds of meters in all directions. The second plane would be circling at eight or ten thousand feet, and the flare ship would try to guide him visually to what looked like the suspected target—a bridge, a road intersection, a truck park, a warehouse, an ammunition dump, whatever. The second pilot would then dive steeply at the target, "pickle" at about six thousand, and pull back on the stick to get back up and away from the coming explosion. In such a maneuver, the plane dropping bombs would usually bottom out at about five thousand feet, sometimes much lower.

All this depended on the actual facts at hand, of course. If the weather was clear and the burning flare gave good sight of the target and the area around it, the attack plane might go much lower to be more sure of hitting his target. If there were heavy clouds and rain right down to the target area and they knew they were in the karst, the pilots were drilled to avoid coming below five thousand feet in the fog, target or no target: The statistics of dueling with the karst gave them no leeway at all.

For the Americans, the Night Owl missions were very, very effective, catching the communists in the open at night, when most of their activity occurred, under cover of darkness. But in the karst, Night Owl missions were also very, very dangerous.

One unit, the 497th Tactical Fighter Squadron out of Ubon airbase in Thailand, flew nothing but Night Owl missions. They flew most of their strikes on the Ho Chi Minh Trail in Laos, which was much more heavily defended by antiaircraft guns than any area in South Vietnam. Still, in one twelve-month period, the 497th had lost seven airplanes to enemy ground fire, and thirteen to the karst. Their pilots had a saying: "If the big guns don't get you, the black karst will."

That meant that, in order to maximize your return on investment, you sent nothing but your very best pilots on Night Owl missions. Still, the losses were horrendous.

At first, Dave had also been a little bit concerned about whether he would measure up to the pressures of combat. But he had never felt the slightest hesitation, and in his fifth month in Vietnam, he truly loved his life as a combat fighter pilot.

A flight of two or more aircraft worked these missions together, hitting enemy targets in sequence as they were guided in by a forward air controller, or FAC. The FAC was another American pilot whose mission was solely directing fire on targets. The FAC was usually flying a light, propeller-driven airplane similar to a Piper Cub, which consumed very little gas and allowed him to stay on station, if need be, for hours. But FACs could also be flying "fast movers," or fighter jets similar to the attacking aircraft, but without the added weight and fuel consumption caused by a load of bombs,

These targets had been determined by intelligence officers as much as a day or more before takeoff, but updates and changes could be relayed to the crew up until the very time they released their ordnance on a target below.

While they talk to each other on a mission, Air Force fighter pilots also use slang terms that are meaningless to an outsider. For instance, when they identify a target, they will convey this by saying, "Tally!" or "I have a Tally!"

The term "Tally" was a shortened version of a phrase that had been borrowed from those most revered of fighter pilots, the men who flew for the Royal Air Force in the 1940 Battle of Britain. Depending on pluck and luck, they threw their Spitfires and Hurricanes with reckless abandon against the waves of German bombers attacking their homeland. The initial British pilot strength in early August 1940 had been over 1,400; a month later, it was down to 840, and they were losing an average of 120 each week.

As we now know, however, their stiff upper lips, laughter in the face of danger, and unwillingness to ever, ever give in finally won the day. These were the men about whom, while speaking for the British people, Churchill later said, "Never has so much been owed by so many to so few." If ever there were fighter pilots deemed by American fighter pilots in the 1960s and 1970s to have been made of the "right stuff," these Brits were they.

During the height of the Battle of Britain, as they moved toward their aircraft for a mission or when they were about to pounce on a flight of German bombers, they would often sing out "Tally-ho!" This indicated to their fellows that they were eager for the chase or were about to attack, but sounded for all the world as if they were involved in some lighthearted hunt to hounds rather than risking, and often losing, their very lives.

So "Tally" is both an American fighter pilot's salute to his heroic cultural ancestors and an indication that he sees his target and is about to attack.

Similarly, when a bombardier drops his bombs or signals the pilot to do so, he no longer says "bombs away"; rather, the modern term is "pickle!"

Just after the turn of the century, winged and motorized craft that could actually carry people through the air were such a new concept that, by the time World War I broke out in 1914, little thought or effort had been given to using airplanes as weapon platforms. At first, even going off to act as spotters, pilots just carried pistols or rifles to defend themselves. As their potential use as warfighters became apparent, these were quickly upgraded to machine guns, whose rate of fire was eventually carefully regulated so that they could fire through the spinning propeller blade without shredding it. They began to shoot each other down with great regularity.

Then someone thought of dropping bombs from airplanes onto targets below. When the U.S. Army first tried this from their observer aircraft in this country, the pilot simply threw an object over the side as he flew some fifty or one hundred feet above at a speed well under fifty miles per hour. The actual facts are by now somewhat confused, but apparently the original objects were either pickles thrown at a basket of some sort or some kind of sandbag thrown at the rather commonly available pickle barrel. In any case, the use of the term "pickle" by a bombardier as he releases his load or, as here in an F-4, informs the pilot that the moment is right to do so, has endured ever since.

Within a few hours of flight from Da Nang, they had topped off with a by-now-routine air-to-air refueling pause at a KC-135 flying fuel tanker and arrived onstation over Cambodia. They dropped down to twelve thousand feet, then made radio contact and hooked up with their FAC, Stormy, also flying an F-4.

"Okay, Flight Two Five, what's your angels?"

In fighter jock talk, Stormy was asking Dave for his altitude in thousands of feet, with one angel being one thousand feet.

Dave, as lead, spoke for both aircraft.

"This is Two Five Lead, we're at twelve, Stormy, and we're just coming up on an airfield."

"Well, if you can see that airfield, you're not too far from the target. What kind of munitions did you bring?"

Jim's voice broke in on the intercom.

"There he is, ten o'clock, way below us and moving in the same direction."

Dave looked down to his left and saw the glint of metal a few thousand feet below them as he spoke.

"Stormy, this is Lead, we just picked you up, we're above you at your four o'clock. We're each carrying four napes and six snakes, over."

"Well, the target you got briefed on, that twenty-three, is still there, and there is also another gun in the same position, we think a thirty-seven or maybe something bigger with radar control. We plastered them with CBUs yesterday afternoon and again this morning, and we silenced 'em, so now we want to knock out the whole site before they fix whatever we broke."

When an antiaircraft gun position was bringing down American aircraft or even just keeping them out of a crucial target area, the most crucial and immediate thing for American pilots to do was to silence it. But a cardinal rule for our dive bombers in Vietnam was that they never get in a pissing contest with a gun on the ground: When at all possible, they were to try to stay out of the gun's range. The first choice, then, for silencing an antiaircraft gun was use of a standoff weapon that could be fired or dropped from outside the gun's range. "CBU" stands for "cluster bomb unit," devastating area weapons usually used in an antipersonnel mode. Each CBU dropped was initially a bomb-shaped pod that in turn would open a certain distance above ground and disperse 130 smaller bomblets over a large, elliptically shaped area, each of which would explode on contact with the ground or anything else it might hit. Here, CBUs had been dropped from an altitude beyond the range of either gun, and as it turned out, had done the trick by destroying exposed crucial elements of the target—gun crews, ammunition stores, whatever. Now, the next day, Dave's flight was to destroy the gun site itself before the anticipated completion of repairs needed to get those two guns back into action.

Stormy continued his guidance. "From the airfield, the target is about half a click to the north of the end of the main runway. There's a lot of clouds below us, but you can see a river beyond our target, and a road just this side of the river, see that?"

"I see the runway and the river, but the clouds . . . I don't . . . okay, there it is, I can see the road now."

"All right, now the gun pit itself is between the road and the river. It looks like it's a clump of bushes or small trees close to the road. I'll put some smoke on him, after that I'll be climbing out to about angels six and clearing you in from there so I can stay out of your way, stand by."

The F-4 is most effective when the pilot and the GIB are able to work together like well-oiled machinery. Gunfighter Two Six and Two Seven, Dave and his wingman, who would operate as "Lead" and "Two" on this station, stayed at eight thousand feet. As they flew in a wide, lazy curve, Dave felt the tension trying to leap up and wash over him, but he held it back. Once they had put in their first strike, he knew, the tension would disappear just as it does in football when you deliver or receive your first solid hit on the field. Until then, he had to occasionally restrain his nerves as the tension built. But to a casual observer, Dave and Jim were preparing for their upcoming dive-bombing run in calm, business-as-usual voices over their intercom that betrayed not the slightest concern.

"Okay, Jim, single drop on both outboards is selected."

The pilot of an F-4 armed as Dave's was had several options for dropping his ordnance. The one Dave selected meant that, on the first pass, he would drop one napalm bomb from each of his outboard stations.

"Roger, 219 mils . . . no, check that, 142 mils for nape."

Jim was telling Dave what setting, in mils, to put on the gunsight, which is right in front of the pilot high in the forward area of the cockpit. The GIB has tables that relate the airspeed of the aircraft, angle of attack, height of release, and type of munitions, and before a bomb run, he tells the pilot how far to move the red pipper, or aiming point, down in the gunsight. This is similar to moving the sights on a rifle to compensate for distance, wind, or other factors that affect the true course of a bullet. The main difference is that, while you move the rifle in your arms to adjust the strike of the bullet, the pilot of an F-4 is in effect flying the rifle barrel.

In selecting a mil setting, the pilot is making a contract with himself that he can be at the precise airspeed and altitude in a diving, rapidly accelerating aircraft at the precise instant that the pipper "walks up" to the target—offset for wind, of course. If any parameter is off, the bomb will miss. The true skill of a pilot on a dive-bombing mission comes into play as he recognizes (or fails to recognize) errors, seemingly insignificant though they may be, and makes lightning-fast decisions to accommodate for them (drop early or late, correct right or left), all the while hurtling down in an aircraft that is moving at more than six hundred feet per second and accelerating toward the ground.

In a dive-bombing attack, the GIB gives the pilot the sight setting, then calls out his decreasing altitude and increasing airspeed, and finally calls the release altitude.

Dave and Jim were making last safety checks as they watched Stormy swoop down and fire a smoke rocket. He was far below them now, soaring off to their left and climbing for altitude as they looked down through the clouds and watched bright purple smoke billow up from the ground. Then he came back up on the radio.

"Okay, Lead, my smoke went in about fifteen meters to the west of the gun pit, it's in that dark green clump down there."

As the Lead, Dave would make the first attack. Near the base of the smoke, he saw a lush green clump of vegetation and knew that was the target.

"I have a Tally. Am I clear?"

"You're clear, Lead."

The FAC acts as a sort of traffic cop, making sure that more than one aircraft doesn't attack a target at the same time, as that could be quite dangerous, particularly if the aircraft were coming in from different azimuths or altitudes.

"Lead in."

That was just his announcement that the Lead aircraft in Gunfighter Flight Two Five was about to roll in and attack the gun site. Their left wingtip popped straight up into the sky and they flipped over hard to the right as they dropped side down. The nose of the aircraft then revolved until they fell face down from the sky. Jim was soon talking.

"Coming through five thousand, airspeed 345 . . . now four thousand, airspeed 385 . . . we're gonna pull out at twelve hundred feet, there, David."

"Roger."

Whatever kind of gun it was they were attacking, so far it was not shooting at them.

"Three thousand, airspeed four hundred . . . coming through two thousand, good airspeed . . . ready, ready . . . pickle!"

Dave and Jim pulled their normal four Gs—four times the force of gravity, exerted against your body as you pull out of a steep dive—as they heard the "crump!" of the napalm behind and below them. They were just climbing out of danger when Stormy came back up on the radio.

"Okay, good shootin' there, Lead, your line was good but you were a little short. Two, you need to add about fifteen or twenty meters to the northwest, toward the river, there, that gun is sittin' in a funny place, I think he's got some high ground protecting him from this direction, that's what caught Lead's fire."

"Roger that, Stormy, I have a Tally, but I can't see Lead, am I clear?"

"You're clear, Two."

"Roger that, Two in."

As they climbed back up, Dave and Jim watched their wingman put his napalm in. It hit beyond the target, leaving a bright green patch between the two greasy strips of guttering flames.

As Two climbed out, he was way too smooth. When you made a strike against a target you thought might be covered by antiaircraft guns, after you released your ordnance you were supposed to jink back and forth, left, right, up, down, so that the enemy gunner couldn't track you and shoot you down; when going against radar-controlled guns, this is crucial. This is what Dave had done, but since the gun they were targeting had not yet fired a shot, Dave's wingman had apparently taken it for granted that there was no live-gun problem. But Stormy was as careful of the F-4s he was controlling as a mother would be of her children near a hot stove, and he was loud over the radio.

"Don't pull out like that, Two! He can see you!"

Two's nose instantly started to jink even as the gun on the ground opened up. The tracers missed and Two really scrambled as he clawed his way back up to safe altitude. Stormy was soon back in his calm, laconic drawl.

"This is not an easy target, Lead, but now we have him bracketed. He's hidin' in that sandpit, almost right between where those two strikes went in, you think you can get him with your other two napes?"

"Rog, I see two little trees there on the edge of a sand-pit, you say that's where he is?"

"Yeah, two little trees right next to him, that's it."

"Okay. Tally. Am I clear?"

"You're clear, go get him, big guy!"

Again the nose dropped as Dave revised his plans with Jim.

"All right, we've got a tough target, so screw it, this time we pickle at a thousand, okay?"

"Roger that . . . coming through five thousand, keep your airspeed up, only got 325 . . . four thousand, 340, crack a burner if you need it."

"No sweat."

"Okay . . . three thousand, 385, that's more like it . . . two thousand, good airspeed . . . ready—pickle!"

After releasing his bombs, the F-4 pilot has to come out of his dive by pulling back pretty sharply on his stick to keep from hitting the ground. But if he pulls *too* hard, the aircraft will start to shudder and stall, and the nose won't come up fast enough. So the best of pilots will dive very low before releasing, then pull out on the edge of shudder. Dave and Jim were right down in the weeds as they skated along the edge, touching that shudder then dancing away, edging back and starting to shudder again and shying away as the ground grew distinct and detailed before them. Within seconds they were clawing back up into the sky, jinking hard as Stormy's shouts surprised them.

"All *right*, Lead! That one was right *on the money!* Great shootin'!"

Dave cracked a smile as he banked hard in his climb and snatched a glance over his left shoulder. The two smoldering smears from the first strikes were now connected by the one he had just put in. The green clump around the sandpit, the two little trees, the sandpit itself had all disappeared in a raging fire.

Two chimed in on the accolades.

"Way to go, Dave!"

Dave felt his cheeks burn a bit as an uncontrollable smile spread across his face. Damn! It felt *great* when you did your job right under pressure! Dave's wingman came in behind him and, in a steeper dive since he was using pinpoint weapons rather than napalm, which covered a wider area, put two Snakeyes into the heart of the fire, and masonry and chunks of metal ballooned up above the ugly black and orange flame bed. Both aircraft made several more attacks, and finally their bombs were just bouncing the metallic rubble inside the gaping, jagged, broken wall around the gun site. No more American planes would be brought down by antiaircraft guns from *this* particular location.

It seemed like a short ride back to Da Nang. When they landed and taxied over to their squadron area, Dave was still happy with his day's work. The rain had let up while they were gone, and now it was still overcast, but not as hot and muggy as it usually was.

Dave was still soaked with perspiration, both from the heat and from the overload of tension that built up on these combat strike missions. He had to almost peel himself out of the cockpit, then indoors to the operations center for the debrief.

Five days later, on August 17, 1970, Captain Dave Ramsay took off on a Night Owl mission, accompanied by another F-4. Dave's weapons systems officer was Major Phillip Wellons, an experienced GIB. The pilot of the other plane was, like Dave, an instructor pilot, Captain Steve

Melnick, and his GIB was another F-4 pilot, Captain Jim Wood. Melnick and Wood were both Air Force Academy graduates, and in terms of raw flying skills, the four of them were probably as fine a team of aviators as ever took to the air together.

The mission of the two planes was in a valley southwest of Da Nang known unofficially, but commonly, to the U.S. military as "Happy Valley." This name had been awarded to the valley in a typical burst of American combat cynicism, largely as a function of the concentration of North Vietnamese troops, weapons, and combat support systems and facilities deployed there, including massive antiaircraft weaponry, much of it radar-controlled.

Their mission was to have lasted less than an hour under the control of a U.S. Marine Corps FAC. As near as can be determined, however, they never made contact with him. Rather, they simply disappeared off the radio net with no warning and never returned to base.

The next morning, spotter planes found their crash sites in Happy Valley, but because of the North Vietnamese presence, it was five days before a Marine reconnaissance team could be inserted on the ground to search for bodies. They recovered some partial remains, which were evacuated, identified, and put inside sealed coffins. The official report noted that the two aircraft had been lost on a combat mission, and that there was "suspected enemy ground fire." But with no surviving witnesses, no one could really ever know for sure what had actually happened.

Captain Bob Ramsay met his older brother's coffin in Oakland, California, and escorted it back to West Point. Dave was born on December 25, 1938. On August 29, 1970, Captain David Leroy Ramsay was buried with full military honors in the West Point cemetery, thus joining the ranks of other West Point graduates who have given their lives for their country.

Captain Robert Benjamin Ramsay was deeply hurt by his brother's death. Say what you will, Dave had been his true hero in every sense of the word. And now he was gone.

After flying B-52s over Vietnam for a year, Bob spent a few years working in the administration of the U.S. Air Force Academy in Colorado Springs, Colorado. Flying in combat over Vietnam was one thing, and he had certainly logged his time there. But sitting behind a desk just didn't thrill him, even in beautiful Colorado Springs. Since his older brother Dave had been killed in Vietnam, his heart just really wasn't in the Air Force anymore, so he resigned his commission in 1973 and went to work for General Motors. Bob had grown up in Boston, and his wife, Bev, was born and raised in nearby Cape Cod. As Bob climbed the corporate ladder, he and his wife would raise five wonderful children.

After a number of years at General Motors, Bob took a job with a tobacco company in Richmond. While he was there, he went to night school at Virginia Commonwealth University and got an MBA in finance. Then he was hired by a big New York City bank.

Bev and the kids didn't complain about city life, and living in the Big Apple was fine. "No, really, dear, it's fine." But some years later a small metal manufacturing company in the middle of Pennsylvania came on the market, and Bob asked Bev what she would think of living out in the country. She was just this side of delirious at the prospect. So he rounded up the money and the financial paper required, and he bought it. For the Ramsays, the next decade was unalloyed family bliss.

Then the big job offer came along. He flew out to Milwaukee for several interviews, and finally the chairman of the board called him with the good news. He would be acting president and CEO for a large metal manufacturing business for six months until the previous president and CEO cleaned everything up and retired. Then he would officially take over and run the whole show as president and chief executive officer.

He and Bev were simply delighted. This was not much different from the work he had been doing in Pennsylvania, just move the decimal point over a few spaces for production and sales receipts. Even though the kids would all be off in college or married, Bob was finally going to make some serious money. And as he would be president and CEO of a considerably larger company, they would both have to get into a social whirl.

So they sold their house and moved to Milwaukee. And sure enough, after six months the chairman of the board changed his mind and decided he wanted to be president and CEO himself. Bob and Bev weren't left completely high and dry because they had had the presence of mind to have a lawyer go over their contractual agreements. But Bob felt as if he had been kicked in the stomach. He worked as a consultant, and he made decent money. He wasn't quite the king of the hill he thought he would be, but they liked Milwaukee and they made the most of it.

A few years later, a lawyer he knew slightly called him up. He told Bob he had been involved in part of the whole business deal that had brought him to Milwaukee and the ensuing disappointment. He had watched him carefully and was impressed by the way he had handled himself. He had made no complaints, expressed no anger, shown no negative emotion at all, even though anger was the least that might have been expected. Then he checked, and he found out that he was a West Point graduate, and that he had flown combat missions over Vietnam. He realized then that, by comparison, the struggle for control of a company by a bunch of greedy men was probably not very important to him. But he told Bob that he had carefully noted his behavior at the time. Now a door of opportunity was opening for a competent businessman with the sort of integrity he had shown, and he asked Bob to come to his office to meet some people and talk.

Bob was a little bit surprised by this call, but you never know. A few days later he went to the lawyer's office at the agreed-upon time, and inside his office he met three white-haired men in business suits. After introductions, the lawyer started to talk.

"Bob, a big pork and sausage producer in the Midwest is now going through a major restructuring. These three gentlemen are senior officers and major owners of that company. As part of their restructuring, it has become clear that they will have to get rid of some of their other businesses and focus their efforts. One of those businesses is a pretty big one. It is a filled pasta manufacturer called Romance Foods, and they have a nice market niche established pretty much across the whole country. They compete primarily against two giants: Contadina Brand, which is owned by Nestlé, and Digiorno Brand, which is owned by Kraft. Now, when you buy a Romance product in a grocery store, it's already fully cooked, all you have to do is heat it up. But if you buy something that sounds the same but is made by their competition, that's just not true, you still have some cooking to do. The advantage Romance has in production is that there are only three systems in the country that can provide what's known as "postpackaging pasteurization," which kills bacteria that might otherwise get into the food product and could cause harm to the consumer. Romance owns two of those systems, and they use them for all their products, so that they are safe to eat right out of the package."

The lawyer paused, the old men smiled, and Bob smiled back. Then he continued.

"Okay, Bob, I think that gives you some insight into the commercial side. But when these men sell this company, they don't want to sell it to just anybody. Their concern is that some big wheeler-dealer corporate baron might get his hands on it and just break it up, sell off some parts and junk the rest. That happens all the time, and if that happened at Romance, why, they could end up with a lot of people losing their jobs. Now this pork and sausage production was originally just one man who worked his way up the hard way. He was very smart and he did very well in business. But all his life he had gone out of his way to promote and protect the people who worked for him. When the employees got into the thousands, he had refused to cut back on his concern over the welfare of the workers, and that has always been part of the business. This is not just their reputation I am talking about, it is the reality of the company that has tried to retain almost a human heart and soul, and it always, always treats its employees with dignity. From what I have seen of you, Bob, particularly in the issue over control of that metal manufacturing firm, I think the personal honor and decency you showed then, combined with your West Point training and your combat experience, are perfect evidence that you would do the right thing if you were able to buy this pasta company."

Bob spoke right up.

"Thank you, I think I would. But how much money are we talking about here?"

The lawyer was silent, and one of the older men spoke up.

"We believe a fair price is X million dollars."

Bob's spirits sank.

"Well, it sounds wonderful, but I'm afraid that takes me out of the picture, I don't . . ."

The same older man spoke up again.

"No, no, you don't need any personal money. The financing is all arranged, we've got the banks lined up, and Romance Foods has an established income stream that will justify a loan to cover the price of purchase and everything else. We just want to make sure we sell it to the right guy, that's all. We never would have heard your name if you weren't a smart businessman, but from the time we learned you were a West Point graduate, and that you flew in the Vietnam War, well, that really was all we needed to know. We just wanted to meet you, that's all. I must tell you, Bob, we are all honored to know a man who has done so much for our country."

Bob had to smile.

"Well thank you, but listen, I didn't do anything, I just . . ."

The three men were quick to quiet him.

"No, no, we know what you did . . ."

"You did well, son . . ."

"You're among friends here . . ."

"Okay, thank you, thank you. Well, this all sounds great but . . . before we go any farther, you need to know something about me . . . I . . . I love the prospect of becoming a pasta king, don't get me wrong. But I'm not . . . how do I say this? I don't think I have a single drop of Italian blood in my veins! Does that matter?"

Everyone laughed, then one of the two older men spoke up: "Don't worry about that, son, 'Ramsay' sounds more

Italian to me than 'Kraft' or 'Nestlé,' and that doesn't matter. All we care about is professionalism and competence, and I think you are just the man we've been looking for."

Bob smiled at this.

"Okay, I'm interested. What do you want me to do?"

"Nothing, Bob. We know your history as a businessman, we just wanted to meet with you face to face, that's all. If we sell the company to you, do you think you would give this company a fair chance of staying together for a while, let the employees have an opportunity to make sure it continues to be profitable?"

"Of course I would! It sounds to me like there would be no reason to break it up. If anything, it sounds like it ought to grow!"

Smiles all around.

"That's what we think too, Bob. Okay, we need to talk some, and then you'll hear back from us in a few days."

When he got home that night, he had decided not to tell Bev about it just yet. Nobody had signed anything, and it might all blow away.

A few days later, he did sign something. And a week later, there was a formal signing of papers at the bank by him, the lawyer, and the three older gentlemen.

So now Bob Ramsay is Romance Foods. Next time you're in a supermarket, go over to the refrigerated pasta section and try some. I think you'll agree, it really is good, even if Bob doesn't have a single drop of Italian blood running through his veins.

The Soul of West Point

In the marketplace of free ideas generated by our most cherished constitutional freedoms, our extraordinary American freedom of speech and of the press, antiwar opposition was really beginning to heat up in the late 1960s and early 1970s. While West Point and West Pointers may not have been physically assailed, there were times when they felt as if that was about to happen. And the preaching in the media became relentless.

The "revealed wisdom" that was increasingly available in print held that the Republic of Vietnam, or "South Vietnam" as it was popularly known at the time, was an artificial state. It had been created by American and other Western powers in the 1950s from the residue of one and a half of France's five colonial possessions in Indochina, built up in unreflecting fear as a bulwark against the advance of Stalinism. And what many Americans had feared most in the wake of World War II and the Korean War was the seemingly relentless march of world communism, a fear widely dismissed by intellectuals in the late 1960s as illusory.

In Vietnam, this cure was worse than the disease, said the opinion makers of the media. The Vietnamese to whom Western powers had handed complete and arbitrary political control over the state of South Vietnam had become totalitarian rulers, men apparently oblivious to the welfare of the people they ruled. And while they may have had a few idealists in their midst at the outset, these men in political control had quickly evolved into a military junta who seemed to care not at all about the freedoms or even the welfare of the people who lived under their rule. When Buddhist monks, for instance, had immolated themselves on the street in public protest against the oppressive rule of these unelected dictators, the tyrants ruling South Vietnam had suppressed dissent with an iron hand. And then they had openly laughed in the world press about the problems caused by "Buddhist barbecues."

To the newspaper and television pundits in New York City, echoed by their supporters in academia, this was not what America represented, and if we had to be involved at all, we should have looked first to the will and the welfare of the Vietnamese people. No matter what we may have thought of communism at the time, America was about personal freedom, and it seemed that we had chosen to support the wrong side, the police state side, in the Vietnamese civil war. How could American Army officers, particularly those who had been educated at West Point to believe in and protect the highest moral and ethical standards, be going off to fight in such a wicked war?

And it is that sort of moral dilemma that allows the outsider to strip the cultural coverings away from West Point and examine it closely as a governmental institution. Is it doing what it is supposed to be doing? It is most important for affected critical observers—the American people, for whose benefit and welfare it exists—to examine the ethical theories it teaches, according to which it hopes to build moral as well as physical courage in its products. The purpose of this institutional effort reaches far beyond simple education in the attempt to establish strong standards of ethical leadership in all cadets, for such is the hallmark of a West Pointer.

The ethos of West Point is difficult to describe in words, and the effort is somewhat like trying to pick up mercury with your fingertips. West Point teaches belief in and devotion to absolute principles. Its motto, "Duty, Honor, Country," captures some of them, while a few lines from its nondenominational Cadet Prayer shed light on more: "Help me to seek the harder right instead of the easier wrong, and never to be satisfied with a half truth when the whole can be won."

The desired moral base of a West Point graduate was written down long ago by Epictetus, the Stoic philosopher: "Do the Right Thing." The essence of the West Point experience is moral, and it is to teach its graduates how to make difficult decisions under pressure that are morally correct. Once the West Pointers know what they must do in order to obtain a given outcome, the hope is that they will then have the moral and physical courage to act so as to attain those ends, whatever the personal cost.

The essence of the moral decision can be synopsized as follows: Whenever you are faced with a challenging moral decision—every day—you have only to reflect upon such issues as time, place, and personal responsibilities to others, and you will quickly know what is the Right Thing to Do. It might be popular or unpopular, it might be easy or hard, it might be legal or illegal. But if you truly believe in your heart of hearts that it is the Right Thing, then the institutional hope is that a West Pointer will see no further moral choice. And so long as West Pointers believe they are Doing the Right Thing, then they cannot be defeated. They can die, but they cannot be defeated. Moral value, says the Academy, is more important than even life itself.

But to establish leadership authority in any individual, that person must quickly acquire a sense of responsibility for group action, which means for the actions of others, even when that assumption of responsibility has results that are not, in some sense, "fair." On the first day of Beast Barracks, every New Cadet learns that he or she has only three permissible answers when questioned by an upperclassman, and those answers are, "Yes sir," "No sir," or "No excuse, sir." The lesson gradually imparted is that when you, your team, or just one member of your team fails to perform as required, the leader must pay a price for that failure. There may be an explanation for that failure, but there is no excuse. And life demands performance, not excuses. Even though a given failure to perform may have been beyond your personal control, you, as leader, are still responsible for it. It may be unfair, but life isn't fair. Get used to it. Stand up and take the hit. Show yourself to be a leader. Absorb the blow without complaint. Grow stronger. Learn.

But West Point is not alone in attempting to build moral and physical courage in our youth, in trying to help young Americans establish principled behavior under pressure as the leitmotiv of their lives. The major difference it represents from other American organizations or institutions, whether they be of a social, religious, cultural, or business nature, is that West Point is in the business of producing Army officers able to adhere to principle under pressure, officers who will lead soldiers and reliably perform their duties in a professional manner no matter the cost. The life of the leader as well as others under his command may one day depend on such predictably professional performance of duty. More important, so might the completion of a mission on which far higher stakes may ride. If our constitutional freedoms are to be defended, therefore, such a moral focus in an official institution of our secular society seems not only appropriate, but even mandatory.

The Vietnam War illustrates an important aspect of this value system. From the first day they arrive, West Pointers swear to uphold the Constitution. Before World War II, Hitler had the entire German military swear an oath of allegiance to him personally. And indeed, that has been the historical norm throughout the world: Warriors' first allegiance was to their leader. But this is not the American way. Except for the few years at the end of the eighteenth century mentioned in Chapter 1, when President John

Adams, a Federalist, used the U.S. Army led by openly Federalist officers to fight against and generally abuse his political opponents in Jefferson's Republican party, the American military has never played a significant political role in our national history.

This is important. Even though individual officers might have agreed personally in the abstract that a particular war was politically the wrong war for America to fight, that it was being wrongly waged or was fatally flawed in some other way, that does not matter. Deciding on the political rectitude of any war, or on the freedom of opponents of a war they might be fighting to profess their feelings, has never been a choice open to American soldiers.

When professional military officers sworn to uphold the Constitution are ordered by America's democratically elected leaders to fight a particular war, they simply obey those orders and fight that war. In so doing, they are offering their lives for their country in a pure sense, one that is without political conditioning, but conforms only to the laws of our land and the Constitution. This necessarily includes their defense of the constitutional right of any American citizen to oppose a war, even a war in which the country might be engaged, and that defense of constitutional freedoms is part of their duty.

It cannot be claimed, of course, that all West Point graduates have always upheld the highest moral standards in all their actions. West Point is a human institution, and its graduates, its commissioned officer staff and faculty custodians, its cadets, and even its potential cadets are all flawed human beings. But those shared flaws and the potentially central role their actions may one day play in our nation's defense only provide more justification for teaching cadets adherence to the highest moral standards in their lives.

West Point's public image has waxed and waned over time, and this is perhaps best seen during the period of the Vietnam War. In the 1950s and middle 1960s, the Great American Public believed West Point to be an elite and highly prestigious educational institution. Its standards were high, and the open competition for presidential and congressional appointments to West Point was fierce. In fact, during that period, there were roughly ten applicants already qualified according to West Point's traditionally high academic, athletic, physical, and medical standards for each appointment ultimately awarded.

During the late 1960s, however, the Vietnam War was opposed first by rebellious youths, then by academics, intellectuals, journalists, and ultimately by the great mass of the American people. This dramatic political change, of course, had a very negative effect on the Army and its uniformed soldiers. These, after all, were the most readily identifiable targets who could be held responsible by American civilians for that wicked, evil war: They were the ones who were fighting it, so they could be criticized for that and that alone until they stopped.

This may have been misdirected criticism, but it reached its mark. And to men in uniform, it hurt.

Ultimately, West Point, too, paid a price in terms of seeing its prestige fall through the floor while a negative image of it was built up in the hearts and minds of the American populace. The competition for political appointments to West Point plummeted in less than a decade, from only one in ten applicants being admitted in the early 1960s, to all qualified applicants receiving appointments in the early 1970s. But the Old Guard was unimpressed.

That's what happens in wartime, they said, most teenaged kids don't really want to risk dying in battle, and during a war, such risk for a military professional is self-evident. So fewer of them want to go to West Point. Don't worry, they said, it will only take a few years of unthreatened peace for standards to go back up and the competition for appointments to once again reach fierce levels.

And that is what happened after the Vietnam War ended.

Many of the officers teaching at West Point in the late 1960s had already served in Vietnam. Some would go back there for second and third tours of duty. Many of the peers of these faculty members had already been killed in that ugly war. And virtually all of the young cadets they taught would graduate, be commissioned, and go to Vietnam in their turn, some to bleed, others to die.

These were not stupid men. Given the challenge of a once-popular war that turned sour at home before their eyes, most simply assumed the responsibilities of their commissions in the Army and performed their duties to the best of their ability. If those duties included fighting and offering their lives—even dying—in an ugly war that increasing numbers of Americans opposed, then that was what they would do. No matter the cost, they would perform their duties: They would Do the Right Thing, for that is the West Point way.

Chapter 12:

Afghanistan—Jason L. Amerine

JASON LUKE AMERINE WAS BORN IN CALIFORNIA on May 6, 1971. Later, his parents both went to college in Hawaii and liked it so much that they stayed. Because of this, Jason grew up in Hawaii, a classic "*Haole*," or Mainlander. His high-school years were somewhat unusual, however, in that he was very much involved in a Junior Reserve Officers' Training Course, in which he excelled, and after graduation he won an appointment to West Point.

His cadet years at the Academy were pretty standard: heavy academics mixed with spit and polish, parades, intramural athletics known as "intramurder," and the usual list of too much to do in too short a time. But he had a not-too-secret longing that came from his earlier years in Hawaii. His JROTC program was one of the few run entirely by U.S. Army NCOs, and two of them had a powerful effect on Jason's life.

The first was Sergeant Major Kenneth Q. Ching, Jr., the senior Army instructor. He saw early on that Jason had the "right stuff" to make it, both at West Point and as a professional Army officer. He also knew how unfocused teenagers often are, so he secured the appropriate paperwork that would at least get Jason considered for a political appointment to West Point. Then he called Jason into his office and ordered him—not "requested" or "suggested," but "ordered"—to sign the papers. Sergeant Major Ching got the administrative ball rolling, and the next thing Jason knew, he had orders to report to West Point in early July 1989, only a few weeks after high-school graduation.

The other key influence came from another JROTC instructor who had been a "Green Beret," a Special Forces soldier in Vietnam. That man, Master Sergeant Howard Noe, became a genuine hero to Jason, and the stories he told an eager teenaged boy about the Vietnam War were just the purest romantic adventure.

These two NCOs worked hand-in-glove to get Jason into West Point and the Army, for they believed he was a most promising young man. And when he arrived at West Point, Jason suddenly had a life plan: More than anything else, he wanted to be a Special Forces leader conducting unconventional warfare behind enemy lines. His one true hope all through West Point was that he would, one day, find a way to join Special Forces, and he even tailored his academic curriculum to that end.

Academic options had changed at West Point during the 1970s, or perhaps I should say that was when they first appeared. Before that time, the standard required curriculum was heavily weighted to engineering. But Jason was fortunate enough to be able to tailor his studies, and he took a total of ten semesters of Arabic during his four years at West Point. When he graduated, his bachelor's degree was in Arabic studies, and he could read, write, and speak Arabic quite easily, a rather unusual asset for a brand-new second lieutenant in the U.S. Army. But he knew that it would be a very good fit with Special Forces, which was the main reason he had chosen that path.

An important part of a West Point education for future Army officers is what's known as Cadet Troop Leadership Training. This normally occurs during two summer months after the cadet's sophomore or junior academic year, and it consists of sending each cadet to an active duty U.S. Army unit. Over that two-month period, the cadets play the role of second lieutenants, usually acting as platoon leaders, a sort of first "hands-on" exposure to the Army life that lies before them after graduation. During the summer after his junior year at West Point, Jason chose an assignment with Special Forces. He went to Fort Campbell, Kentucky, and spent eight weeks with the 5th Special Forces Group (Airborne). Once he was finally on the ground and playing the role of a Special Forces leader, Jason, as he himself had predicted, truly fell in love with the whole concept of unconventional warfare.

But even after graduation, Special Forces was still far away. No brand-new second lieutenants could even apply for Special Forces, and Jason knew he had to prove himself as a soldier before unconventional warfare would even become an option. After graduation leave, Jason attended the Infantry Officers' Basic Course at Fort Benning, Georgia, jump school, and Ranger School. But he had some glitches in Ranger School, and for whatever reason, he was part of the 20 percent or so of each class who fail to earn their Ranger tab. He went off to his first assignment as an infantry platoon leader sorely singed and determined to one day heal that wound. But more immediate things awaited him in Panama. Soon after he took over as an infantry platoon leader in the 5th Battalion of the 87th Infantry, trouble loomed large.

Haitian refugees came flooding out of Haiti onto U.S. shores in 1994, and the American military was heavily involved in rounding them up and sending them home. Fidel Castro saw this as an opportunity to make major political capital, for he knew the United States would not turn away refugees from one of the last remaining communist countries. So in the summer of 1994, he emptied his prisons and mental hospitals, put the inmates on boats, and sent them north to America.

The political result in the United States was complex. First, we sent a force into Haiti to try to calm things down. Next, we rounded up the Cuban refugees and held them in military camps, the first at the U.S. naval base at Guantanamo Bay on the tip of Cuba. But that small area quickly filled up, so about four thousand Cubans were shipped from Guantanamo to Panama. And soon enough, they launched a major riot.

At first, the American position was to keep back, and the rioters set up their own little fiefdom inside the camp. But it didn't take long before the situation got out of hand, and the decision was made to breach the camp and put down the rioters. Jason's platoon was among those who went in on September 8, 1994, and they met a true firestorm of resistance. As part of their construction of the camp, the Army had sown hillsides with rocks the size of baseballs to prevent erosion, and the Cubans hurled these lethal missiles at the American soldiers. The stones shattered the plastic defensive shields carried by the soldiers, and soon enough American teeth, then bones, began to break.

Twelve of the twenty-three men in Jason's platoon who went into the camp were evacuated as casualties, among some two hundred American casualties from retaking the camp that day. But there were no American fatalities, and attention at home was fixed on Somalia, where sixteen American Rangers had been killed. As a result, there was very little press coverage, but Jason was deeply involved in some heavy-duty violence from a mass of very angry people directed at him and at his men.

After two years in Panama, Jason returned to Ranger School and, on his second try, ended up the officer honor graduate, based on performance on patrols, and the Merrill's Marauder Award winner, based on peer ratings. His next duty assignment was in Korea. There, he served in Panmunjom as executive officer of the United Nations Joint Security Force Company, a Korean Army unit of 220 tough infantrymen. All the soldiers in this company, including the company commander, were Korean. But Jason enjoyed this year in a foreign army tremendously, and he learned a great deal. With that year in Korea under his belt, it was time for Jason to take the Infantry Officers' Advanced Course at Fort Benning. Upon graduation, he finally was ready to go after the golden ring: Special Forces.

After all the correct paperwork had been submitted and cleared, the first hurdle was Special Forces Assessment and Selection. This was three weeks of torture at Fort Bragg intended to weed out the weaklings. Jason cleared that hurdle easily, then entered the Special Forces Officer Qualification Course. This was a six-month course, and Jason followed its completion with six months of intensive Arabic-language studies. This was followed by two weeks of Survival, Escape, Resistance, and Evasion School before Jason was given command of an operational "A" detachment at Fort Campbell, Kentucky.

The normal mission of an A team is to train indigenous recruits as soldiers and assemble them into a military unit capable first of self-defense and later of offensive operations. His first A team was Operational Detachment A-572. An A team normally consists of a dozen men with a captain as commander and a warrant officer as executive officer. The rest of the team consists of NCOs, and first and foremost is an E-8 master sergeant. This team sergeant is usually an experienced man of around forty years of age with more than twenty years in the Army under his belt. The remaining NCOs are E-7 sergeants first class or E-6 staff sergeants, usually tough men in their late twenties and thirties whose areas of expertise are focused as follows: one intelligence sergeant, who assembles and interprets all intelligence leads; two weapons sergeants, who know all the weapons in the world and do the actual tactical training of local troops; two communications sergeants, who establish and maintain radio contact under difficult circumstances, both with higher authority and with subordinate units; two medical sergeants, who are able to handle any and all medical emergencies up to and including minor surgery; and two Engineer sergeants who are masters of construction and demolition and are also responsible for feeding and resupplying the team. Additionally, all team members are cross-trained in at least one other specialty.

During Jason's first assignment with Special Forces, he and his team deployed twice to California and once to Kuwait. After a year, he left 572 and took over command of ODA 574. The main difference between these two teams was their means of insertion into a given operational area. His first team, ODA 572, simply walked in carrying their rucksacks and gear, but ODA 574 entered vertically by parachute, using something called "Military Free Fall." This means the team members leave the aircraft at high altitude, many thousands of feet up, and fall free until reaching precisely the right point above the earth, when they open their parachutes at only hundreds of feet of altitude. This means of entry is nearly impossible to detect, even for an alerted force. It also is just the slightest bit dicey for the guy who is falling like a rock until he opens his chute just before plowing in. But these guys just loved the occasional high-risk thrills that came with their job.

ODA 574 entered Afghanistan in October 2001 and linked up with Hamid Karzai and his soldiers. Jason was in command, but he had no warrant officer second in command. One other minor variation was that he also had a combat control technician from the U.S. Air Force to augment the abilities of his two communications sergeants.

Hamid Karzai is a well-educated man who speaks fluent English and had been a political refugee until September 2001. Driven from Afghanistan in 1996, he had found refuge in Pakistan. There, he and a few colleagues had planned their eventual return to their homeland and the armed overthrow by the Afghan people of the unpopular Taliban regime. A member of the Afghan majority tribe, the Pashtun, he had long opposed the religious dominion over the country exercised by the Taliban. This political party had based its rule of Afghanistan on an extreme Muslim view since the late 1990s and enforced its dictates and laws by the application of life-and-death force against the Afghan people.

This extreme fundamentalist Muslim rule was quite harsh on ordinary Afghans. While extreme religious customs practiced in other foreign lands largely go unnoticed within the United States, the Taliban rule of Afghanistan was suddenly perceived to be a direct threat against the secular world of the West after the terrorist attacks of September 11, 2001, in New York City and Washington, D.C.

Most Taliban members came from fundamentalist Muslim students in the post-Soviet years, men who had not fought against the Russians. They took advantage of the political anarchy after the Soviets left and the United States abandoned its support of the guerrillas, seizing political power and refusing to give it up, even as their oppressive movement became increasingly disliked. Karzai's original goal was to return to Afghanistan and help small towns or villages overthrow their Taliban masters. If he was able to launch such a low-level revolution, he hoped the political antipathy of the people would spread and eventually drive the Taliban from power at the national level.

When ODA 574 first established contact with Hamid Karzai in early October, they provided the promise of all that would be needed for the growth of a substantial rebel force: weapons, ammunition, food, even modest amounts of cash if that was the lubricant required. These were all delivered by parachute as needed, and Jason was able to deliver in a matter of hours, not days. Gradually, these American Special Forces soldiers helped train a significant rebel force armed with small arms from the former Soviet Union: AK-47 submachine guns, rocket-propelled grenades, and PKM machine guns that fired chain-linked ammunition.

As his force grew, Karzai was constantly on the phone informing other disgruntled tribal leaders of what he was doing and asking them to join him. Once his rebel force had grown to about two hundred fighters, the people of the small city of Tarin Kot put a rope around the neck of their Taliban mayor and hung him from a lamp post. While this city has only a few thousand inhabitants, it is the regional capital of Oruzgan Province, where the Taliban began. After the people had strung up their Taliban mayor, Karzai's force entered Tarin Kot on November 16, the first day of Ramadan, and took over peacefully. The Taliban heard about the mayor's death and the smallish rebel force that had taken over the town, but they apparently had no idea that American Special Forces were on the ground with Karzai.

The Taliban immediately raised a force to retake Tarin Kot and started moving north from Kandahar in various vehicles. Their plan at the time, as Karzai's men would later learn from prisoners, was to move into Tarin Kot against what they thought would be slight, if any, resistance. Once they had retaken the town, they planned to randomly select Afghan families, shoot all the members, then drag their corpses out in front of their houses and leave them in the street as an example of what lay in store for those who opposed the Taliban.

That evening, soon after his forces took over Tarin Kot, Karzai was hosting Jason at a dinner with other Afghan tribal leaders in the governor's residence. Then he got the warning by cell phone that some five hundred Taliban soldiers were moving toward them in about eighty vehicles, and he immediately shared this information. Jason wanted to leave then and look to establishing defensive positions around the threatened parts of town, but Karzai and the others would not hear of it. There will be plenty of time for fighting, they insisted, but for now stay here and drink some green tea with us.

Eventually, Jason was able to leave, and he spent most of that night with members of his team trying to get Afghan rebel defensive positions set up covering key roads and wadis that gave access to the town. He also got in touch with the U.S. Air Force and was assured that all the airpower he could use would be waiting for him overhead the next morning.

Just before dawn, he moved south of town to a ridgeline overlooking the exit from a mountain pass into the Tarin Kot Valley, an area perhaps forty miles wide and fifty miles long, surrounded on three sides by immense mountain ranges. Jason's team was with him, as well as perhaps thirty or forty of Hamid Karzai's rebel soldiers, and they were watching the road that came out of a pass in the end of a mountain box perhaps ten miles to their south. Within a few hours, a long line of vehicles appeared at the pass. Jason and his men had already set up their laser target acquisition equipment, which looks not unlike a large camera on a tripod. While his Air Force communications sergeant got on the radio with the forward air controller (FAC) loitering overhead, one of Jason's soldiers looked through a laser target designator and adjusted the sight on the lead vehicle. He then fixed a laser beam, invisible to the human eye, right between the headlights of the lead vehicle while his Air Force commo sergeant got an F-18 laden with "smart" bombs to roll in. The pilot released the bomb some distance above them and pulled back up to altitude, but the bomb followed the laser into the radiator of what looked like a five-ton truck with an immense antiaircraft gun and a dozen armed Taliban soldiers in its bed. In a burst of flame and molten metal, the truck and its contents were instantly converted into little more than a scorched steel frame surrounded by a billowing cloud of hot dust. Even ten miles away, the noise of the explosion was stunning.

The vehicles in the Taliban convoy lurched to a stop for twenty seconds or so, then moved forward onto the valley floor once again. They were a mixed assortment, ranging from large trucks similar to the lead vehicle and bearing artillery or antiaircraft guns all the way down to mini Toyota pickups, but all were loaded with armed Taliban soldiers, and Jason's team used several target designators to steer bombs onto them. After the first half-dozen or so had exploded without a single miss, the Taliban column halted once again.

But then Jason heard people yelling and engines roaring into life behind him and turned to see his allies beginning to race away. The rebel soldiers who had come up on the ridge with them were plainly terrified by the Taliban convoy, and they were all jumping into their vehicles and heading back to town. He and the other team members ran for the trucks, yelling and screaming at the rebels that the Taliban would be stopped and killed right there. But they weren't heard, and a quick backward glance told them that the Taliban vehicles had started pouring out of the mountain pass once again.

Jason had a decision to make, and he realized that it was just too risky for the Americans to stay where they were with no local support. The rebel soldiers were clearly not going to stick around, and since they were their only ride back to town, the decision was easy: The Americans scooped up their equipment and loaded it in the rear of the last truck, then hopped in and headed back to Tarin Kot.

Once there, Jason ran into Hamid Karzai's headquarters building and quickly briefed him. Then he and his team members "borrowed" four vehicles and drove around the edges of the town, making sure the rebels were manning the defensive positions they had set up the night before. This done, they grabbed their target designators and radios and headed south again. By now, Taliban vehicles had overrun the ridge that Jason and his team had occupied during the first strikes. So they stopped a few miles south of town and set up on a small hill about eight miles north of the ridge. The Taliban vehicles were more spread out now, but the Americans quickly set up their tripods and brought in the air strikes once again.

As the laser-designated bombs hit the vehicles, Jason methodically targeted the ones closest to his position and worked his way back. Suddenly, he heard from team members left back in Tarin Kot that they were being attacked by Taliban infantrymen from the east. This was not good news, as the valley was covered with numerous shallow wadis, basically dry streambeds, that offered concealed infantry approaches into Tarin Kot.

Since Jason had been forced to return to town after the first air strikes, he couldn't be sure that the Taliban force had not broken into smaller elements, with one group continuing south on the main road while other elements split off and moved down these wadis to either side of town in order to attack from there. Indeed, that might be what was happening right then. He had at least set up those rebel defensive positions with that in mind, but he had to be careful that Tarin Kot did not fall to a Taliban infantry attack behind him while he was busy trying to destroy the convoy moving up the main road.

By this time, perhaps one hundred rebels of the two hundred in Karzai's force had joined him on the hill south of town. He sent most of these men back to defend Tarin Kot and, through his interpreter, told them that no more than half should be committed to the fight on the east side of town. The other half should report to Karzai's headquarters to serve as a reserve force. He and the other team members with him continued to destroy the Taliban trucks. After an hour or so, the remaining trucks in the convoy retreated into the pass.

About that time, he heard from Tarin Kot that the Taliban infantry attack from the east had been beaten back, and there was no longer any hostile fire from that sector. Jason was relieved to get that news, but he also told the Air

Force that the Taliban convoy seemed to be moving back into the narrow pass. He still was able to target a few vehicles or what he thought were dismounted enemy positions, but he could see F–16's and F–18s diving low, followed by explosions in the mountain pass. Clearly, U.S. aircraft from the Air Force and the Navy were having a field day!

When Jason got back to town, he learned that some sixty to eighty rebels had held off the attack from the east, and the Taliban force never gotten closer than several hundred meters from town. The whole defense of Tarin Kot that day had taken about four hours, and the effectiveness of air strikes called in by Special Forces teams operating on the ground with laser target designators was simply breathtaking.

Jason counted more than thirty destroyed Taliban vehicles in the Tarin Kot Valley later that day. After this thunderbolt crushing of the Taliban convoy, Hamid Karzai told Jason that the Taliban force was broken. ODA 574 then interdicted all other Taliban efforts to come north from Kandahar in convoys of any size: Within a few weeks, they destroyed another forty to fifty Taliban vehicles loaded with soldiers or armaments in other parts of Oruzgan Province.

Meanwhile, Jason's Special Forces team reinforced the defenses of Tarin Kot as Hamid Karzai's small rebel group grew into a much larger force. Karzai was constantly on his cell phone with tribal leaders, coordinating military movements as they switched their allegiance from the Taliban to him. Jason was in constant contact by radio with his commanders and, as the senior American on the ground, explained the political and military reality as best he could. He asked his higher authority to convey the sensitivity of the situation to the political decision-makers in Washington, urging them to give Karzai room and time to build his anti-Taliban force as the Afghan people turned to him. He explained that Karzai never wanted to be seen as a military leader of the Afghans; rather, he wanted to enable the Afghan people to rise up and overthrow the Taliban town by town. Karzai considered himself merely a representative of the people who wanted peace, for that was all he wanted himself.

Eventually, the United States decided to give Karzai the time he needed while ensuring that ODA 574 and their on-call air support protected him. After Tarin Kot, Karzai built a much larger force, negotiated surrenders, and most of Oruzgan Province in the south central part of Afghanistan came under his control within days. The Pashtun tribes make up the majority of the Afghan population, and although Karzai is a Pashtun himself, he sought a governmental structure that was built along national rather than ethnic lines.

By December 3, Karzai's force had grown to powerful proportions, and he planned to move south and pressure Kandahar. His first move was some thirty miles south to Damana, which is still twenty miles north of Kandahar. He sought to mass his forces at Damana, then negotiate for the surrender of Kandahar, the last major city under the political control of the Taliban. Karzai was confident that the Taliban in Kandahar would surrender, but he nevertheless prepared for a siege.

For this movement, it was agreed that Jason and five of his team members would take the lead with around one hundred guerrillas, while his team sergeant and the other half of ODA 574 stayed with Karzai and the main body that would move more slowly behind them. Jason, in essence, would be conducting a very aggressive reconnaissance in force, moving both day and night. But while Jason and his team had night vision goggles that turned night into day, the one hundred rebels who would be called upon to do any infantry fighting involved did not, so night movement was conducted very judiciously.

Jason and his force began their movement in civilian pickup trucks on November 30, and always stayed a few hours ahead of the main body. There is a major river nearly a half-mile wide between Kandahar and Tarin Kot called the Arghandab, across which there is only one bridge, a massive reinforced concrete structure. It was the only way across a wide river, and as far as troop movement north and south was concerned, control of that bridge was of crucial importance. As they moved south, Karzai the politician wanted Damana, but Jason the soldier wanted the bridge.

They passed through Damana on December 3, but Jason kept pushing for the bridge. As they moved, the rebels would normally clear every ridge. Then they hit the final ridgeline before the bridge, just above the town of Sayyd Alma Kalaya. The guerrillas dismounted from their vehicles, moved to the crest of the ridge, and became engaged in a fierce firefight. After a few minutes, Jason saw them come back down off the ridge, obviously retreating. Climbing out of his own vehicle with an M-4 carbine on which was mounted an excellent telescopic sight, he grabbed the translator and started running up the ridge, waving his arms and shouting for the guerrillas to follow him.

He got to the crest and fell forward into a prone position, easing his head and weapon forward through the weeds. Below him, some two hundred yards away, was the town, and gunfire winked from some of the windows in the houses. But perhaps four hundred yards away, there was a small hill in the middle of town, on top of which was some sort of fortification. Five or six Taliban soldiers were standing in the open on this hilltop, two of them firing rocket-propelled grenades blindly over the ridge toward Jason's guerrillas, while others sprayed automatic fire from their AK-47s in the same general direction. Evidently, this was what had driven his guerrillas off the crest of the ridge.

Jason estimated the range at four hundred meters and used that distance with his telescopic sight. Then he took careful aim at a man about to launch another RPG and fired. He noticed, in the lower half of his telescopic sight, a puff of dust at the feet of his target. So he ignored the reticle inside his sight, instead instantly using the old "burst on target" trick he had learned long ago: He simply moved his weapon until the place in his scope where the puff of dust had appeared was centered on his target's torso. He squeezed off another round and the target fell like a sack of wheat. Two other Taliban soldiers bent to help him as the others stopped, shocked, and watched them. Jason carefully sighted one of these figures and dropped him with his third shot.

The remaining Taliban soldiers on the hill glanced briefly in his direction, then turned and ran like rabbits, including the two who had been ministering to the first man shot. Jason was surprised to hear cheering from the side and behind him. Only when he looked around did he realize that the guerrillas had followed him back up onto the ridge, but now they were just watching him rather than firing themselves.

The gunfire from the hilltop in the middle of town had ended, so Jason looked for targets at closer range. He quickly saw muzzle flashes and fired one round at the dark window from which they appeared. He never knew if he hit anything inside that house or not, but no more muzzle flashes appeared in that window. He then started engaging other windows marked by muzzle flashes and, through his interpreter, encouraged the rebels to do the same.

Within a very few minutes, the few Taliban left alive in Sayyd Alma Kalaya were running the other way. Jason and his men descended the ridge into town and took control unopposed. Eventually, they even walked up the hill and into the bunker where the two Taliban soldiers had been hit. There were no bodies, but Jason did find two large pools of blood. By this time, he could see that his force was simply too disorganized to take the bridge that day, so he decided to spend the night in defensive positions in Sayyd Alma Kalaya.

Well after dark, the Taliban came across the bridge in force. They encircled half of the town, and for a while it looked as if they might surround Jason's entire force. Many of the rebels started running back toward Damana, but one group of about thirty loyal fighters led by a man named Bari Gul stayed with Jason and the Americans. They used a variety of optics, night vision goggles, and laser designators to bring in overwhelming air power. In addition to fighter-bombers dropping laser-directed bombs, Jason also was able to employ AC-130 gunships. These are basically C-130 propeller-driven cargo aircraft armed with six miniguns and a 105-mm cannon. The aircraft flies in in a slow and steady circle, and each of its miniguns is able to fire down at a rate of six thousand rounds per minute, either singly or in concert, while the cannon fires conventional 105-mm artillery rounds directly into targets below. The Taliban forces that had dared move against Jason and his Argonauts were turned into hamburger, and the survivors fled south across the bridge before the first light of dawn.

The next morning, Jason took sixty rebels and half his

team to seize a hilltop on the north side of the bridge. As they approached that hilltop, the Taliban opened up from positions in the trees along the riverbank on the north side of the bridge as well as from positions south of the river. These positions included caves along a ridge south of the river, and Jason's team hammered them all with air strikes. One of his team members, Sergeant Wes McGirr, was shot through the neck, but he was evacuated by helicopter, and the wound was not fatal. Enemy fire died down after the air strikes, and that afternoon, the first element of an American command team was landed by helicopter and took control of the operation.

With a lieutenant colonel finally on the ground, the responsibility for a lot of as-yet-unuttered and intangible responsibilities was removed from Jason's shoulders for the first time. Jason and his team were ordered to spend the night back in Sayyd Alma Kalaya, several miles away. While he thought this was a big mistake, that oversight of the bridge should be maintained through the night to preclude another Taliban incursion, Jason was not consulted, and his protests were ignored. So he decided to shut up and do what he was told.

No Taliban came across the bridge that night, and Jason and his team got some sleep for the first time in quite a while. Next day, the remainder of the headquarters team arrived with letters, packages of cookies, and other goodies from ODA 594's wives, sort of like Christmas "Care packages." While they were reading letters, an American bomb, called in by the headquarters team and intended for a Taliban target on the other side of the river, hit Jason's hilltop.

The strike was deadly. Two team members were killed instantly: the team sergeant, Master Sergeant Jefferson

Davis, who was remembered as the father of the team family, and Sergeant First Class Dan Petithory, everyone's older brother. Bari Gul and four of his loyal Afghan warriors also were killed. The other members of Jason's team were wounded, five of them seriously. Jason himself had his thigh slashed open by shrapnel and both eardrums burst. The whole team was quickly evacuated by helicopter, then airplane, and soon received expert medical care from American doctors. Within days, they were back in the United States. Ironically, on the day the bomb fell on ODA 574, the Taliban dispatched a delegation to surrender Kandahar to Hamid Karzai in Sayyd Alma Kalaya.

Most of the team members faced lengthy hospital stays, but within a few months, Jason had his eardrums surgically repaired and the wound on his thigh closed up with stitches. Before even that basic medical care was received, he was back to red hot and raring to go. But that is as it should be, for Captain Jason Amerine is a professional soldier, and he is "on duty" all the time.

Epilogue:

The Heart of West Point

IN MANY WAYS, THE 1991 TRIUMPH OF DESERT STORM lifted the cloud of guilt and regret associated with Vietnam from the Army, especially at West Point. Thereafter, the military training occurred in the wake of a vibrant victory, not a shameful political defeat, and the new spirit this engendered put wings on the officers teaching and training cadets.

The Cadet Leadership Development System is something that was developed in the late eighties and early nineties, primarily by my West Point classmate Larry Donnithorne, who has a doctoral degree in education from Harvard and worked for the superintendent as his long-range planner. It is a superb system, and it prepares cadets for the Army much better than anything we had. There is a new thrill loose at West Point, and the future of cadets in the Army is once again filled with excitement and adventure.

One central philosophical issue still lurks menacingly at the base of the United States Military Academy, however. That issue calls into question how appropriately individuals at West Point and within the ranks of the Army, and perhaps especially members of Congress, are filling their custodial roles to take care that the purpose and the mission of the Academy be appropriately met. Is West Point doing what our national leaders from the Founding Fathers through to those of the present day want it to do?

We can state the question rather simply: Why did West Point come into being, and why does it continue to exist? The immediate and almost self-evident answer is that it came into existence in order to train officers who would later lead the U.S. Army, and that it persists for the same reason. But an answer that straightforward can be deceptive, for over time, the institution that came into being at West Point has gradually evolved into something that does other things as well as train officers to fight and win wars, things that may even handicap and limit in ways generally not recognized, let alone understood, its ability to fulfill its primary purpose, to perform its fundamental mission.

According to the West Point Public Affairs Office as we enter the twenty-first century, the *purpose* of the United States Military Academy, the reason it exists, is "to provide the nation with leaders of character who serve the common defense"; its *mission*, that which the Army requires of it to achieve its purpose, is "to educate and train the Corps of Cadets so that each graduate shall have the attributes essential to professional growth throughout a career as an officer of the regular Army, and to inspire each to a lifetime of service to the nation."

These, of course, are self-descriptive definitions written by officers filling custodial roles at West Point, and they have changed over the years, though subtly. But however slightly, these differ in their implementation from the purpose and mission originally desired.

West Point responds, of course, to the dictates of our democratically elected civilian leaders, the president and members of Congress, who are tasked by the Constitution with commanding and supporting the Army. But throughout our history, our civilian federal government has for the most part left the specific organization, administration, and maintenance of military schools to the services themselves. When our political leaders feel so moved, however, they speak right up—as was the case in recent years when the Army was told to expand the number of civilians on the West Point faculty or to reduce the number of cadets admitted. Members of Congress have most recently been asking why so much money is spent on West Point despite the fact that it was not the source of commission for a large majority of the Army's top uniformed leadership, its general officers.

When West Point was established in 1802, it was the only such school for the formal training of the officer corps that would lead America's armies. West Point's first fifteen years were rather confused and unproductive, but in 1817, Superintendent Sylvanus Thayer and the disciples he brought with him tried to establish a systematic American study of war. They sought to fuse elements of land war and maritime defense into a strategy for America's military protection and advancement of her national interests, thus curing the worst ills from the War of 1812.

In a nation not immediately threatened by foreign foes and unhappy with standing armies, however, West Point had to provide some beneficial public service that justified its existence in peacetime. Thus it became America's first, and until well into the second half of the nineteenth century, its most important engineering school. The period from 1840 to 1860 is remembered as West Point's "Golden Age," when its graduates were the engineers who built much of the physical infrastructure of young America.

But West Point graduates also came to dominate the leadership of the Army, an unspoken tradition that endured until the late twentieth century. During the Civil War, the commanders of both sides in almost all the major battles were West Point graduates, as were, at the end of World War I, thirty-four of the thirty-eight American corps and division commanders in France. During the World War II era, four of the five men elevated to five-star-general rank to command the largest American army in history were West Pointers.

Recent times have seen dramatic change. In 1966, when I was commissioned, virtually all of the three- and four-star generals and the great majority of the one- and two-star generals were West Point graduates. In 1984, West Pointers made up only 37 percent of all active-duty general officers. In 1994, the proportion of all active-duty Army generals who are West Point graduates had fallen to 29 percent. The last three chairmen of the Joint Chiefs of Staff of the twentieth century, and so the highest-ranking generals in the U.S. military services, were Army generals Colin Powell, John Shalikashvili, and Henry Shelton, and none of them were West Point graduates. At the beginning of a new century, only four of the eleven four-star Army generals are West Pointers. One need not be a gifted intellectual to discern trend lines.

Over time, programs have grown up that initially trained and commissioned reserve officers—those forces that would be called up to support the regulars in dire times. The Reserve Officer Training Corps, or ROTC, on many college campuses, and Officer Candidate School, or OCS, which trains and commissions worthy enlisted soldiers, are the two main programs. Traditionally, it was difficult for such reserve officers to obtain regular commissions, while all West Pointers received them at graduation. Since about World War II, however, ROTC programs have produced large numbers of officers who eventually obtained regular commissions.

Most discussion now heard about the United States Military Academy at West Point seems to be commentary attempting to assess the relative value of West Point graduates compared to officers commissioned from other sources. Some find them better, some worse, some indistinguishable. Those who hold the latter two opinions, of course, naturally call into question the need for the Army to maintain a highly selective and expensive institution that today fails to perform a role it filled in earlier times: that of producing the great bulk of officers who will rise steadily in grade and as generals lead the Army into the future.

This is an even more important issue now that Congress has changed the rules on regular commissions: From now on, *all* new second lieutenants, including West Pointers, will be commissioned in the reserves; regular commissions will be awarded selectively on the basis of merit and only after some years of active duty.

A not-too-subtle question now arises: Should West Point change to accommodate the new and ever-changing face of the Army? If so, how? Is it time for West Point to take on a new challenge, as it did under Thayer, to provide a sorely needed service for America that is of value beyond producing an annual cohort of second lieutenants? How can West Point be made maximally productive for the ever-smaller Army and the nation?

Some numbers don't lie: West Point's relative importance as the source of our Army's general officers, an unwritten but powerful American tradition, is steadily slipping away. When confronted with this fact, the standard response of institutional West Point has been to ignore the changed source of the Army's top leadership as a nonissue. Instead, complex numbers and charts are presented showing West Point graduates as a group to be marginally superior to officers commissioned from other sources, and reassuring the argument that West Point's singular importance remains: that it serves as the source of the highest moral and ethical standards for the officer corps. West Point builds in its cadets, the argument goes, the highest personal standards of character, standards of principled performance under pressure, of "Doing the Right Thing" no matter the personal cost. Upon commissioning, it is said, West Pointers will then reinforce these standards throughout the Army by the "inkblot" principle.

I will accept that West Point graduates as a group may be marginally superior, but that is predictable: The qualities and promise of newly admitted cadets are routinely so high that anything less would be rather a disappointment. And I have no doubt that the ethical training at West Point is indeed of the highest order. But let's not exaggerate—personal honor is an innate quality, and few institutions beyond one's family can take credit for it. West Point may stress and sensitize its students to the concept beyond virtually any other institution of higher learning, but its graduates remain human beings with flaws.

I think the answer to West Point's dilemma of decreasing relevance to the Army lies in revisiting its purpose and its mission and *expanding* the role West Point plays in formal education. I would now like to propose an idea that would more fully and realistically perform West Point's traditional function of teaching professional skills to young officers, dramatically reduce the longstanding-but-senseless rivalry between officers who graduated from West Point and those commissioned from other sources, make use of the sunk capital investment in buildings and facilities at West Point built to accommodate a Corps of Cadets some forty-four hundred strong but now on a downward slope, and, given the latter resources (as well, perhaps, as facilities not fully used at the former Ladycliff College now known as "South Post," or even at nearby Stewart Air Force Base), perform all of this at relatively modest cost. This is a concept that could dramatically enhance the value of West Point to the parent Army and at the same time increase the benefits accruing to the American people.

What I propose is a graduate school for Army officers at West Point. At present, the Army is the only branch of service that does not have its own graduate school: The Navy has the Naval Postgraduate School in Monterrey, California, and the Air Force has the Air Force Institute of Technology at Wright-Patterson Air Force Base in Ohio. The Army occasionally sends its officers to these two fully accredited and highly respected schools rather than to civilian universities, and this is the most cost-effective education available: These military schools cost the Army about eight thousand dollars a year for each graduate student, while Harvard or Tulane or Vanderbilt, for example, all cost around twenty-two thousand dollars.

But this is more than just trying to match the prestigious institutions of the other services. We are talking about equity, about allowing the benefits of a West Point education to extend beyond the small circle it now reaches to those who have shown their mature commitment to careers as professional soldiers—members of a group West Point should, by all rights, be teaching. It is common knowledge that many of our best soldiers are men and women who never realized how much they would enjoy the Army until they were well into their twenties or thirties, when education at West Point, for them, was far beyond realistic consideration. But why not give these individuals a sort of *"repechage,"* or "second chance," to mark their mature professional commitment to a career in the Army with a graduate degree from West Point? A graduate school at West Point would allow consolidation of effort, achieve economies of scale, and limit capital investment in buildings and support facilities simply by making use of what already exists there, at South Post/Ladycliff, and at Stewart Air Force Base.

In the second half of the twentieth century, many American universities developed engineering departments that later became world-renowned. Indeed, the graduate schools of engineering departments at such well-known academic institutions as MIT, Cal Tech, and other national universities have become the recognized source of engineering developments that have changed the face of the world. It does not seem probable, therefore, that West Point could hope to reassume the role it played for most of the nineteenth century as the premier engineering school in the nation. But in what fields might it expect to emerge as a true leader?

That a graduate school in a given field could not expect to become recognized in short order as a major leader in that field should not serve as justification to avoid its establishment. The benefits available at the school, after all, should accrue to the students and, ultimately, to the class of people those students, once they have completed their educations, will serve. Engineering should be included, therefore, among the disciplines considered by the Army's leadership in the event it elects to investigate establishing a graduate school at West Point. The same can be said for other fields of study, ranging from the technical field of environmental engineering to a more erudite focus on strategic studies. But there is one field or area that, given the history of West Point's establishment in 1802 and its two sequential centuries of service to our nation since, seems most appropriate, and that would be a combination of military history and leadership.

It may seem somewhat strange to American civilians, but it was not until the last quarter of the twentieth century that cadets were able to make any significant choices in their field of studies at West Point. Over the preceding seven-eighths of West Point's history, almost all the classes cadets took were required, and the curriculum was heavily weighted toward hard sciences and engineering. Indeed, having graduated in the class of 1966, it remains quite clear in my memory that I had only one elective course in the second semester of my junior year and one in each semester of my senior year. The other classes I took over four years were taken by all other cadets as well.

Since the Army's Corps of Engineers dominated West Point politically over that same period, it is perhaps not too surprising that it tried to make engineers out of all cadets. And despite the fact that all cadets were being educated and trained to serve as officers, ideally for a full career period, the academic focus remained on the narrow field of engineering. This remained true for nearly two centuries, even though fewer than 20 percent of each class would choose to be commissioned into the Corps of Engineers at graduation. Military history, on the other hand, the heart and soul of the profession that lay before every cadet, was all but ignored until the cadets' senior year. And even then, over most of the period between the Civil War and the Vietnam War, the required curriculum only offered one course each semester, the first on Napoleon, the second focused primarily on the U.S. Civil War.

Many West Point cadets who might have been masters of the liberal arts, but were unable to manage the heavy mathematical load required, failed academically and were dismissed—and failure of any single course was mandatory grounds for dismissal. That seems too bad, for the loss was not just to the individual cadet concerned, but oftentimes this rigidity no doubt meant the loss to the Army of the service of a potentially fine officer. Fortunately, those days are over, and since the 1970s, cadets have been able to choose majors from among an array of different fields of study. West Point was opened up somewhat, and by establishing a formal graduate school of Military History and Leadership, I would have it open more.

I believe the Army should select a few hundred senior captains or junior majors, men and women in their early thirties, and assign them to West Point for two years of formal education. The students who would enter this graduate school would have already spent a decade or so in uniform, and have shown themselves to be officers of the highest character and promise just to win a place in the class. And I also believe that there should be some sort of rule that no individual soldier would be allowed to win more than one degree from West Point, so that officers who had been there for their undergraduate degree would not monopolize all the openings and would let other officers learn at West Point too.

There are any number of unused or underused large buildings at West Point, including the large installation formerly known as Ladycliff College, which West Point inherited and now vainly tries to fill with museum materials, archive storage, and a large gift shop. The families of these officer-students could live on post, or fifteen minutes away at Stewart Field in the large housing developments that were emptied in the last twenty years when that former Air Force base was closed. While enrolled, these students would go to parades, football games, wrestling matches, swimming meets, graduation ceremonies—West Point would become their school too! During their final semester, each student would be required to write a significant thesis. The curriculum would necessarily be rigorous, and some would predictably fall by the wayside, thus disrupting or redirecting their careers. And that's too bad, but in an effective academic environment, that's life.

A large number of those who receive undergraduate degrees from West Point leave the Army once their original commitment is up. But given their age and commitments at the outset, virtually *all* of those who receive master's degrees could be expected to serve full careers in the Army. Statistically, it would seem that a much larger proportion of each class of graduate students could be expected to eventually become general officers than of the corresponding undergraduate class. Seen in this light, a graduate program at West Point can perhaps be of even *greater* service to the Army than the undergraduate program.

The West Point graduate school would neither displace nor diminish the value of the undergraduate program already in place at West Point. In fact, it should cause the academic reputation of West Point to grow. I think a fair analogy would be to Harvard, already recognized as an excellent school when it offered only undergraduate courses. That Harvard later established top graduate schools in a number of fields only enhanced the value of a

Harvard undergraduate degree. And the same has been true for state universities. There are public universities in some states with established reputations of academic excellence that, at the turn of the century, allow them to be ranked among the top thirty to fifty universities in the nation. But in every case, it was because of their graduate schools that they were able to acquire such reputations, and those reputations made them all the more attractive to undergraduate students. This has often resulted in the somewhat anomalous situation of competitive students from one state seeking admission to a public university in another state simply because it was known to be a better academic institution. And so it would be with West Point.

I believe that, as the curriculum of this graduate school developed, small numbers of officers from other services might be allowed to attend as well. And as its reputation grew, one might expect to feel pressure for the admission of officers from allied countries, and perhaps even civilian governmental employees. Military history is taught in precious few American colleges or universities, and leadership in almost none, save, perhaps, in a somewhat different format in large graduate business schools. But military history is, or should be, the heart and soul of a truly professional military officer. And no matter what you call it, leadership is the key skill of any competent military officer, a skill that can be learned and yet is too often ignored as an academic discipline, even at West Point. And so the graduate school at West Point might come to life at an opportune moment and enhance both the image and reputation of the entire institution.

It is a commonplace that large organizations failing to respond to the pressures of a changing world court self-induced strangulation and eventual suicide. It is a fact that

West Point, clinging hard to tradition in the face of an ever-evolving Army and public environment, is losing its luster. At present, the image of West Point is slowly sliding from widely acknowledged prominence in the middle of the last century to what is often and increasingly seen by the American public that pays the bills as marginal relevance. It seems highly unlikely that, unless substantive change occurs, more "business as usual" will recover that highly favorable image. But if a graduate school such as that I propose above were to be born there, it is not at all unrealistic to think that, in twenty or thirty years, West Point might attain an image analogous to that of Harvard Business or Law or Medicine and become recognized as the top school of military history and leadership in the world.

The marks of top military leadership everywhere have always included initiative, flexibility, adaptability, independence, the freedom to adjust plans in the face of a changed opportunity or threat and to take risks in order to win greater victories. These are the enduring elements of military success. Why, then, should a key American military institution like West Point fail to exercise these cardinal military virtues while seeking to optimize how it performs its duty both to the Army and to the nation at large?

If we rigidly refuse to consider steps such as those outlined here or other ways to open West Point up in a way that would cause it to serve a wider section of the Army and the nation, beyond a group of promising teenagers, we must recognize the risks we run: Congress might react to such rigidity by taking stronger action on its own. It would be a sad outcome to see the diminution of the role, or even the disappearance, of West Point caused by its own institutional rigidity and inability to accept the need for productive change.

Across the short two-centuries-plus of our nation's existence, we have fought nine major wars in as many generations. We love peace, but we thrive on war.

In the wake of the Cold War, the U.S. Army has essentially been converted from a conscripted force preparing to fight World War III into an all-volunteer expeditionary force that is now often sent to perform myriad missions. While the threat to our civilian population posed by the clenched nuclear fist of actual or potential adversaries has been largely reduced or eliminated, the threat of "conventional" war on a smaller scale endures. And the duties and responsibilities of our professional army—to fight and win our nation's wars—remain the same. In order to better prepare the leadership of the army, a graduate school in military history and leadership at West Point would educate an even larger number of professional office's for national service. In so doing, the U.S. Military Academy would expand the role it plays and the service it provides to the american public.

When military threats to our national well-being appear, West Pointers will be expected to step forward, offering their lives for our country. They will thus continue to set the standard and lead the way. They will be "on duty" all the time, trying always to Do the Right Thing. For that is the way of West Point Warriors.

Notes

THE UNITED STATES MILITARY ACADEMY (USMA) at West Point maintains a major library collection, where it also keeps unusually extensive records of all its graduates. Within the library are the archives, where all official records for West Point and all cadets can be found. The library also houses a "Special Collections" division, where the personal records of all cadets and graduates are found. But there are other repositories as well. Nearly every West Point graduate since the Academy's establishment in 1802, for instance, has had his death noted by an unofficial obituary. These are now published in *Assembly*, the bimonthly alumni journal published by the USMA "Association of Graduates" (AOG). These obituaries sometimes run several pages for noteworthy individuals, but are generally six hundred to eight hundred words in length, and regularly include a summary of the individual's military career and civilian life. The materials on which these obituaries are based are often housed either in the official West Point library Archives or Special Collections or in the records of the Association of Graduates.

The USMA library, then, complemented by holdings of the AOG, has extensive collections of official historical records, after-action reports, and publications, as well as letters, diaries, and other personal papers belonging to or describing various graduates and events in which they figured. These events, of course, take place both in war and in peace, and while peace lasts much longer than war, the events that merit recording at USMA tend to occur more commonly in wartime.

These records begin with the establishment of the USMA and the roles played by its graduates in leading the U.S. Army through the first decade of the nineteenth century and the War of 1812. They continue through all the subsequent wars in which America has fought: the Mexican-American, Civil, and Spanish-American wars in the nineteenth century, then on to World Wars I and II, the Korean War, the Vietnam War, and various other police actions and rescue missions across the rest of the twentieth century. At the beginning of the twenty-first century, of course, we have already sent our soldiers to fight—and win—in Afghanistan. As Plato is reputed to have said, "Only the dead have seen the end of war," so this record-keeping of combat experiences can be expected to continue apace.

As our nation's first engineering school, however, West Point has also played a major role in the technical world, and her graduates have been central in such matters as building railroads, digging the Panama Canal, setting up and maintaining the Tennessee Valley Divide, and landing on the moon. Although her role as the source of engineers crucial to our national defense has faded somewhat in the second half of the twentieth century, her role as a source of warrior leaders endures.

But the scale has changed dramatically, complicating West Point's task of record-keeping. During the last decade of the nineteenth century, West Point classes ranged from fifty to seventy graduates each year, while in the decade before the Civil War, the average class size was in the low forties. In the first century of its existence, 1802–1902, just over four thousand cadets graduated from West Point, while during the second hundred years, the count hovers around fifty-five thousand.

During the nineteenth century, the maintenance of records for the relatively small number of graduates of what was widely perceived as a prestigious institution was not a terribly difficult task. By the end of the twentieth century, however, the growth of West Point classes had expanded to the point that some nine hundred cadets graduate each year. The maintenance of extensive personal records on each graduate has therefore been affected. The publication of an official *Biographical Register of West Point Officers and Graduates,* for instance, which was renewed every ten years, ended in 1950. But a *Register of Graduates,* published by the USMA AOG and containing only brief biographical summaries, was started in the 1940s and is still updated and published every year.

The research that produced this book was primarily drawn from the USMA library Archives, the library's Special Collections, and the records and archives of the AOG. Information was sought from those sources on virtually all graduates whose stories are narrated herein. In addition, there are many other publications widely available in the world outside West Point. And while I was particularly dependent on the written record for those West Point graduates long dead, the same is not true for West Pointers who graduated in the twentieth century.

I am particularly indebted for their extraordinarily supportive assistance to an array of individuals at West Point.

Within the USMA library, these include the USMA archivist, Suzanne Christoff, and her assistant, Alicia Mauldin; Special Collection librarians Judy Sibley, Sheila Biles, Deborah McKeon Pogue, and Allen Aimone, and manuscripts curator Susan Lintelmann. Within the Association of Graduates, I was bountifully rewarded in my research effort by Lieutenant Colonel (retired) Julian Oleniczak, the editor in chief of *Assembly*, by Cheryl West, the managing editor, by Jade Newman, the *Assembly* memorials editor, and by Sylvia Graham, the editor of the *Register of Graduates*.

Additional sources of information for various chapters are recorded below.

Prologue

All the material in the Prologue is based on personal experiences, letters written in Vietnam by Art Parker to his wife, Connie, and to me, and extensive interviews with Connie.

Chapter 1

There are many books that cover the foundation and the early days of West Point. In addition to materials found in the West Point library (both Archives and Special Collections) and in my own Princeton dissertation, "African American West Pointers in the Nineteenth Century," I used *Duty, Honor, Country* by Stephen Ambrose, *Where They Have Trod* by Ernest Dupuy, *To the Point* by George Pappas, and *West Point: A Bicentennial History* by Theodore Crackel. An essential source for understanding Jefferson's establishment of the U.S. Military Academy is another key text I used, *Mr. Jefferson's Army*, also by Dr. Crackel.

Chapter 2

In addition to the texts cited above for Chapter 1, I found useful material in *History of the United States Army* by Russel Weigley, and in *School for Soldiers* by Joseph Ellis and Robert Moore.

Chapter 3

The best recounting of Grant's experiences in Mexico is no doubt that in his autobiography, *Personal Memoirs of U.S. Grant*. There is, unhappily, no autobiography of Robert E. Lee from which to draw similar accounts. However, there is a lengthy biography entitled *Memoirs of Robert E. Lee* by Armistead L. Long, West Point graduate and military secretary to General Lee during the Civil War. It contains a great deal about Captain Lee in the Mexican-American War, as does *Robert E. Lee* by Douglas Southall Freeman.

Chapter 4

The Spirit of Old West Point by Morris Schaff, who graduated from West Point in 1862, contains enormous detail on cadets who were at West Point between 1858 and 1862, both during their days at the Academy and also later in life. O'Rorke's attack up the flank of Little Round Top and subsequent death leading his men in a charge down into the advancing Confederate ranks is there vividly recounted. Schaff also records the actions of "the Gallant Pelham" at Fredericksburg and his later death at Kelly's Ford. More detail on both men is to be found in the West Point Archives and Special Collections, and *Colonel John Pelham, Lee's Boy Artillerist,* by William W. Hassler, is quite thorough. A wonderful book entitled *They Lie Forgotten* by Mary Sergent commemorates O'Rorke and

Pelham, as well as other cadets at West Point between 1856 and 1861. Ms. Sergent did quite thorough research into these cadets, including extensive contact with their families and their descendents, from whom she obtained some extraordinary records and materials.

Chapter 5
All the material in this chapter is taken from my dissertation, "African American West Pointers in the Nineteenth Century," or draws upon research I did in writing it.

Chapter 6
There are many books about MacArthur and Patton, and I was fortunate enough to be able to use what I believe are the best works on their subjects: For MacArthur, I used the splendid *Old Soldiers Never Die* by Geoffrey Perret as my primary source, while for Patton, I used the excellent *A Genius for War* by Carlo D'Este.

Chapter 7
For Benjamin O. Davis, I was able to use his truly wonderful and powerfully moving autobiography, *American, an Autobiography*, as well as a book about his father, Benjamin O. Davis, Sr., entitled *America's First Black General*, by Marvin Fletcher. For Red Reeder, I used his autobiography, *Born at Reveille*, supplemented by four personal interviews, and interviews with his wife, Dort, who told me things Red never would've revealed about himself.

Chapter 8
For the story of Joe Clemons on Pork Chop Hill in Korea, I had a wealth of resources. I relied primarily on

personal interviews with Clemons, backed up by the book *Pork Chop Hill* by S. L. A. Marshall, and the movie *Pork Chop Hill,* in which the part of Joe Clemons was played by Gregory Peck.

Chapters 9–12

The rest of the stories told in the last chapters of this book are all based on personal interviews with the subjects and their friends and relatives. The only exceptions to that rule are for Rocky Versace and Dave Ramsay.

Nick Rowe told of Rocky Versace's heroism in great detail in his wonderful memoir, *Five Years to Freedom.* The Special Forces Command at Fort Bragg, North Carolina, was engaged over several years in a laborious effort to secure the Medal of Honor for Rocky. The Friends of Rocky Versace collaborated closely with them and supported their efforts, principally through the massive amounts of research done and materials obtained by Duane Frederic. Finally, a bill authorizing this award was passed by Congress, and it is expected that President Bush will present the Medal of Honor to Rocky posthumously at a White House ceremony in the spring of 2002.

Many of those who worked to advance Rocky's cause have been of great help in my research for this book, with special thanks to Steve Versace, Mike Heisley, John Gurr, and Duane Frederic. The sense of loss among his friends endures.

The same is true for Dave Ramsay, of course, and I have recorded extensive interviews with his brother Bob Ramsay, and his widow, Elizabeth Ramsay. In addition, Elizabeth was kind enough to share with me letters and voice tapes Dave sent her from Vietnam. Included in the tapes was a special recording Dave made of a combat operation. He was able to do this by having his crew chief connect a small tape recorder to the F-4 intercom system, so that everything Dave said, whether to his GIB or to others over the radio, was recorded. This particular tape recording is the source of the combat mission reported in the body of the text, and all words in quotation marks are taken from that tape recording. As to the events occurring inside the cockpit and the specific mechanics of the F-4 flying on an operation, I am indebted to Lieutenant Colonel (retired) Jack Jannarone, USMA 1965, who flew F-4s in Vietnam and is now a pilot for United Air Lines. To Lieutenant Colonel (retired) Mark Berent, who flew F-4s and other aircraft in Vietnam and then wrote the "Rolling Thunder" series of novels about The Vietnam War. And to my father, Colonel (retired) Thomas M. Carhart, who began his military career flying P-38s in World War II and ended it in command of a wing of F-4s flying out of Yokota Air Force Base in Tokyo, Japan.

Bibliography

Books

Ambrose, Stephen A. *Duty, Honor, Country: A History of West Point.* Baltimore: Johns Hopkins Press, 1966.

Berlin, Ira, ed. *The Black Military Experience.* New York, Cambridge University Press, 1983.

Black, Lowell D. and Sara H. *An Officer and a Gentleman: The Military Career of Lieutenant Henry O. Flipper.* Dayton, Ohio: Lora Company, 1985.

Burns, James M. *The Vineyard of Liberty.* New York: Knopf, 1982.

Carroll, John M., ed. *The Black Military Experience in the American West.* New York: Liveright, 1971.

Coffman, Edward M. *The Old Army: A Portrait of the American Army in Peacetime, 1784–1898.* New York: Oxford University Press, 1986.

Crackel, Theodore J. *Mr. Jefferson's Army.* New York: New York University Press, 1987.

———. *West Point: A Bicentennial History.* University Press of Kansas, 2002.

Davis, Benjamin O., Jr. *American, an Autobiography.* Washington, D.C.: Smithsonian Institution Press, 1991.

D'Este, Carlo. *A Genius for War.* New York: HarperCollins, 1995.

Dupuy, Ernest R. *Men of West Point: The First 150 Years of the United States Military Academy.* New York: William Sloane Associates, 1951.

————. *Where They Have Trod.* New York: Frederick A. Stokes & Co., 1940.

Elkins, Stanley M., and Eric McKittrick. *The Age of Federalism.* New York: Oxford University Press, 1993.

Ellis, Joseph, and Robert Moore. *School for Soldiers.* New York: Oxford University Press, 1974.

Fletcher, Marvin E. *The Black Soldier and Officer in the United States Army, 1891–1917.* Columbia, Mo.: University of Missouri Press, 1974.

————. *America's First Black General.* Lawrence, Kans.: University of Kansas Press, 1989.

Flipper, Henry O. *The Colored Cadet at West Point.* New York: Homer Lee & Co., 1878.

————. *Negro Frontiersman.* El Paso, Tex.: Texas Western College Press, 1963.

Freeman, Douglas S. *Robert E. Lee.* New York: Charles Scribner's Sons, 1935.

Grant, Ulysses S. *Personal Memoirs.* New York: Charles L. Webster & Co., 1885.

Hassler, William W. *Colonel John Pelham, Lee's Boy Artillerist.* Chapel Hill: University of North Carolina Press, 1960.

Long, Armistead L. *Memoirs of Robert E. Lee.* New York: J. M. Stoddard & Co., 1886.

Marshall, S. L. A. *Pork Chop Hill.* New York: William Morrow & Co., 1956.

McPherson, James M. *Ordeal by Fire.* New York: McGraw-Hill, 2nd edition, 1992.

————. *Battle Cry of Freedom.* New York: Oxford University Press, 1988.

Pappas, George S. *To the Point.* Westport, Conn.: Praeger, 1993.

Paret, Peter, ed. *Makers of Modern Strategy.* Princeton, N.J.: Princeton University Press, 1986.

Perret, Geoffrey. *Old Soldiers Never Die.* New York: Random House, 1996.

Reeder, Colonel Red. *Born at Reveille.* Queechee, Vt.: Vermont Heritage Press, 1994.

Rowe, Nicholas. *Five Years to Freedom.* New York: Ballantine, 1984.

Schaff, Morris. *The Spirit of Old West Point.* New York: Houghton Mifflin, 1908.

Sergent, Mary. *They Lie Forgotten.* Middletown, N.Y.: Prior King Press, 1993.

———. *An Unremaining Glory.* Middletown, N.Y.: Prior King Press, 1997.

Weigley, Russel F. *History of the United States Army.* Bloomington, Ind.: University of Indiana Press, 1984.

Government Publications

American Military History. Washington, D.C.: U.S. Army Center of Military History, 1989.

Proceedings, In the Case of Henry O. Flipper (Deceased), U.S. Army Board for Correction of Military Records, 17 November 1976.

"Regulations for the U.S. Military Academy at West Point," New York: Baldwin and Jones, 1868.

Unpublished Dissertations and Theses

Andrews, Richard L. "Years of Frustration: William T. Sherman, the Army, and Reform, 1869–1883." Unpublished Ph.D. dissertation, Northwestern University, 1968.

Carhart, Thomas M. "African American West Pointers In the Nineteenth Century" Unpublished Ph.D. dissertation, Princeton University, 1998.

Denton, Edgar III. "The Formative Years of the United States Military Academy, 1775–1833." Unpublished Ph.D. dissertation, Syracuse University, 1964.

Dillard, Walter S. "The United States Military Academy, 1865–1900: The Uncertain Years." Unpublished Ph.D. dissertation, University of Washington, 1972.

Harris, Theodore D. "Henry Ossian Flipper, the First Negro Graduate of West Point." Unpublished Ph.D. dissertation, University of Minnesota, 1971.

Morrison, James L., Jr. "The United States Military Academy, 1833–1866: Years of Progress and Turmoil." Unpublished Ph.D. dissertation, Columbia University, 1970.

Index

About the Author

TOM CARHART graduated from West Point in 1966. He served as an infantry platoon leader with the 101st Airborne Division in Vietnam and was awarded two Purple Hearts for wounds suffered in combat. He left the army and earned a law degree at the University of Michigan.

After one year as the Editor of "European Taxation" in Amsterdam, he was a policy analyst at the Rand Corporation in Santa Monica, California. He next worked as an international corporate lawyer in Brussels before serving in the Department of the Army as a civilian policy analyst and an army historian. During the 1990s, he earned his Ph.D. in American and military history at Princeton University.

The author of three earlier books (*Battles and Campaigns in Vietnam*, Crown, 1984, in paperback as *Battlefront Vietnam*, Warner, 1991; *The Offering*, Vietnam memoir, Morrow, 1987; and *Iron Soldiers*, U.S. Army unit in Iraq War, Pocketbooks 1994), he presently lives in Washington, D.C. area with his wife and two children, where he writes and teaches a course on the Civil War at Mary Washington College in Fredericksburg, VA.